THE MAKING OF WOMEN TRADE UNIONISTS

Gender and Organizational Theory Series

Series Editor: Emma Jeanes,
School of Business and Economics,
University of Exeter, UK

The aim of this series is to provide research monographs and edited volumes on all topics within the area of gender and management, broadly defined. The series is intended to encompass different perspectives within feminism (for example liberal, post-structuralist and Marxist) as well as the interplay of feminist perspectives with other forms of identity and discourse. The series also aims to provide books that explore notions of masculinities in an organizational context.

Forthcoming titles in the series:

Gender and Communication at Work
Edited by Mary Barrett and Marilyn J. Davidson
ISBN 0 7546 3840 5

Masculinities and Management in Agricultural
Organisations Worldwide
Barbara Pini
ISBN 0 7546 4734 X

The Making of Women Trade Unionists

GILL KIRTON
Queen Mary, University of London

ASHGATE

Published by
Ashgate Publishing Limited
Gower House
Croft Road
Aldershot
Hampshire GU11 3HR
England

Ashgate Publishing Company
Suite 420
101 Cherry Street
Burlington, VT 05401-4405
USA

Ashgate website: http://www.ashgate.com

British Library Cataloguing in Publication Data
Kirton, Gill
    The making of women trade unionists. - (Gender and
    organizational theory)
    1.Women labor union members 2.Labor unions - Officials and
    employees
    I.Title
    331.4'78

Library of Congress Cataloging-in-Publication Data
Kirton, Gill.
    The making of women trade unionists / by Gill Kirton.
        p. cm. -- (Gender and organizational theory)
    Includes bibliographical references and index.
    ISBN 0-7546-4569-X
    1. Women labor union members. 2. Women labor union members--Great Britain.
    3. Labor union members--Great Britain. I. Title. II. Series.

    HD6079.K57 2006
    331.88082'0973--dc22

                                                        2005037630

ISBN 0 7546 4569 X

Printed and bound by Athenaeum Press, Ltd.
Gateshead, Tyne & Wear.

Contents

List of Figures and Tables

Figures

Tables

List of Abbreviations

Amicus	Union formed of merger between AEEU and MSF
AEEU	Amalgamated Electrical and Engineering Union
ETUC	European Trade Union Confederation
MSF	Manufacturing, Science and Finance
NALGO	National and Local Government Officers' Association
NASUWT	National Association of School Masters and Union of Women Teachers
NUT	National Union of Teachers
RIO	Regional Industrial Officer
RWO	Regional Women's Officer
SERTUC	Southern and Eastern Region TUC
TGWU	Transport and General Workers Union
TUC	Trades Union Congress
UNISON	Local government workers' union
USDAW	Unions of Shop, Distributive and Allied Trades Workers
WEA	Workers Educational Association

Acknowledgements

I owe an enormous debt of gratitude to all the women I interviewed for this research, who were so kind and enjoyable to talk to. Thanks are also due to the two unions – MSF and TGWU – for co-operating with this research and providing me with the information and access necessary to complete the fieldwork, especially: Sarah Howard and Jennie Scott-Reid of MSF, and John Fisher and Jeneva Reynolds of TGWU. I am also grateful to the MSF and TGWU tutors who participated in the interviews, but also kindly let me observe their classes.

I also thank academic colleagues who guided me in this research, particularly Geraldine Healy and Al Rainnie and also Anne-Marie Greene. All the discussions and conversations over the years of the fieldwork and writing helped me to formulate my ideas and interpretation. Finally, I thank my family for their support.

In memory of Bill Carey

Preface

This book explores the making of women's lay trade union careers in Britain. It examines how and why women embark on a union career path, specifically considering family, work and union influences. The book focuses on women's engagement with one form of women's separate organizing – women-only union courses. It considers the possibility for women-only courses to strengthen trade union and gender identities so that in turn this form of women's separate organizing might encourage increased female participation. The book also looks into how women's lay trade union careers develop over time within their family, work and union contexts and the degree to which women utilize gender-conscious strategies with the potential to work towards gender transformation of trade unions. The research presented in this book is based on detailed qualitative case studies carried out within two large, male-dominated British trade unions – MSF[1] and TGWU between 1999 and 2002. The study responds to the call for greater attention to the social processes of industrial relations (Kelly 1998). Further details of the fieldwork and the research sites can be found in the Appendix and in Chapter 4.

The background to the book's discussion is the long period of membership decline in Britain (1979–1997) and the union movement's focus at the start of the twenty-first century on strategies for survival and renewal. However, this debate transcends the national context to resonate with the predicament of unions in most of the developed world (Howell 1996). With the trend of the last two to three decades of labour market feminization predicted to continue and combined with overall restructuring of the labour market, commentators suggest that trade unions in many countries need to develop strategies to reach workers beyond their traditional male-dominated manufacturing and public sector bases (Ledwith and Colgan 2002). In response to this context, the global industrial relations literature has explored ways in which unions might revitalize themselves by becoming more democratic and encouraging greater membership participation (e.g. Briskin and McDermott 1993; Colgan and Ledwith 2002a; Curtin and Higgins 1998; Heery et al 2000; Hunt and Rayside 2000). This has prompted both greater policy and academic attention to

---

1 Towards the end of the period of fieldwork for this study (on 1st January 2002) MSF merged with male-dominated AEEU (ten per cent female) to create the new 'super union' Amicus with approximately 1.1 million members. Because of the change in size and membership composition and for the sake of clarity, the union is referred to in this book as MSF. The merger is now consolidated and the union is divided into 22 sectors and the name MSF is no longer used. In addition the GPMU merged with Amicus in 2004. By 2005 Amicus had closed the MSF education centre, Whitehall College, and along with it 'Women's Week', the national women's school, one of the central research sites of this study.

women, who are now an undeniably important source of members for most British unions (Howell 1996; Sinclair 1996).

The feminist industrial relations literature is at pains to point out that women are under-represented in union decision-making structures from the local level of workplace representatives, to paid officials, to executive bodies (e.g. Cunnison and Stageman 1995; McBride 2001), producing what Cockburn (1995) has termed a 'democracy deficit'. Again, this is not an issue confined to the British context, but a more global one (Colgan and Ledwith 2002a), even manifest in the more gender-egalitarian countries such as Sweden (Curtin and Higgins 1998). The literature on women and trade unions highlights the negative impact of the absence of gender democracy on bargaining agendas and outcomes (Dickens 1997; Colling and Dickens 2001). In particular there is concern that 'women's issues' are not adequately addressed by the traditional male-defined trade union bargaining agenda. Feminist authors argue that women are a specific constituency with gender specific employment needs and concerns which unions need to respond to if they are to be successful in recruiting and retaining women (Cockburn 1995; Cunnison and Stageman 1995; Kirton and Healy 1999). The failure to address women's specific concerns in turn produces and reinforces women's lower favourability to trade unions and lesser willingness to participate (Sinclair 1996; Walters 2002). It is also posited that unions need to develop more inclusive processes and structures to encourage greater female participation (Cockburn 1995; Munro 2001; Parker 2002). However, this is no easy task. The literature identifies considerable barriers to women's union participation at the levels of work, home and union, including the gendered division of domestic work, the organization of women's work and the organization of trade union work (Briskin and McDermott 1993).

There is now a growing research literature focused on the strategies the unions are using to work towards gender democracy, particularly the various forms of women's separate organizing. Separate organizing is designed to redress the gender democracy gap in trade unions by encouraging and empowering women (for example, women-only courses) and by establishing structures, which give women as a group power and resources (for example, women's committees). There is far more published research on women's self-organized groups and on women's committees (e.g. Cockburn 1995; Colgan and Ledwith 2000; Healy and Kirton 2000; Colgan and Ledwith 2002; Humphrey 2002; Parker 2002; Briskin 1993) than there is specifically on women-only courses (Greene and Kirton 2002; Kirton and Greene 2002; Kirton and Healy 2004).

Overall there is only limited consideration of the links between union education and the renewal debate (Croucher 2004) despite the fact that many union educational initiatives are designed to support the aim of revitalization. However, education is a significant area of trade union activity. Bridgford and Stirling suggest that trade union education is a 'key resource for the construction of trade unionism' (2000:5), whilst Holford sees union education as a 'vital catalyst as the movement tries to come to terms with new realities' (1993:12). Similarly, Munro and Rainbird (2000) argue that trade union education encourages a greater identification with the union and can lead to active participation in union activities, thus having the potential to strengthen workplace activism. However, despite obvious links, there have been few attempts to marry the study of this area of trade union activity with the debates surrounding gender democracy.

Presentation of the research

Chapter 1 outlines the broad theoretical background and 'sensitizing devices' (Giddens 1984) underpinning the research and argues that the gender 'blind' or gender neutral orientation of traditional, mainstream industrial relations research is unable to develop our knowledge of women trade unionists. Therefore the study is located within what can be termed a feminist industrial relations paradigm, which draws on the strengths and insights that mainstream industrial relations theories combined with feminist theories can offer.

Chapter 2 looks at the position of women in trade unions, focusing particularly on women's participation and activism. The main barriers to women's participation are outlined, including the gendered division of domestic work, the organization of women's work, the organization of trade union work and the masculine construction of trade union agendas. There is also discussion of the individual and collective identities that influence orientations to participation. Finally, there is a detailed discussion of women's separate organizing as a feminist strategy towards gender democracy.

Chapter 3 situates the discussion in a historical context and outlines the history of women's separate organizing and women-only courses in Britain. The analysis shows that early developments were mainly a response to women's external exclusion from mainstream, male dominated trade unions and later developments to their internal exclusion from the structures of power and enablement. Women-only courses became a more politicized, proactive vehicle in the late 1970s under the influence of second-wave feminism and are now an established form of trade union education.

Chapters 4 to 7 are based on the case study research. Chapter 4 provides an examination of the case study unions' education provision and approach to educating women, concluding that women-only courses are situated in a dynamic and evolving context where key actors play an active and central role in shaping the educational offering to render it more appealing and useful to women. Through the analysis of quotes from interviews and more detailed illustrative stories of four women, Chapter 5 considers the broad range of influences that stimulate women's union participation and the structural barriers and constraints they encounter in the family work and trade union environment. Chapter 6 explores women's motivations for attending and their experiences and perceptions of women-only courses. The analysis is organized around key themes and processes of women-only courses: 'safe space', shared learning and privileging 'women's issues'. The Chapter shows how women's gender and trade union orientations are shaped by the courses, such that the courses can be characterized as a significant experience in a woman's trade union career.

Chapter 7 uses data gathered in second interviews with MSF and TGWU women to explore how women's union careers unfolded over a two year period following their attendance of a women's school. The analysis shows that while some women failed to realize their intentions or aspirations for a union career, because family/personal life, work or union stood in their way, the majority went on to sustain and develop their participation, albeit often in non-linear, qualitative and personal ways.

Chapter 8 brings the themes of the study together in the context of the debates presented in Chapters 1 to 3. With no direct influence on union decision-making without doubt women-only courses are a weaker form of separate organizing. However, the detailed case study research in MSF and TGWU reveals women-only courses to be very valuable to trade union women individually and collectively. The courses shape and strengthen the gender and trade union identities of participants, fostering the collective identification thought necessary to promote and sustain participation. Further, the gendered discourses of the women's schools also encourage participants consciously or unconsciously to act in ways that influence the gender democracy project. The study also reveals the complexities of women's lives, often involving balancing roles in the family, work and union, but that it is possible for women to break the vicious circle of gender inequality through their individual and collective actions.

Chapter 1

Theoretical Background

The purpose of this chapter is to provide the reader with the broad theoretical framework used for interpreting the research presented in this book on women's trade union participation. The research is located within the field of industrial relations, a field with a strong empirical tradition, an emphasis on research useful for policy-making and characterised by under-theorisation (Marsden 1982; Hyman 1994; Kelly 1998). It would be erroneous to argue that theory has no place within policy-oriented research. Theoretical concepts can be regarded as 'sensitizing devices', which are useful for thinking about research problems and the interpretation of research findings (Giddens 1984: 326). This chapter outlines and discusses the 'sensitizing devices' underpinning the research presented in this book. The chapter is organized into three main sections. The first section considers industrial relations theory, the second section considers feminist theory and the third section outlines how industrial relations and feminist theories combined can be used to make sense of women's lived experiences of work, union and family.

Industrial relations theory

Class is the principal concept used within sociology to theorize social inequality and it is the dominant theoretical influence within industrial relations. Theoretical concepts borrowed from neo-classical economics have also influenced industrial relations research in relation to explaining employers' and employees' labour market behaviour and the genesis of collective organisation and action (e.g. Hartley 1992; Klandermans 1992).

The main approaches to conceptualising and understanding class were set out by Marx and Weber (Bradley 1996). Classic Marxism's approach focuses on the dichotomous relationship between capital and labour and the antagonism that this inevitably produces. The Weberian model is more pluralist; it arranges clusters of occupations together as social classes and forms the basis for theories of class fragmentation. Both approaches have been traditionally utilized within class analysis to explain the subordinate position of women (e.g. reserve army theories, Beechey and Perkins, 1987) and black workers (e.g. segmented labour market theories) (Bradley, Erickson et al. 2000).

Class is undoubtedly a fundamental and essential concept for thinking about how and why people come to be in particular occupations and how and why they come to join and participate in unions. However, class theory provides inadequate explanation of the gendered social divisions and gendered power relations shaping women's employment behaviour and their willingness to participate in unions (Walby 1986; Beechey and Perkins 1987; Walby 1990; Cockburn 1991; Bradley 1996; Pollert 1996; Gottfried 1998). Walby labels class theory as a 'malestream' perspective (1990: 7): it is at best gender-neutral and at worst gender-blind (Cockburn 1991).

From a gender perspective, there are three main errors within both neo-Marxist and neo-Weberian approaches to class. First, an over-concentration on the capital-labour relation, with inadequate attention to the gendered division of household work and the gendered impact this has on employment patterns (e.g. Walby 1990; Bradley 1996) and willingness to participate in trade unions (e.g. Colgan and Ledwith 1996). Doing away with class inequalities would not get rid of all gender inequalities. Second a failure to deal with the way that gender has historically divided the working class. There is a tendency to ignore the trade union role in constructing women's inequality and to valorize uncritically the role of trade unions in advancing the interests of a genderless working class. For example, the assumption that men are breadwinners and women homemakers underpinned the trade union movement's historical ideal of a 'family wage', which did little to achieve equal pay for women, even holding back the project. At the same time, a unitary, class-based conception of trade union interests is also responsible for the unions' historical lack of interest in recruiting and representing women, who were not until relatively recently regarded as proper workers (e.g. Beale 1982; Cunnison and Stageman 1995). Trade union victories have in fact often been victories for men, which women could only vicariously enjoy based upon their associations with men as fathers and husbands. The third error is a function of the first two: women tend to be invisible within traditional class analysis and men are regarded as gender free beings (Hansen 2002).

These errors mean that class theory is unable to address sufficiently the three main features of gender relations in employment, (i) the gender pay gap (ii) gender segregation (iii) women's lower rates of employment participation (Walby 1990). Neither can it explain the three main features of gender relations inside unions, (i) women's historically lower levels of membership (ii) their lower rates of participation (iii) their under-representation in decision-making. Thus the consequence of the gender-blind theoretical underpinning of much industrial relations research is that gender-blind knowledge is produced (Wacjman 2000). Much industrial relations research is potentially less useful to policy-makers (and to academics) than it should be, as it fails to explain sufficiently women's experiences at a time when women are almost half the workforce and an important source of members for trade unions.

Nevertheless, it is necessary for gender research to engage with concepts of class. There are undoubtedly class variations in the way that gender is experienced; i.e. men are not all equally privileged, while women are not all equally subordinate (Cockburn 1991). In the feminist sociological literature there have recently been calls for greater sensitivity to gender within class analysis (Walby 1997) and to class within gender analysis (Bradley 1999). This book adopts a broad conception of class, where it is seen as a 'complicated set of economic, political and cultural relationships arising from the way societies organize the production of goods and services' (Bradley, Erickson et al. 2000). This conception allows for gender to be held as one modality in which class is lived.

With regard to neo-classical theories, these are generally utilized to explain the preferences and choices of workers. To summarise it is argued that in making employment choices female workers take into consideration their domestic responsibilities (primarily childcare), as well as their personal preferences, skills and abilities (Anker 1997). In addition, the neo-classical approach stresses the importance of human capital (most notably education and training) in determining occupational status (Becker 1971). Thus, any gender differences in labour market outcomes are not problematic because they are the consequence of gendered individual preferences and choices; that is of rational choice (Walby 1990). Some industrial relations authors borrow neo-classical theories to explain willingness to join or participate in trade unionism (e.g. Klandermans 1992; Hartley 1992). For example, Hartley (1992) argues that rational choice theory is appealing because it is based on subjective perceptions, beliefs and values and therefore can help to explain variation in union joining where employees are in similar objective circumstances. However, it is important not to overlook gender differences in employment and occupational contexts and to take account of the fact that women's 'choices' will undoubtedly be influenced by their roles in the home and family. What is needed is an approach that examines the exercise of 'choice' within the context of wide-ranging structural constraints. One other danger is that the neo-classical approach avoids the need to confront the gendered power relations within the union movement and means that it is possible to 'read off' from women's lesser participation, their lesser interest or belief in trade unionism.

Thus, one of the main weaknesses of neo-classical approaches is that there is a failure to take account of the structural factors that shape individual choices and preferences in relation to employment and union membership/participation (Procter and Padfield 1999; Healy 1999). For example, because women are typically the primary carers in the family and take main responsibility for household chores, their expressed choices and preferences usually reflect the necessity to perform a 'juggling act' of paid employment and unpaid work in the home. This argument is reflected in the fact that single, childfree women have very similar employment patterns to men. Similarly, most female trade union activists are 'atypical' (Cockburn 1995) – older women with no or adult children – suggesting that mothers of young children, who are 'time poor' have little excess time and energy to engage in union activism. Neo-classicists acknowledge gendered differences, but contend that they are the outcome of rational choice, rather than a function of the structural constraints faced by mothers (e.g. Hakim 1991). Overall then, rational choice theory has only limited value for a gendered analysis, although it does offer a theoretical opening for examining how and why women exercise choice.

Feminist theory

From a gender perspective the two dominant influences on industrial relations theory leave explanatory gaps and this necessitates utilisation of feminist theory. Feminist theory is a broad 'church' which has evolved and continues to evolve. The concept of patriarchy lies at the heart of classic approaches developed in the 1960s and 1970s. Theorising patriarchy was an important first step towards redressing the failure identified by feminists, of social theory, particularly class theory, to account adequately for women's inequality (Acker 1989). However, in the late 1970s feminist theorists began to construct a substantial critique of patriarchy, outlined below, (see also the early papers in Hennessy and Ingraham's (1997) collection) and as an explanatory theory patriarchy has over time fallen into disuse. Nevertheless, it is worth engaging with the concept and the critique because it has shaped the contours of feminist thought and it certainly influenced the early feminist critiques of trade unionism.

Walby's work on patriarchy summarises the development of the concept (1986; 1989; 1990) and the four dominant ways of understanding patriarchy, which emerged in the 1970s: radical feminism, Marxist feminism, liberalism and dual systems theory (1990: 3–5). She explains how the different schools of thought frame the 'problem' of women differently. Within radical feminism, patriarchy exists as an independent social system. The central focus is on sexual practice, sexuality and male violence against women. Critics of this interpretation of patriarchy are concerned about a tendency towards essentialism and biological reductionism (Acker 1989). In contrast, Marxist feminism holds that patriarchy derives from capitalism, such that men's domination over women is a by-product of capital's domination over labour. Here, critics contend women's inequality cannot be reduced to capitalism (Acker 1989; Barrett and Phillips 1992). This interpretation also fails to highlight how working class men (trade unionists, for example) might benefit alongside capitalists from patriarchal social structures; further, it offers no explanation for gendered divisions within pre-capitalist societies. Liberalism does not depend upon overarching social structures to explain women's inequality. Instead, the focus is at the micro level, upon detailed instances of prejudice against women, together with the attitudes, which reproduce such prejudice. The perspective is criticised for its failure to deal with the embeddedness of women's inequality and the interconnectedness between its different forms: the gendered division of domestic and paid labour, for example (Walby 1990). Dual systems theory is a synthesis of Marxist and radical feminist theory, sometimes referred to as socialist-feminist theory (Calas and Smircich 1996): here both capitalism and patriarchy are important in the structuring of gender relations. There is disagreement among dual systems theorists as to whether the two systems operate as one (capitalist patriarchy), or whether they are separate, although interconnected systems.

Walby attempted to rescue the concept from its critics by producing a model of patriarchy consisting of six partially interconnecting structures: paid work, housework, sexuality, culture, violence and the state (1990: 16). Walby's model addressed two major early criticisms of patriarchy (Acker 1989). First it acknowledged that patriarchy pre-dates capitalism, therefore she did not suggest that as a social system it grew from or was created by the forces of capitalism. Second it recognised that under capitalism the form of patriarchy changed, thereby highlighting that patriarchy exists in no constant or fixed form and is therefore spatially and historically contingent (Walby 1986). Walby (1990) also identified a third social structure – racism – in order to counter black feminists' emerging criticism that the combined structures of capitalism and patriarchy were unable to deal with black women's experiences. For example, black feminists argue that it is important to recognise that as a retreat from a hostile employment situation, the home may not be the central site for black women's subordination; rather it could represent a site for resistance and solidarity against racism (Anthias and Yuval-Davis 1993).

The concept of patriarchy undoubtedly enabled feminist theorising to advance by, for example, helping us to see and understand how men's concerns and interests have come to dominate and define public and political agendas (Cockburn 1991), those of trade unions included. It also exposed how patriarchal attitudes create stereotypes of women, which, amongst other things, deny their capacity to be leaders, whether in employment as managers (Kanter 1977) or in trade unions (Ledwith et al. 1990). In short, the concept of patriarchy helped provide the tools with which to challenge neo-classical and functionalist explanations for women's inequality and to fill the gap left by traditional class analysis. However, the criticisms of patriarchy were not fended off by attempts such as Walby's (1990) to proffer a more multi-dimensional understanding; instead the critique became more fundamental.

The contemporary critique of patriarchy is part of a wider one of universal theories and a shift towards postmodernist thought as the new orthodoxy in the social sciences (Flax 1992; Bradley 1999). One of the main criticisms, of particular relevance to this book, is that as a concept it merges explanation with description and collapses into a form of abstract structuralism, losing the tension between agency and structure necessary to understand complex social processes (Acker 1989; Pollert 1996; Gottfried 1998; Bradley 1999). Paradoxically, the in-depth, qualitative research of feminist social scientists, influenced by patriarchy, exposed the very limitations of the concept for understanding the complex and fluid nature of gender relations. Abstract structuralism did not seem to help feminists to understand women's lives (Acker 1989; Bradley 1999; Gottfried 1998), because once gender relations are analysed in context of lived experiences the 'static oppositions' of capital and patriarchy disappear (Pollert 1996: 646). Thus, an analytical approach capable of exploring the complexity of gendered social processes and relations and their in-built linkages to other social dynamics is thought necessary (e.g. Acker 1989, Bradley 1999, Gottfried 1998).

Not only is an abstract structural model now widely considered to be unhelpful in understanding women's inequality, but it is also questioned whether patriarchy is actually a social system, which sits alongside capitalism. Pollert (1996) argues persuasively that patriarchy does not constitute a social system in the way that capitalism does, so the concept is analytically redundant. Whilst capitalism contains an internal dynamic which drives the system, and ensures its survival, patriarchy has no such internal dynamic. There is, she says, '*no necessary internal connection between men and women as gendered subjects which defines a self-perpetuating material dynamic or economic/social system*' *(*1996: 643). Pollert goes on to illustrate her case in very simple terms: '*Capitalists could not become "good capitalists" by ceasing to exploit wage labour; they would cease to be capitalists*' (1996: 643, original emphasis). In contrast, men and women can and do alter their material and ideological relationships with one another and this is exposed when research takes place at the level of lived experience.

Black feminist theorists also argued (hooks 1989; Anthias and Yuval-Davis 1993), that as a single reified structure and a universal theory patriarchy is insufficient to explain differential experiences among diverse women. Patriarchy is unable to take on how multiple oppressions cross cut and interweave, so that, for example, a black woman's experiences are qualitatively different from a white woman's and cannot simply be analysed as 'double oppression', with a theory for gender oppression and a separate theory for race oppression.

However, despite the various well-founded criticisms of patriarchy, it has proven a useful conceptual tool in order to underscore the specificity of women's employment and to make women visible within the analysis of the capitalist-labour relation and abandoning it altogether contains dangers (e.g. Acker 1989). A move to a (possibly more anodyne) 'gender analysis' may weaken the connections between political issues and theoretical analysis, which made the development of feminist thought possible in the first place. Pollert (1996), on the other hand, counters this argument by asserting that the continuance of patriarchy to inform feminist analysis carries its own dangers, namely those of failing to engage with people and of losing sight of class. An attractive compromise struck by many academics (for example Bradley 1999; Cockburn 1991; Gottfried 1998; Pollert 1996; Walby 1997) is to continue to use the term adjectivally (i.e. patriarchal) to describe specific situations and circumstances, whilst keeping sight of class and race difference. Moreover, adjectival use of the concept does not elevate it to a social structure, but sees it more as a relation or dynamic.

The critique of patriarchy is now substantial and it is clear that it cannot provide a universal explanation for women's inequality. The debate surrounding the utility of the concept has reached a cul-de-sac, with most authors having abandoned it as a universal theory. Even Walby, one of the most prolific theoretical writers on the subject largely abandons the label in her later work '*Gender Transformations*' (1997). Along with other authors, she continues sporadically to use the term adjectivally, rather than as a noun, but does not enter into a detailed discussion of its continuing appropriateness/utility or otherwise. Instead, she uses the term 'gender regime' after making passing reference to the six patriarchal structures she outlined in her earlier work (1997: 6). Bradley (1996: 7) confronts the dilemma concerning abstract structuralism and states clearly that she prefers to employ the term 'dynamic' rather than 'structure' to convey the evolving nature of sets of relationships.

What does this departure from patriarchy mean for feminist theory? Many authors have chosen postmodernist feminism over the traditional feminist lenses outlined earlier because it addresses issues of women's diversity, difference and subjectivity. Postmodernism has become enormously influential in the social sciences generally and has had a huge impact on feminist theory; it is therefore worthy of more detailed attention. Postmodernism is not persuaded by 'meta-narratives' and therefore postmodernist feminism abandons patriarchy, although it does engage with women's oppression (Hearn and Parkin 1993: 154–5). Its strength is that it does this within a paradigm which focuses attention on a multiplicity of oppressions (based on gender, sexuality, race, class, age, disability, and so on), their complexity, inter-relationship and changing nature. However, it is worth noting that traditional (modernist) feminist thought has also become more sensitive to diversity within social categories, such that the concern to expose a diversity of subjective experiences among women was not invented by postmodernists. Importantly, within postmodernism 'femininities' and 'masculinities' are not reduced to biological sex categories, but are de-essentialised (Stabile 1997) so that either sex can display feminine and masculine characteristics and meaning that women are not cast as all the same.

The weaknesses of postmodernism are first that it denies the existence of a dominant set of social categories (class, gender and race, for example, as in the modernist project) (Bradley 1999; Walby 1992), which are regarded as overly simplistic by postmodernists (e.g. Hearn and Parkin 1993). Second, within postmodernism there is a de-emphasis of economic relations and of the material experiences and consequences of oppression (Bradley 1999; Flax 1992; Hearn and Parkin 1993; Pollert 1996). Third, power is diffuse and detached from class (or gender) relations (Pollert, 1996) and is present in all social relationships; it is not derived from economic or sexual divisions (Pringle and Watson 1992).

Postmodernist feminism focuses on issues of sexuality, subjectivity and textuality (Barrett 1992), emphasising the importance of language and discourse, not just in describing the world, but in constituting social reality (Pringle and Watson 1992). For example, postmodernists focus on the social or discursive processes, through which femininities and masculinities are produced, sustained and reproduced (e.g. Alvesson and Billing 1997). The essence of postmodernist social analysis is captured by Derrida's famous statement, '*Il n'y a pas d'hors texte*' (there is nothing outside the text) (in Barrett 1992: 209). This does not literally mean that nothing exists, rather that 'things' have no significant meaning outside the systems of rules and conventions (discourse) by which they are constituted. Therefore, postmodernists seek to examine the minutiae of the various discourses that constitute the subject or object of analysis.

Barrett (1992: 216) posits that postmodernists have exposed the flaws of Marxist and liberal thought, but she suggests that whether they can offer a more useful alternative is a 'much vexed question'. Critics of postmodernism would suggest not (e.g. Pollert 1996). Thompson (1993: 202), for example, contends that postmodernism '*represents a retreat from engagement by sections of the intelligentsia*'. Some of the linguistically convoluted and impenetrable postmodernist literature seems to have little application to a project for social change, such as feminism. Maynard (1994: 19) goes so far as to state '*paradoxically, although everything is about the subject, no one in postmodern analyses actually appears to <u>do</u> anything. Subjectivities are seemingly overdetermined by the discourses in which they are constituted, and thus lacking in both intentionality and will*' (original emphasis). She goes on to argue that deconstructing social categories through language does not cause the significance of those categories in shaping personal and subjective experiences to disappear.

An alternative approach is to side step the rather sterile debate on patriarchy and to avoid the relativist pitfalls of embracing postmodernism wholeheartedly by adopting a more general feminist lens (e.g. hooks 1989; Walby 1997) through which to analyse patriarchal and gender relations at the level of lived experiences. This then has the potential to lead away from the notion that there are necessarily three structural pillars – patriarchy, capitalism and racism – which explain women's inequality and emphasise instead sets of lived relationships (Bradley 1996) that can be seen as gendered and racialised. Within such a general feminist lens it is possible to see material consequences and outcomes as arising from these sets of lived relationships, but also to see gendered discourses as an integral element to their production and reproduction.

Feminism meets industrial relations theory

The above discussion has outlined and discussed the main theoretical influences or 'sensitising devices' on the research presented in this book. The research draws on the strengths and insights of industrial relations and feminist theories to inform the analysis, summarised as follows.

With regard to influences from industrial relations theory, class is an essential but limited tool when researching women, because of its inability to deal with the specificity of women's experiences. Further, it is important for research on women to avoid the pitfalls of earlier attempts to gender traditional class analysis, where the heterogeneity of women and their lived experiences (as in reserve army thesis and dual labour market theory) were underplayed and theorising consequently proved overly deterministic. However, the view taken here is that the capital-labour relation and class positioning remain central to understanding women's employment and their relationship to trade unionism and also that it is important to recognise that gendered experiences inevitably contain class dimensions.

Neo-classical approaches have provided a useful focus on individual choices and preferences, but are severely weakened by their failure to acknowledge the embeddedness of the social constraints influencing individual women. However, women are 'knowledgeable agents' (Giddens 1984) and generally act in ways, which to them appear rational according to the (albeit constrained) options open to them (Purcell 1979). Therefore, the research does examine rational choice and human capital issues as this proves a useful way of ensuring that women are constructed as active (albeit constrained) agents.

To overcome the weaknesses of traditional class analysis and to rebut neo-classical claims that individuals exercise free choice, feminist theory has relied heavily on the concept of patriarchy. Without doubt patriarchal theory was an important development, but one which more recently has rightly been subjected to a substantial critique, largely because it presents an overly structural and deterministic account of women's oppression, allowing little room for more fluid gender relations. However, there is support among feminist authors for retaining the adjectival form of 'patriarchal' (e.g. Bradley 1999; Gottfried 1998) to underscore '*the concrete ways in which male power legitimises authority in capitalist organisations*' (Gottfried 1998: 465). Pollert (1996) meanwhile prefers more concrete descriptive terms, such as male-dominated. Pollert's preference for greater precision is justified to the extent that it is important not to overuse 'patriarchal' because it can take on a slogan-like quality, which does little to advance serious feminist scholarship. On the other hand more concrete terms are not always applicable to the specific contexts and situations and broader terms, such as 'gendered', if overused sometimes have a somewhat anodyne or benign flavour, which does not quite capture the force or causal nature of patriarchal relations. There is therefore a midway, adopted in this book, between abandoning the use of 'patriarchal' altogether and describing all social structures and relations with which women are involved as patriarchal. Pollert talks about the 'poverty of patriarchy', but equally it is possible to argue that without the concept, feminism as a political project would be impoverished. Feminist sociological analysis is after all about more than documenting and explaining women's experiences. It is also a 'live' political project concerned with making women visible as a sex category and advancing their interests as an oppressed social group; as such it requires a feminist vocabulary of which patriarchy is part. The most recent turn in feminist theorising has been postmodernist feminism. Although it has remained fairly marginal to industrial relations theory and research, postmodernism is recognised by some writers as potentially relevant and useful (e.g. Kelly 1998). It is in its concern with social change that traditional feminist analysis most differs from postmodernist approaches (Flax 1992; Pollert 1996). That said, postmodernist and feminist theorising share many affinities; both reject the Enlightenment concept of a unitary self and question the concepts of neutrality and objectivity (Flax 1992). Further, although postmodernist feminism offers a way to side step the problem of patriarchy, the researcher could go forever round in circles exploring the ways multiple identities manifest and are created and recreated without ever touching base with 'reality' or with material consequences. Informing the analysis contained in this book is the belief that it is possible to attempt to integrate the strengths of modernist analyses with the insights of postmodernism (Bradley 1999: 3). More precisely, it is possible to recognise the importance of discourse in shaping experiences or 'reality', at the same time as holding on to a belief that concrete social and material realities must be at the centre of the analysis.

Language and discourse do matter because they are the tools social actors use to describe their worlds, to persuade and influence others, to change or reinforce attitudes or values. However, there are 'real' differences 'out there' (Bradley 1999: 21) between women and men and among women which social researchers need to explore.

Chapter 2

Women and Trade Unions: An Overview

This chapter outlines the main features of women's trade unionism. The context of the research is the UK and therefore the discussion focuses on British patterns. However, women's under-representation in trade unions is a phenomenon affecting most countries in the developed world and therefore much of the discussion has salience beyond the UK (for example see collection of articles in Colgan and Ledwith 2002).

Union membership has generally been falling across the developed world in recent decades, largely as a consequence of economic restructuring; in particular the decline in the traditionally highly unionised manufacturing sector, a growth in the lower unionised service sector and increasing levels of 'atypical' employment (Howell 1996). British trade union density has fallen massively from its peak of 55 per cent in 1979 to around 29 per cent today (Brook 2002), resulting in a steep decline in collective bargaining coverage and reduced union power and influence over government and employers. This has occurred against a turbulent context of industrial restructuring, political hostility from the Conservative government of 1979–1997 and the introduction of a host of legislative interventions restricting and constraining trade union activities. Membership decline has now more or less stabilised and (at best) lukewarm relationships exist between the union movement and the Labour government of present, together with more enabling legislation in the form of a recognition procedure under the Employment Relations Act (1999) and 'labour friendly' European social policy. The prospects for and processes involved in British union renewal have been extensively debated in the literature (Bassett and Cave 1993; Fosh 1993; Farnham and Giles 1995; Kelly and Waddington 1995; Waddington and Kerr 2002; Heery et al 2003). Here, the interest is in the policy responses that this debate has triggered.

The long period of decline and the more recent period of relative stability of a shrunken movement have prompted fundamental reassessment of the traditional *modus operandi* of the trade unions, which had centred on representing the interests of male workers in heavy industry. Of particular note, the unions have increased the level and scope of their organizing efforts, seeking to reach previously unorganised workers and groups of workers with historically and/or currently lower rates of unionisation. (For example, see Heery and Abbott's (2000) discussion of unions and the 'insecure workforce' and Waddington and Kerr's (2002) discussion of unionisation among young workers). Indeed, in the face of social and economic changes, rather than as a result of strategic reorientation, it is evident that the characteristics of the 'typical' or 'paradigmatic' (Howell 1996) British trade unionist have changed over time. Little over a decade ago, the 'typical' trade unionist was a male, full-time, manual worker in the private production sector. Today, the 'typical' British trade unionist is just as likely to be female as male, more likely to be non-manual than manual, more likely to work in services than production and in the public sector, but the one constant, more likely to work full-time (Sneade 2001).

As the traditional, male membership base has declined, so the male dominated unions have become less important within the British trade union movement and the TUC specifically (Colling and Dickens 2001). In contrast, membership in female dominated public sector unions (e.g. NUT, UNISON) has remained relatively stable and therefore some unions have risen in importance within the movement and the TUC. These changes have prompted 'top-down' initiatives to recruit under-represented groups and 'bottom-up' pressure to democratise and to become more inclusive of diverse constituencies, especially women. There is now widespread recognition in the British and European trade union movements that renewal and regeneration, involves recruiting and retaining more members and also revitalising policies and agendas to represent membership diversity, where women are especially important simply on account of their numbers (ETUC 2002).

This constitutes an important strategic reversal since British unions have long been criticised for failing to prioritise women workers' concerns and needs and for being wedded to a unitary, white-male biased conception of members' interests (Cockburn 1991; Rees 1992; Dickens 1997). It is now indisputable that British unions need women if they are to secure a future for themselves in a restructured economy and therefore addressing women's needs and concerns is no longer a policy choice, but a necessity. The above discussion of the context of women's employment has shown that British women's patterns and experiences of employment are different from men's: in particular the strong tendency to work part-time and to be located in different occupations and industries poses recruitment, organizing and operational challenges to unions. To recruit, represent and bargain for women, it is necessary to enter previously neglected territories and debates.

Female membership

Rates of union membership in Britain are historically markedly gendered, but the gender membership gap, of an enormous twenty-five percentage points in 1979, has now closed with equal proportions of women and men now in membership (29 per cent) (Hicks and Palmer 2004). This has occurred because the rate of decline since 1979 has been much slower and less marked in female dominated areas of employment than in male dominated and while men's membership is still declining, women's is rising very slightly. Women are dispersed across British unions and of the largest ten TUC unions, two are female dominated (UNISON and NUT), and in a further two (USDAW and NASUWT) women are a narrow majority of members.

Women comprised 41 per cent of total TUC membership in 2001 compared with 29 per cent in 1979.

Examining British union density by a range of intersecting individual characteristics, women with higher level qualifications are the most likely to be union members, part-time workers are among those least likely to be members, and black women are more likely than black men to be members (Sneade 2001). This indicates that gender alone does not determine propensity to unionise; class position, age and ethnicity are also salient factors, while the structure of employment impacts on opportunity to unionise.

However, the relative importance of gender (and other demographic characteristics, such as ethnicity) for unionisation compared with occupational and other structural characteristics, is contested. For example, feminist critics argue that groups of workers (such as women and part-time workers) with historically lower rates of unionisation are not intrinsically difficult to organise (e.g. Boston, 1987; Cockburn 1991; Cunnison and Stageman 1995), as is sometimes suggested (e.g. Kelly 1998). Rather union efforts to recruit these groups have not historically been concerted enough, because they have until recently *actively chosen* to focus on male-dominated occupations and industries.

Another interconnected strand of the critique draws on evidence of workers' perceptions and experiences of trade unions and argues that there are gendered variations (Healy et al. 2004; Kirton 2005). For example, Sinclair's (1995) study of the influence of sex on rates of unionisation, finds that the male-female membership differential is partly attributable to women's lower favourability to trade unions and their dissatisfaction with their experiences of unions, especially unions' approaches to part-time workers. Similarly Walters' (2002) research finds that female part-timers felt the union was less effective and they were less likely to have been asked to join. This is worrying because the evidence (discussed in Chapter 3) shows that unions failed in the past to address the issues of most pressing concern for women, (Boston 1987), but contemporary studies continue to suggest similar neglect, indicating that the lessons of history might not have been learnt. While it might be argued that the unions' current interest in recruiting women is at least in part instrumental, the changed internal environment in British unions (i.e. the presence of a critical mass of more radical feminist women) renders the contemporary context quite different from earlier periods.

Women's participation and activism

There are a number of different ways of defining what counts as participation and activism. Fosh (1993: 578) makes a distinction between 'formal' (e.g. attending meetings, voting in elections) and 'informal' participation (e.g. reading the union journal, interacting with the shop steward). Conceptually, this multi-faceted definition is a useful way of exploring women's participation because it allows for a variety of different contributions to union life. This definition is likely to show that there is more participation than is commonly thought, especially among women who are less likely to attend meetings and take on the steward role, as we see below. Importantly, it allows for a distinction between people who do not attend union meetings because of lack of interest and those who take an active interest in the union, but have other reasons for not attending, time constraints imposed by family responsibilities perhaps. From a policy perspective this could prompt new ideas for how to increase women's participation, particularly in more formal ways. The drawback of Fosh's dualistic definition of participation is that it is not clear where the steward/representative, committee member roles fit in. Implicit is a further distinction between members who participate and activists that is reflected in Terry's (1995: 203) description of UK unions as resourced by 'unpaid volunteer activists, sometimes referred to as shop stewards', and typifies the traditional understanding in the trade union movement of activism as synonymous with office holding. The problem with this approach is that women become less visible and numerous, as activism becomes elite and role-based, which denies the participation and contribution of many (women) members.

Klandermans (1992) also stresses the multi-dimensional nature of activism, but distinguishes between those who are active, but do not hold office from those who do hold positions. Therefore for Klandermans activism and participation appear to be synonymous, but more importantly activism is a continuum, rather than a static state of being. Examples of activism among non-office holders include disseminating information, recruiting new members, attending meetings, voting in elections and reading union newsletters. The problem with this approach is that more or less every type of union activity becomes activism from the fairly passive kind (e.g. reading union newsletters) to the highly active office-holding, which is conceptually muddy as well as unhelpful from a policy perspective.

To build on the strengths, but minimise the weaknesses, of the above approaches the informal/formal distinction is employed in the book, but office holding/committee participation is included in the category of formal participation, (rather than as a separate category of activism). In this way the categories of informal and formal are themselves multi-faceted.

The picture in the unions across the developed world is one of women's under-participation relative to their share of membership (see Colgan and Ledwith 2002). Whilst little is known about levels of informal participation, levels of formal union participation among all members in Britain are notoriously low (Fosh 1993; Sinclair 1996), but lower still among women. Overall attendance at meetings is estimated as low as ten per cent (Rees 1992) and union elections are often uncontested (e.g. Fosh 1993), suggesting low levels of voting. In Sinclair's (1996) study, approximately 21 per cent of male workers attended union meetings regularly, whilst 13 per cent of female members did so. In order to compare like with like (i.e. full-time men with full-time women), Sinclair controlled for the predominance of women in part-time employment and found the significance of sex to be reduced, but nevertheless important. This insight is useful to a degree because it shows that *if* women were employed in the same objective circumstances as men, they would still participate to a lesser extent, so we need to think about why this is. However, as discussed above, the structure of employment *is* gendered, which means that we need ways of exploring women's participation that allow for the interconnection between sex categories and existing gender structures. Approaches to understanding willingness to participate are discussed later.

When it comes to decision-making structures the overall picture in trade unions throughout the developed world is of women's under-representation (Ledwith and Colgan 2002). In Britain over the last fifteen years or so progress has been made (Healy and Kirton 2000) especially on national executive committees, pointing to a degree of redistribution of gendered power in the unions. By 2002 of the ten largest TUC-affiliated unions, five had achieved women's proportionality on the executive committee and TUC delegation (Labour Research 2002). However, among the much larger ranks of paid officials and workplace union representatives (i.e. those who carry out the everyday work of the unions), women remain considerably under-represented. Research suggests that the growth in the number of paid officials in some unions should speed up a process of gendered transformation (Kirton and Healy 1999), while mergers and staff contractions tend to reduce the numbers of women and put back the project of transformation. Armed with a more radical feminism than their less numerous female predecessors, the present generation of paid women officials are pressing for the types of changes necessary to promote women's participation (Heery and Kelly 1990; Kirton and Healy 1999).

Explaining women's lesser participation

How is women's under-participation accounted for? Is it simply the case that all those willing to participate do actually participate, or do some members never translate willingness into action, and if not, why not? To explain gendered patterns of participation the global feminist sociological literature emphasises barriers and constraints, particularly the gendered division of domestic work, the organization of women's work, the organization of trade union work and the masculine construction of trade union practices and agendas (e.g. Briskin and McDermott 1993; Colgan and Ledwith 2002). This approach counters the old patriarchal arguments that women are inherently more passive (see Purcell 1979) or uninterested because of their lack of attachment to paid work (Cunnison and Stageman 1995). Meanwhile, the social psychological literature draws on rational choice theories and on theories of group identification (Klandermans 1992; Kelly and Breinlinger 1996; Kelly 1998). Both approaches are potentially illuminating, because in their different ways they separate *willingness* to participate from *actual* participation and allow for an investigation of the psychological and contextual factors, which might prevent the translation from one to the other.

The gendered division of domestic work

Recent European evidence (e.g. Fagan and Burchell 2002; Windebank 2001) shows that women continue to take the main responsibility for running the home and caring for the family, whether they work full or part-time and whether or not they have children. One consequence of women carrying the 'double burden' of paid work and household work is that they are 'time poor' with little spare time to participate in public life. It is now generally recognised that women's union participation is constrained by traditional gender roles in the home (Colgan and Ledwith 1996). In Britain, research has found women who lead traditional lives are less likely to participate (especially to become representatives), in contrast to men in the same objective circumstances (Walton 1991; Lawrence 1994).

This is mirrored in Kirton and Healy (1999) where most senior union women were 'atypical', meaning older, childfree and often partner free. These women are more able to give the necessary time, effort and commitment to trade union participation, while women with dependent children and partners are more likely to be 'time poor'. Of course, we have to allow for a life cycle effect whereby women might lead a traditional life for a period and a less traditional one later in the life course. This is a point that emerges from Cunnison's (1987) analysis of women's union participation over the life cycle. She suggests that women's working lives typically conform to a pattern of three fairly distinct phases and that it is during the third phase, when children are older, and women are possibly divorced that they are most likely to become union activists. On the other hand, women leading traditional lives are more likely to become active if they have supportive partners, especially during the child-rearing phase (Lawrence 1994; Ledwith et al. 1990). This indicates that some re-negotiation of the division of household labour is necessary and possible for some women. The relative importance of gender relations in the home is likely to vary over time and space; that is to be context specific. Research needs to be sensitive to contextual variation. For example, the three phase argument is less applicable to professional women who have a greater tendency to retain work continuity over the life course, and who constitute a large proportion of British female representatives (Cully et al. 1999). In contrast, for the many British women who 'choose' to work part-time to balance work and family life when children are young, it would seem counterintuitive to take on a 'third job' (i.e. become a union representative).

As discussed above, the gendered division of domestic work is temporally and spatially persistent and women's increased employment participation has not significantly altered this pattern; indicating that there has been no revolutionary transformation of gender relations in the home. Trade union policy interventions, such as provision of childcare or help with childcare costs, are designed to help women manage their different roles in order to overcome this significant barrier to participation, while accepting its existence. In this sense 'family friendly' measures constitute a short equality agenda (McBride 2001). There is some evidence, though, that once women become politicised through union participation, they are less likely to comply with traditional gendered domestic arrangements (e.g. Cockburn 1994; Jones 2002).

The organization of women's work

Focusing solely on women's family/household roles leaves a gap: even when enabling policy prescriptions are implemented (e.g. meetings in places and at times to suit women, childcare provision, etc), women's increased union participation does not necessarily follow. This has puzzled many male trade unionists and can easily lead back to blaming women's apathy, or to rational choice explanations, i.e. women choose not to get involved, so the main barriers to women's participation lie beyond the control of the union.

Another, but not opposing, feminist perspective highlights the organization of women's paid work as a barrier to participation. Research has established an association between the lower level and type of work that women generally do and lesser participation in unions. There are two main arguments. First, that women's paid work is less likely to develop skills necessary for trade union participation, confidence, public-speaking, participating in meetings, etc (e.g. Cockburn 1991; Lawrence 1994). Consequently when women become active, they often talk of feeling 'out of their depth' (Kirton 1999) and at a disadvantage compared to men. Second, it is argued that the organization of women's work provides fewer opportunities for the construction of a collective identity because it is often socially isolated and closely supervised. Part-time work in particular provides less opportunity to participate, because union meetings are more likely to be arranged to suit a full-time norm and part-time workers are less likely to receive paid time off for trade union duties (Munro 1999: 199).

Thus, men dominate in local union hierarchies precisely because they dominate the hierarchy of labour (Munro 1999: 25); in other words the gender segregated and unequal nature of the labour market produces a form of trade union organization which excludes or marginalises women and their gender specific interests. Historically, the British trade union movement has been quite apathetic about campaigning and bargaining to improve women's employment conditions (Bradley 1999), although the gender pay gap is less pronounced in unionised employment in Britain (Metcalf 2000).

The organization of trade union work

In view of the organisation of women's work and their role in the home and family, provision of childcare, whilst important, is very limited with regard to its ability to enable increased women's participation. Recognition of this has led to a greater policy and theoretical concern with longer equality agendas (Cockburn 1989) and what happens to women once they do participate, for example how the masculine culture and *modus operandi* act as constraint (e.g. Kirton 1999; Healy and Kirton 2000; McBride 2001) and how women seek to cope with or to challenge this situation.

Some practical aspects of the organization of trade union activity reflect historical male domination, (discussed further in Chapter 3), including for example, the timing and location of meetings, which are generally organised to suit male employment patterns, rather than the female pattern of juggling work and family (e.g. Rees 1992). Rather than providing childcare to enable women to adapt to the male norm, a better solution might be to make adaptations to the way trade union work is organized. Most British unions claim to have reviewed meeting arrangements (see for example the SERTUC survey of 2000) to make them more 'woman-friendly', but the extent to which such a policy commitment is reflected in the practice of local branches is highly questionable. Women still appear to complain that meeting times and venues are not convenient (e.g. Bradley et al. 2005; Munro 1999). The decentralised structure of British trade union organization means that national policy is not universally translated into local practice.

Another aspect of the organization of trade union work reflecting men's relative 'time wealth' is the extraordinary level of commitment required for both paid and 'lay' roles, which is addressed by a number of authors (Watson 1988; Cockburn 1991; Colgan and Ledwith 1996; Kirton and Healy 1999; Franzway 2000). Writing about the Australian union movement, Franzway (2000: 259) draws on the concept of the 'greedy institution' to underscore that union activism demands not only a considerable time commitment, but also a commitment to particular sets of values, which demand 'libidinal' energy. Since the family is another greedy institution, and by definition it is only possible to serve one greedy institution at a time, women especially face conflicting demands. Similarly, Watson's (1988) study of British trade union officers exposes the 'long hours culture' of paid trade union work and unsurprisingly the vast majority of her interviewees were men. One of the gendered consequences of the 'long hours culture' is, of course, women's relative absence from the ranks of paid officials.

The trade union agenda

The global trade union movement has been subjected to extensive feminist criticism for failing to bargain and campaign vigorously enough on 'women's issues' (e.g. Briskin 2002; Cobble and Bielski Michal 2002; Cockburn 1991). However, there has been a noticeable shift in the understanding of what constitutes a trade union issue, with sexual harassment, domestic violence and women's health issues now more likely to feature in trade union policy in many countries (Briskin 2002). In addition, the notion of a unitary set of 'women's issues' has been rightly called into question (Colgan and Ledwith 2000; McBride 2001). However, it is possible to acknowledge women's diversity, while arguing that there are sufficient common experiences among women to make it possible to identify a range of work interests specific to women (Munro 2001: 468). Various studies have found that whilst women share many bargaining concerns with men, they prioritise issues differently (Cobble and Bielski Michal 2002; Healy and Kirton 2002; Waddington and Kerr 2002). For example, women stand to benefit disproportionately from bargaining on certain specific issues such as equal pay, maternity leave and pay, childcare arrangements, sexual harassment, measures to reduce gendered barriers to career progression, part-time work etc.

'Women's issues' are easy for unions to neglect or ignore when women are absent from or marginal within the union hierarchy. In the words of Dickens et al. (1988: 32) *'the absence of women at the table has to be part of the explanation for the absence of women on the table'*: the problem then is circular. When women are present there does appear to be at least some gendering of the union agenda. For example, within MSF (Kirton and Healy 1999) senior union women have adopted woman conscious strategies with the twin objectives of transforming patriarchal union culture and union bargaining agendas. Heery and Kelly's (1988) study of British paid women officials shows that female representatives do make a difference to the conduct of trade union work because they prioritise issues such as equal pay, childcare, maternity leave and sexual harassment in collective bargaining. Conversely, where there is continued neglect and subordination of women's interests, women become alienated from their unions and their lesser participation is reinforced (Crain 1994; Cunnison and Stageman 1995; Munro 2001).

Individual orientations to participation

The discussion so far has highlighted gendered barriers and constraints to women's union participation. Social psychological approaches are useful in helping to explain why some individuals participate, whilst others do not, despite being in the same objective circumstances. Kelly and Breinlinger (1996: 20–25) identify three individual characteristics, which influence patterns of participation. The first concerns the 'locus of control'. Here greater participation may be seen as a way of gaining power and control and is of particular importance for those who feel (or are) relatively powerless, such as women, working class or black people. The second is closely related to the first and concerns 'political efficacy', the feeling that the individual can have an impact on the political process. There is some evidence that people who feel efficacious participate at higher levels (see also Bulger and Mellor's (1997) discussion in the US context) and also that those with lower levels of formal education and women perceive themselves as less efficacious. The third characteristic concerns 'individualist-collectivist' orientation, which drawing on Hofstede's (1980) work is defined as the extent to which one's identity is characterised by personal choices, goals and achievements or by the nature of the groups to which one belongs. Kelly and Breinlinger (ibid.: 25) hold that these individual characteristics provide some insight into general influences on behaviour, but that these factors have only limited value in predicting or accounting for participation in specific instances. For this task we need to explore motivations in context and consider how willingness to participate is mediated by observations/experiences of actual participation and intersects with different group identifications. Healy et al. (2003), for example, consider the cross-cutting aspects of ethnicity and gender and how these influence the experiences of work/union and orientations to participation of minority ethnic women.

Rational choice theories attempt to investigate motivations in context, taking the individual as the unit of analysis when seeking to explain willingness to participate and emphasising members' goals or what they expect to gain from participation as motivating factors (Kelly 1998). Klandermans (1992: 187/8), for example, suggests that individuals are active partly because participation satisfies important needs, either intrinsic or expressive, such as socialising with other people, engaging in interesting activities. However, he argues expressive goals are less important to workers than the instrumental value of participation or the expectation that it will help them achieve an extrinsic goal, such as improving pay and conditions.

While this approach allows for an exploration of the context of individuals' decisions, the main criticisms are its emphasis on *individual* decision-making processes and the neglect of *social* processes, which also influence patterns of participation (Kelly and Breinlinger 1996) and the in-built assumption of individuals as self-interested agents (Kelly 1998). There is also a tendency towards gender neutrality, which is unhelpful when studying women. The findings of Kirton's (1999) study of senior union women in one UK union, for example, lend support to all three strands of criticism. It shows that social support networks (gendered social processes) are vitally important in sustaining senior union women's participation over time. Women in the study stayed active despite encountering many obstacles to the achievement of their immediate goals. They did so not out of pure self-interest, but out of a belief in their ability to make a difference to women members and workers in the longer term.

Trade union and gender identities

This leads to discussion of how social identity impacts on orientations to participation. The literature on social identity is now enormous and draws on both psychological and sociological approaches, providing complementary insights. From a social psychological perspective an important sense of self derives from the groups and categories to which we belong and self-identification with a group promotes the perception of a commonality of interests (Kelly and Breinlinger 1996: 34–5), which could stimulate participation in a relevant group. This implies that from a number of groups to which they might belong, individuals consciously choose which groups to identify with. This approach avoids the pitfalls of reified social identities. For example, a black woman might self-identify with black people as a group, but not with women; therefore she would see her commonality of interests lying with black people, rather than with women and might become involved in a black political group. Of course, the 'right' to self-identify with a particular group is often contestable; e.g. what constitutes 'black'? Therefore the concept of belonging is far from straightforward.

From a sociological perspective social identities derive from the 'various sets of lived relationships in which individuals are engaged' (Bradley 1996: 24). Here, a black woman could not escape the fact that she is a woman, even if she chooses to privilege her 'black' identity. This approach suggests that social identities are not simply a question of self-identification, rather to a large extent an objective fact. However, it is the lived realities of social identity that would define perceived commonality of interests, meaning that people can experience or live their multiple identities differently.

Despite a different emphasis, both perspectives suggest that group memberships or social identities will influence patterns of participation in collective action. Bradley identifies 'three levels' of social identity: passive, active and politicised (1996: 25) and in doing so offers a solution to the question of whether social identity is a matter of self-identification or objective fact:

> "Passive identities" are potential identities in the sense that they derive from the sets of lived relationships (class, gender, ethnicity and so forth) in which the individuals are engaged, but they are not acted on. Individuals are not particularly conscious of passive identities and do not normally define themselves by them unless events occur which bring those particular relationships to the fore... . "Active identities" are those which individuals are conscious of and which provide a base for their actions. They are positive elements in an individual's self-identification although we do not necessarily think of ourselves continually in terms of any single identity... . When identities provide a more constant base for action and where individuals constantly think of themselves in terms of an identity, we can describe it as a politicised identity. "Politicised identities" are formed through political action and provide the base for collective organization of either a defensive or an affirmative nature. (Bradley, 1996: 25–26)

In this approach it is possible for different identities to intersect and to be or to become more or less salient in specific circumstances. For example, a black woman might be a teacher: this would be her occupational identity, which she is conscious of (it is an 'active' identity) and which from time to time might cause her to get involved in her union, perhaps participating in industrial action during a dispute. However, it is her black identity that is politicised and provides the base for constant action as expressed by her involvement in a black member group. This example illustrates the dynamic, fluid and intersecting nature of different identities, which may influence different patterns of participation over time, but not determine them. This multi-layered conceptualisation of identity is utilised later in the book to characterise the interviewees' identity affiliations (see also Kirton and Healy 2004).

If as Bradley (1996: 212) argues the construction of identity is a political process, how and why do different identities become active or politicised? Cunnison and Stageman (1995: 16) emphasise the material base for the construction of women's gender identity. They identify three elements as particularly significant: patterns of child rearing, patterns of care and service, and the experience of subordination. The problem with this understanding is the implication that all women experience these three elements in uniform ways. This is contrary to the growing body of literature, which highlights women's diversity and the many different ways in which women experience social realities and their gender (Charles and Hintjens 1998; Yuval-Davis

1998; Colgan and Ledwith 2000). These authors argue that the identities available to women are constructed within specific power relations, which provide the framework of choice, so class, 'race' and ethnicity for example, cross cut gender. The latter approach then acknowledges the material basis of subordination at the same time as allowing for heterogeneous women's 'realities'.

According to Bradley's (1996) approach the lived relationships women experience produce practices and discourses, which promote awareness of gender, causing a gender identity to become active. However, there is no necessary relationship between awareness and participation in collective action, as Bradley (1996) recognises. Kelly and Breinlinger (1996), drawing on Tajfel and Turner (1986), suggest three possible strategies in response to awareness of inequalities and in pursuit of a positive social identity: individual mobility, social creativity, and social change/competition. The latter two are collective responses, although social creativity is less transformative, as it might seek to promote the greater value of stereotypical feminine qualities or traditional female roles and could lead to participation in the 'other women's movement' (Sommerville 1997), pro-life groups for example. In contrast, social change/competition has more radical aims and could occur through involvement in feminist politics/groups and the adoption of a feminist identity.

Gender democracy in trade unions

Although women trade union members clearly have the right to vote in union elections and to stand for election themselves, the picture of women's under-representation in the democratic processes and structures of trade unions in most developed countries points to a gendered 'democracy deficit' (Cockburn 1995). The global trade union movement is seeking to tackle this with a review of union structures and practices (e.g. Cobble and Bielski Michal 2002). What democracy means within the trade union context is contested and is historically contingent (Nicholson et al. 1981). Over the last decade or so, the idea that democracy exists *de facto* where a small group of individuals is elected to represent the membership, has come under pressure from industrial relations (Terry 1996; Morris and Fosh 2000) and feminist authors (e.g. Cockburn 1991; 1995; Colgan and Ledwith 2002; Healy and Kirton 2000; McBride 2001; Rees 1992). The former are concerned generally with the opportunities members have to influence union decision-making, whilst the latter argue that trade unions cannot be said to be democratic if women lack influence and are absent from decision-making. From this perspective, representative democracy can be characterised as democracy without 'voice'. A grassroots (Morris and Fosh 2000) or participatory (Terry 1996) model is now the widely held ideal in the British trade union movement, with a heavy emphasis on direct forms of collective decision-making, rather than indirect representative forms. However, because unions have oligarchic and bureaucratic tendencies (Healy and Kirton 2000, McBride 2001) which can lead to the ongoing exclusion and marginalisation of women, even this might constitute an imperfect model for gender democracy.

The question is how can unions achieve gender democracy? One approach is to focus on the *structures* of democracy and to explore the types of structural change that would result in increased female participation and 'voice'. Structural changes might include a change in union rules and procedures surrounding office holding, for example, length of membership required to stand for election, the number of consecutive terms that a post can be held for and so on. Such changes can be regarded as liberal measures, as ways of letting women in, of increasing their numbers. As Cockburn (1995) points out though, it is important to distinguish between women's representation as individuals in a sex category and their representation as an oppressed social group. When women are present in democratic structures as individuals, they do not necessarily speak *as* and *for* women, which suggests that the mere presence of women does not automatically change the nature of the democratic processes and outcomes (e.g. Munro 1999). A more radical measure is separate structures for women, which aim to ensure women's representation as an oppressed social group, discussed in more detail below.

An alternative approach is to focus on the *processes* and *outcomes* rather than the structures of democracy. Young (2000), for example, is interested in why, even when formally included in democratic institutions some people find that their views are not listened to or taken seriously. She refers (2000: 55) to this process as 'internal exclusion' as opposed to 'external exclusion'. She argues that 'a theory of democratic inclusion requires an expanded conception of political communication, both in order to identify modes of internal inclusion and to provide an account of more inclusive possibilities of attending to one another in order to reach understanding'. This is very apposite in the trade union context, where certain social groups including women, ethnic minorities, disabled people and lesbians and gay men have complained not only of external exclusion, but also of internal exclusion (Colgan 1999; Kirton and Healy 1999; Humphrey 2002). The processes of internal exclusion are often enacted by majority groups by virtue of their greater knowledge of the 'rules of the game' (McBride 2001), that is union jargon, procedures and rule books (e.g. Cockburn 1991, Lawrence 1994). Linked to this, participants of meetings are often intimidated into accepting the position of the most vocal, so that even the physical presence of a group cannot be taken as a sign of democratic outcomes.

Despite its imperfections, Young (1990: 92) argues that participatory democracy has both instrumental and intrinsic value, because it requires that a diversity of interests are voiced and because it provides an important means for the development of capacities for thinking about one's own needs in relation to the needs of others. Thus, 'democracy is both an element and a condition of social justice' (ibid.: 91). From this perspective, it is imperative that unions develop strategies towards gender democracy.

Strategies towards gender democracy

Strategies to encourage women's participation were called for by the TUC in its 1979 'Charter for Equality for Women within Trade Unions' and most British trade unions have now implemented a raft of liberal and radical (Jewson and Mason 1986) reforms. Efforts to democratise are also occurring in many other countries (Trebilcock 1991; ETUC 2002). Liberal measures include, provision of childcare, gender-monitoring, women-only courses, women's officers, and new approaches to conducting union business (e.g. adjusting the timing and location of meetings). Radical measures include, reserved seats for women on governing bodies and on union delegations, electoral reform (proportionality), women's conferences, women's committees (Kirton and Greene 2002). The initiatives, which can be classified as liberal aim to 'level the playing field' with the creation of fair procedures and the dismantling of gendered barriers such as lack of childcare provision or trade union skills. The radical initiatives involve direct intervention to recast union government, for example the creation of reserved seats for women on governing bodies and to give women influence on union decision-making via women's committees and conferences (Kirton and Greene 2002). Women's separate organizing is a significant element of the more radical measures.

Women's separate organizing Women's separate organizing has become a widespread strategy within trade unions in Europe, North America and Australia (Colgan and Ledwith 2002). In 2000 13 of 27 UK unions provided some form of women-only groups (SERTUC 2000), suggesting widespread acceptance in the union movement of the strategy of women's separate organizing. The strategy has delivered gains for women: a comparison of UK trade unions between 1987 and 1997 shows a shift from a liberal approach towards more radical forms of separate organizing and a greater representation of women in union structures over time (Healy and Kirton 2000). Feminist authors have shown a great deal of interest in women's separate organizing, generally agreeing that it is a key mechanism in developing a long equality agenda (Colgan and Ledwith 1996; McBride 2001; Kirton and Greene 2002; Parker 2002). First, because it allows under-represented constituencies to come together in a safe environment (Briskin 1993) to develop their own priorities and agendas, which can then be fed into the mainstream. Second, because it legitimates the representation of women as an oppressed social group, which is key to changing the nature of what counts as trade union business. However, it is not inevitable that the latter will result.

Briskin's work has been particularly influential in developing conceptual approaches to understanding women's separate organizing. She (1993: 94–97) considers three possible claims: that separate organizing is a form of 'ghettoisation', that it is necessary to correct the 'deficits' in women, and finally that it is a pro-active positive appropriation of women's experiences. The ghetto model assumes that integration into male dominated structures on the same terms as men is the strategic aim, and that gender differences are fundamentally insignificant. From this point of view women's structures are ghettos to keep women quiet, ineffective and talking only to each other. Thus, separate organizing could be used as a strategy by the male-gendered oligarchy to maintain the status quo. It might actually legitimate the confining of 'women's issues' to powerless domains and ensure that these issues continue to be seen of marginal importance to the mainstream business of unions (Healy and Kirton 2000; Humphrey 2002). This description evokes some of the early forms of women's separate organizing following the merger of women's unions into the mainstream movement in the late nineteenth and early twentieth centuries (see Chapter 3). However, it cannot be assumed that this interpretation of women's groups is simply one of a bygone age. For example, Parker's (2002) study found mixed outcomes and that there remains tensions between women's groups and the mainstream.

The deficit model recognises the significance of gender and the need for separate organizing, but the emphasis is on women changing or on correcting women's inability to function in the male dominated movement. Briskin (1993: 96) cites the example of some women's courses, arguing that courses that focus on 'changing women' by increasing their confidence and developing their assertiveness lack the politicised content of a proactive model, which she considers problematic. Briskin's understanding assumes that following a course the now more confident and assertive women become integrated within the male norms and co-opted to the masculine agenda, rather than having become politicised through the process of becoming more confident. That this situation is the case is far from clear or inevitable.

The proactive model is informed by recognition of the gender-specific character of experience in employment, the home and wider society (as discussed above). Women must organise collectively to bring their gender specific knowledge to the mainstream to effect democratic change. In line with this, McBride (2001) finds that women use separate organizing to talk about issues not normally on the trade union meeting agenda, such as domestic violence and sexual harassment. She suggests that women's groups provide women with a constant source of authority and influence on mainstream structures, pointing to a gendering of the union agenda as a possible outcome of the more proactive model.

Briskin (1993) clearly believes that the proactive model offers the greatest potential for transformation. However, there is some evidence that current forms of women's separate organizing are underpinned by both deficit and proactive models to the extent that some women's groups may seek to work alongside mainstream, male dominated structures, whilst others seek to fundamentally recast trade union decision making processes. Parker's (2002) study finds that the objectives of women's groups reflect a pragmatic and gradual pursuit of change shaped by the constraints of the existing union framework, suggesting that a 'pure' model of either type is unlikely to dominate the strategic orientation of women who engage in separate organizing.

Despite, or possibly because of its potential for transformation, the strategy of separate organizing, although now widely accepted, remains controversial among men and women trade unionists alike. Measures such as reserved seats and separate courses are often charged with being tokenistic or patronising gestures, which rather than leading to democratic transformation might simply marginalise the issues and the people involved (Briskin 1993; Humphrey 2002; Kirton and Greene 2002). This criticism is a contemporary permutation of old dilemmas discussed in Chapter 3 and invokes the question of whether separate organizing is perceived as a feminist political tool or as an aim. A more recent criticism is that separate organizing embodies essentialised notions of women, which denies women's diversity and their heterogeneous interests (see Colgan and Ledwith 2000). Reflecting shifts in feminist theorising (discussed in Chapter 1), it is, for example, now recognised that trade union women are divided by factors such as class, age, 'race', ethnicity, as well as by occupation and political affiliation, which means that separate organizing needs to be capable of addressing within-group diversity. Within the trade union movement a further (again longstanding) criticism is that separate organizing dilutes unity and solidarity (the cornerstone of trade unionism), and is a distraction from 'real' union business (e.g. Humphrey 2002; McBride 2001). From this point of view it is politically unacceptable and resource draining, especially in a period when unions in many countries are struggling to survive.

Alternatively, to rebut these criticisms, it can be argued that inequalities are historically embedded in the structural and cultural fabric of trade unions and to redress these requires the empowering environment of separate structures (Briskin 1993). Whilst the heterogeneity of women cannot be denied, it is also possible to argue that there exists enough commonality of interest based on a shared experience of gender specific oppression to make it possible to identify a women's union agenda (Munro 1999). Further, that unity within diversity is both possible and desirable (Young 2000; Briskin 2002) and that unions must reinvent themselves as pluralist organizations in order to survive.

To accomplish its aim of working towards gender equality, separate organizing must meet certain preconditions, which Briskin (2002: 37) summarises as maintaining a (delicate) strategic balance between autonomy from the traditional structures and practices of the union movement and mainstreaming into those structures. The former creates opportunities for trade union culture and practices to be deconstructed and reconstructed, whilst the latter is necessary to prevent further marginalisation or ghettoisation of women. With regard to the form of women's separate organizing at the centre of the research presented in this book – women-only courses – it is unclear where these feature in Briskin's framework. Drawing on the idea of 'strategic balance' though, it could be argued that women (tutors and students perhaps) must have autonomy over the curriculum of women's courses (i.e. it should not be men who decide how and what women learn). But women must also have some influence on mainstream union courses so that as women participate more widely their experiences are positive. Thus, equally important as the structural arrangements, as indicated by a number of studies (e.g. Colgan and Ledwith 2002; Healy and Kirton 2000; Parker 2002), will be the way that women as agents of change act on both mainstream and women's structures to head in the direction of gendered transformation. Women-only courses are given more detailed attention in Chapter 3.

This chapter has identified key themes relating to women's trade union participation that are relevant to the research presented in this book. It has also discussed the micro level concepts and theories, derived from the feminist industrial relations paradigm discussed in Chapter 1.

Chapter 3

Women's Trade Unionism
in Historical Context

In order to situate the research in a historical context, this chapter steps back in time and outlines the history of women's trade unionism and trade union education in Britain. There is a more detailed discussion of how and why women-only courses emerged and evolved and came to be widely seen as a necessary element of British trade union education and equality strategies. The final section of the chapter discusses the contemporary nature of women-only courses.

The chapter draws mainly on existing historical literature, but also makes selective use of primary historical evidence[1] because the historical literature on women in unions has little to say about trade union education and the historical literature on trade union education has little to say about women. Similarly, empirical industrial relations research conducted much before the late 1980s was generally gender blind. For example, a 1970s study on the training of trade union officers (Brown and Lawson 1973) tantalisingly informs the reader that the sample included eight women in a survey of 175. But, the text is peppered with references to the male gender of the officers surveyed and the reader learns nothing about the women involved. The omission of a gender perspective on union education was partly rectified in the early 1980s when a series of articles in the practitioner oriented *Trade Union Studies Journal* began to address the issue of educating women.

A short history of women's trade unionism and separate organizing in Britain

It is impossible to understand how and why women's separate organizing, in particular women-only courses, emerged without a sense of the extent of women's marginalization within the trade union movement. As can be seen from Table 3.1,

---

1 The primary documents consulted were 36 annual reports of TUC women's conferences in 1926 and 1931–1966 and two reports on trade union education in 1920 (TUEEC 1920) and 1930 (Millar 1930). The existing literature covered the later period. The TUC's approach to educating women trade unionists is the focus primarily because of the enormous task involved in finding out what, if any, provision individual unions had, bearing in mind that the intention is to outline a historical context, rather than conduct historical research *per se*. TUC provision was taken as a barometer of how the movement generally approached women's trade union education in different periods, although of course initially some women's unions no doubt provided courses which would have been *de facto* women-only.

women workers have historically been an important source of members to British unions, yet the trade union movement has not always welcomed them into membership and has historically neglected women's needs and concerns (Boston 1987). Initially women responded to male hostility and external exclusion by organizing separately; it was not therefore a matter of feminist principle, rather separate organizing was widely seen as a temporary necessity, or as a form of 'interim separatism' (Colgan and Ledwith 1996). The tensions and dilemmas surrounding women's separate organizing never entirely dissolved and throughout the history of women workers' organization there has been considerable debate on the issue (Cunnison and Stageman 1995).

It was women who spearheaded early campaigns to unionise women and generally into separate unions either because of men's refusal to admit women to the appropriate industrial/occupational union or because there was no appropriate union, since men had prioritised the formation of unions in male dominated employment. For example, Emma Paterson founded the Women's Protective and Provident League in 1874 (to become the Women's Trade Union League (WTUL) in the early 1890s). The League, whilst not a trade union itself, was set up to help establish individual unions for women employed in bookbinding, millinery, mantle-making and other skilled sewing trades (Drake 1984: 11). It was a response to male opposition to women's entry to trade unions, but its ultimate aim was acceptance into the male dominated movement (Boston 1987). Accordingly, the League actually favoured the opening of men's unions to women, rather than separate unions for women, but wherever this was opposed it sought the support of men in the forming of women's unions (Soldon 1978: 17). Where women were admitted to 'men's' unions, women's sections or branches were often formed, but frequently functioned under male officers (Soldon, 1978: 60). This was an example of internal exclusion and proved an effective way of segregating women and marginalizing their concerns at the same time as keeping surveillance on their activities.

At the beginning of the twentieth century the proportion of women in paid employment outside the home was still very small (about thirteen per cent) (Boston 1987: 64), although of course working-class women took paid work into their homes. Nevertheless, a number of white-collar women's unions were formed in the early 1900s (Soldon 1978: 53), as was the National Federation of Women Workers (NFWW) in 1906. The latter was an attempt to establish a general labour union for women belonging to unorganised trades or not admitted to their appropriate union. An enormous increase in female trade union membership occurred during the First World War during which women substituted for male workers. By the end of 1918 the female membership of trade unions stood at just over one million, representing about seventeen per cent of total membership (Drake 1984: 111). During the war women had been encouraged to join the general unions, but the ranks of the NFWW had also swelled from 5,000 members to 80,000 by 1918 (Soldon 1978: 85). The union movement overall was still almost exclusively run by men, regardless of the proportion of women members, although a very small number of women had started to appear on the committees of some mixed sex unions (Soldon 1978: 56).

Table 3.1 Women and men trade union members in Britain 1900–2000[2]

Year	Female M'ship (000s)	Increase In Women %	Density Women %	Male M'ship (000s)	Increase In Men %	Density Men %	Women as % of Total M'ship
1900	154	–	3.2	1,869	–	16.7	7.6
1910	278	44.6	5.3	2,287	18.2	18.6	10.8
1920	1,342	79.2	23.9	7,006	67.3	54.5	16.0
1930	793	(69.2)	13.4	4,049	(73.0)	30.8	16.3
1940	1,119	29.1	17.6	5,493	26.2	40.3	16.9
1950	1,684	33.5	23.7	7,605	27.7	54.6	18.1
1960	1,951	13.6	24.1	7,884	3.5	53.6	19.8
1970	2,583	24.4	31.2	8,089	2.5	59.0	24.2
1980	3,771	45.9	39.9	8,468	4.4	65.0	30.8
1990	3,752	(0.5)	32.0	6,195	(36.6)	43.0	37.7
2000	3,350	(12.0)	28.9	3,884	(59.5)	29.9	46.3

For women workers, the end of the First World War brought with it widespread unemployment as employers, supported by trade unions, discharged women from jobs in factories and offices and a marriage bar was imposed in the public sector (Boston 1987, Cunnison and Stageman 1995). Union bargaining strategies now emphasised the importance of the 'family wage' for the male breadwinner. In essence the end of the war brought with it a return of the attitude that a woman's primary role was that of wife and mother (Boston 1987: 132–145), although the

---

2   Figures provided in Table 3.1 relate to the membership of all registered trade unions and not just those affiliated to the TUC. This is to avoid skewing the data at points in time when female-dominated unions (such as NALGO) first joined the TUC. Further, because of the limited historical literature on women in trade unions, data presented in the table had to be gathered from a range of sources; therefore the only way to ensure consistency and comparability across the periods was to cover all registered trade unions. Sources: 1900–1960: Bain, G.S., R. Bacon, and J. Pimlott (1972) 'The Labour Force', in A.H. Halsey (ed) *Trends in British Society Since 1900*, London: Macmillan. 1970/1980: Waddington, J and C. Whitston (1995) 'Trade Unions: Growth, Structure and Policy', in P. Edwards *Industrial Relations*, Oxford: Blackwell. 1990/2000: *Labour Market Trends* (2001: 433–441).

war had shattered the myth that women were incapable of skilled work. Against this relatively hostile climate, union women were organizing themselves inside the movement to push their cause forward indicating that separate organizing had become a political tool in response to internal exclusion, although criticism of the male hierarchy was muted (see Drake 1984). Drake (ibid.: 213) identified the chief function of women's advisory councils as 'education and propaganda', describing them as a 'practical training ground' for inexperienced women, indicating that the ultimate goal of women's separate organizing was to enable women to take up positions in mainstream structures. So far we can see that early forms of women's separate organizing constituted what Briskin (1993) would characterise as initially a ghetto model and later a deficit model.

During the two decades of falling membership from 1920–1940, the TUC was keen to recruit women in order to stem the overall decline in membership. However, the movement lacked leadership for women and there were few efforts by the male leadership to make recruitment campaigns appeal specifically to women (Boston 1987: 157). The WTUL had achieved its goal of merger with the TUC in 1920 and women were subsumed within the male-dominated organization. Nevertheless, in response to pressure from some trade union women and a motion at the 1923 TUC conference, women were afforded recognition within the TUC by the establishment in 1922 of two reserved seats on the General Council, and in 1926 of an Annual Women's Trade Union Conference (Boston 1987: 157). However, the conference was not a women-only structure. On the contrary, the male-dominated National Women's Group of the TUC tightly controlled it (TUC 1926: 3). By now women's position in the union movement was an uneasy one between separation and unity (Boston 1987).

There were no further women's conferences until 1931 when the renamed Conference of Unions Catering for Women (CUCW) was held, organised by the newly established National Women's Advisory Committee of the TUC. The significance of the change of name should not go unnoticed: the new name confirmed that the conference was *about* women and their interests rather than *for* women as a women-only structure. Women workers, because of their lower pay, continued to be viewed by men in the trade union movement as a threat to male rates of pay, especially as during the economic slump of the early 1930s men's employment decreased at a far greater rate than did women's. However, the perceived solution now was to engender greater solidarity between men and women by drawing more women into the male dominated unions (Soldon 1978: 135). Congruent with this there was opposition to women's separate organizing (Boston 1987: 162).

By 1940 a sizeable proportion of total union membership, union women's position was strengthened during the Second World War through further membership gains (arising from the mass employment of women). A new, albeit small, body of militant women stewards emerged who used the women's advisory structures of the TUC and of some individual unions as a vehicle to press their demands (Cunnison and Stageman 1995: 28), indicating a shift in the orientation of women's separate organizing. However, their claims had a liberal emphasis on equal treatment, meaning 'same' rather than 'different', with equal pay the principal concern.

By 1950 many women had left paid employment as the wartime nurseries disappeared, whilst others had returned to their former lower status, low skilled jobs. Women's primary role was once again seen by employers, trade unions and wider society to reside in the home. The trade unions showed no real commitment to acting on women's employment issues – nurseries, equal pay, and rights of married women to equal employment opportunities were all issues that received scant attention by the movement.

Throughout the 1950s an increasing number of married women entered paid employment, although the growth was concentrated in part-time, sex-segregated work, which enabled women to conform to the prevailing conservative and traditional ideology and enabled unions to continue to prioritise the 'family wage'. There was a considerable numerical and proportionate increase in women's membership, but they still only constituted about a fifth of total membership (see Table 3.1). The relatively low level of female unionisation was attributed largely to apathy and lack of trade union consciousness among women (Boston 1987: 247): in other words, the unions blamed women.

Between 1964 and 1970 women accounted for an enormous seventy per cent of the increase in members of TUC trade unions[3] and this was to be important for the development of a vocal and assertive women's voice within the movement. However, despite or possibly because of, considerable growth in women's membership, unions showed little direct concern to recruit more women into union decision-making. For example, although in 1967 women comprised around half of the membership of the public sector union NUPE, the union sent a delegation of twenty-four men to the TUC annual conference (Boston 1987: 265).

A strike by TGWU Ford women machinists in 1968 is widely regarded as pivotal in the history of women's trade unionism in Britain: it was led by women and was about women's working conditions. It has been described as the point at which feminism in the British trade union movement became significant (Boston 1987: 278–279). The so-called 'new-wave feminism' underpinned the emergence of a new understanding by trade unions of the need to widen their policy agendas to include the specific concerns of women and to introduce structural change to encourage women's participation (Cunnison and Stageman 1995). The 1970s witnessed a number of changes in the trade unions, which were to herald the beginnings of gender equality in the movement. These included: an unprecedented increase in women's union density to almost forty per cent in 1980; an increase in women's share of total membership to around thirty per cent; the drawing up in 1979 of the TUC *Charter for Equality for Women within Trade Unions*; an increase in the influence

---

3   It is important to note that rather than representing new union members, much of the increase in women's membership of TUC unions during the 1960s and early 1970s is attributable to the new affiliation of some female dominated unions, such as NALGO in 1964.

of women's separate organizing in the wider union movement; and an increase in women's representation in mainstream decision-making structures. Not all women supported women's separate organizing, but there was now more unified support than ever before and a widespread belief that it was an effective political tool, if not an end in itself (Boston 1987).

This brief history of women in British trade unions highlights the longstanding existence of a context of internal and external structural constraints inhibiting women's equality within employment and the unions, coupled with evidence of women's struggles to direct their own destiny, largely via separate organizing, within the trade union movement. Importantly the historical picture shows how the contemporary participation of women in unions, outlined in Chapter 2, has been socially constructed over time by various actors, including women themselves. The chapter now turns specifically to explore how women-only courses came into being in the context of the emergence and evolution of general trade union education provision.

Laying the foundations for internal exclusion: women-only courses 1900–1945

This section shows how the foundations were laid early on within context of male domination for women to be excluded from the decision-making processes shaping the birth and evolution of trade union education provision.

Although some British trade unions began providing schools and classes as early as the 1840s, before the First World War, the term 'trade union education' would not have been recognised. Instead, the debate centred more generally on questions of 'working class' education, with providers offering subjects as diverse as economics, history, geography, psychology and philosophy against a context of poor general educational provision (Holford 1993). A number of 'external' labour movement organizations developed the earliest provision, whilst individual unions' expenditure on education was minimal (McIlroy 1980) and TUC involvement was distant. The Workers' Educational Association (WEA), founded in 1903, was at the forefront of developments, together with the Central Labour College (CLC) and later the National Council for Labour Colleges (NCLC), founded in 1909. Ruskin College, Oxford, established in 1899 also had strong links with the trade union movement.[4] With regard to the participation of women in the nascent trade union

---

4 The unions were involved in the governing bodies of both the WEA and Ruskin College, as it was intended that students would be working class and drawn mainly from unions. The unions provided (and still provide) scholarships to Ruskin College – many of today's trade union leaders and paid officials are Ruskin *alumni*. By 1909 there was a strong element among some Ruskin students of dissatisfaction with the lack of socialist content in courses and suspicion of the college's paternalist traditions. This led to the establishment of the Central Labour College and subsequently the NCLC. By contrast with the WEA and Ruskin, whose tutors were mostly university lecturers, the NCLC drew its tutors from former and current students, creating a form of autonomous working class education.

education provision, the literature is generally silent. However, given the overall union context described earlier it is fairly safe to assume that working class meant male.

The women spearheading the early campaigns for women's equality within unions were mostly middle-class and relatively well educated. For example, Emma Patterson (1848–1886) was the daughter of a teacher, Sylvia Pankhurst (1882–1960) the daughter of a barrister, and Mary Macarthur (1881–1921) the daughter of a shop owner (Boston 1987). Their own class position would not necessarily have inclined them towards perceiving (lack of) educational provision for working class women as a major issue impacting upon their organization and this might have contributed to the relatively slow development of consideration of women's access to union education. That said it was soon recognised by male trade unionists that women needed to have better access to union education courses if they were to become more involved in the unions (Drake 1984: 42).

There were further significant developments in trade union education in the years immediately following the First World War. The WEA formed the Workers' Educational Trade Union Committee (WETUC) in 1919, which was the first scheme designed specifically for trade union members, which the unions ran themselves through their own structures (Holford 1993: 47–8), providing a range of weekend and summer schools. Because of their marginalization in the trade union hierarchy, women had little say in these developments, although the National Federation of Women Workers provided special summer and weekend schools for women (TUEEC 1920: 9).[5]

The question of how best to educate women into trade unionism more generally was discussed at the first Women's Trade Union Conference in 1926, where one woman speaker, supporting a resolution calling for parents to educate their children in the principles and values of trade unionism asserted:

> I am hoping we shall be able to educate our shop stewards and collectors, because if we got [*sic*] a proper system of educating our shop stewards and collectors we would have a larger percentage of women in our ranks than we have to-day [*sic*]. If the men would do their share the girls would have receptive minds instead of being antagonistic as they are to-day [*sic*]. (TUC 1926: 22)

The speaker did not call for women's courses, but her contribution does indicate that women were beginning to articulate their dissatisfaction with the lackadaisical attitudes of male trade unionists towards women. By the early 1930s, when greater effort was being applied to representing women and their interests, there were

---

5   Although early provision was biased towards catering for the needs of working class men, there was some, albeit limited, formal educational provision specifically for working class women. Hillcroft College, Surrey, founded in 1920 and loosely associated with the unions, was a residential, women-only college designed to serve educationally disadvantaged women, i.e. those who had left school at fourteen and who had worked since leaving school. The TUC offered *one* annual scholarship at the college.

women within the TUC arguing specifically for women's courses. Although, as stated earlier, the CUCW was not a women-only structure, it was a forum where 'women's issues' could be legitimately discussed. One important outcome was a motion to the 1931 CUCW[6] that women's courses should be piloted within the TUC (TUC 1931). In response the TUC began providing women-only schools from 1932 onwards, first experimenting with the holding of two weekend schools. It is evident from CUCW reports that members of the National Women's Advisory Committee tutored on women's schools, although it is not clear that tutors were *exclusively* female.

In 1933 it was reported at the CUCW that the weekend schools had been deemed a success and a motion was put to make them permanent and to extend the numbers. This was agreed in 1934 against some male opposition (TUC 1934). The subject of women-only schools continued to feature on the agenda of the CUCW, suggesting continued controversy and in 1936 their purpose was clarified:

> The general purpose in holding special schools for women is to bring together women in the various localities who are likely to carry on the work of trade unionism in their locality and give them enthusiasm and inspiration. (TUC 1936: 13)

In 1938 such schools were described as highly successful in fulfilling their purpose of encouraging women's participation (TUC 1938).

In summary the period from around 1900 up until 1945 witnessed the birth and subsequent formalisation of a system of trade union education. The emphasis on gender neutral constructions of working class education laid the foundations for women's exclusion. From the beginning of the twentieth century working class men gained access to education through organizations such as the WEA and by the 1920s were honing their trade union skills within the TUC education scheme. Working class women and women trade unionists were catered for less well. TUC courses specifically for women first began in 1932: ironically this was a period of defensive and conservative leadership in the movement as a whole (Boston 1987: 155). This suggesting that this innovation proposed by the male dominated CUCW was a less than radical one and that is was probably more about keeping the now more vocal women quiet, indicative of a ghetto model of women's separate organizing (Briskin 1993).

---

6   The CUCW reports have a running agenda item 'Educational Facilities', where numbers of women attending various schools are reported and where on occasion conference's discussion of women's union education is reported. These were scrutinised in an effort to discover orientations and attitudes towards educating women and are drawn upon as a resource in the chapter.

Consolidating internal exclusion: women-only courses 1945 – late 1970s

It was during the period 1945–late 1970s that external contextual events and internal decision-making consolidated women's exclusion from the growing trade union education provision. The 1945 election of a Labour government and its pursuance of harmonious industrial relations provided new opportunities for the trade union movement to expand its education provision. Attention in the domain of industrial relations increasingly focused on collective bargaining and in response the education provision of the TUC and of individual unions began to concentrate on the areas deemed necessary for trade unionists to participate in that process (Smith 1982). To the extent that overall provision grew, this was an exciting period for trade union education. However, for women, underrepresented as they were among union representatives and officers, the evolving provision had little to offer. For example, the 1950 CUCW noted that although the numbers of women attending TUC courses were higher than the previous year, they remained low (TUC 1950).

The TUC continued to hold its women's weekend schools in the 1950s, but the scale of special provision was very small, reaching only tiny numbers of union women. In 1950, for example, a total of 211 women attended TUC Women's Department Schools (TUC 1951). In 1952, reportedly 'anxious to stimulate the interest of women', the TUC arranged a special Women's Summer School at Ruskin College Oxford. The 1952 CUCW stated:

> It is not intended that this special facility should discourage affiliated organizations from nominating women as students from general schools. It was hoped that the experience of a TUC school for women would help to encourage women members to participate in the general courses and then to take a greater part in trade union affairs. (TUC 1952)

This and other CUCW reports of the 1950s indicate ambivalent and sometimes contradictory attitudes towards this form of women's separate organizing on the part of both female and male trade unionists. For example, the following year, 1953, a motion put to the CUCW on women's summer schools rekindled the controversy over whether special women's courses should be a temporary or permanent provision as agreed in the 1930s. Male and female speakers in favour of temporary status believed that separate education for women was necessary, but that the ideal was for women to take part in general schools. Speakers in favour of permanent status emphasised the continuing need to positively encourage women's participation. Supporters lost and the motion was carried to the effect that women's schools should be considered a temporary experiment (TUC 1953), suggesting little support for a feminist principle of women's separate organizing.

In 1954 the CUCW reported on a survey of 'Service to Trade Unions by Women Members'. The survey noted the scarcity of women on National Executive Committees, but stated that all the participating unions 'declared or implied that full opportunities for women already existed', implying that women did not choose to get involved and there was no need to give special encouragement. The report states:

A few [unions] stated categorically that it was the responsibility of the women to exercise their rights and one union even remarked that it was not particularly desirable or necessary to give special encouragement. (TUC 1954)

Only one of the responding unions (which were not named in the report) held women-only courses. Two unions mentioned domestic responsibilities and lack of time as deterrents to women's attendance at general courses, but there was no discussion of how these barriers could be surmounted or removed. This is unsurprising given the dominance of conservative social values during the 1950s, despite the influx of women into the labour market. The survey also reports on 'an interesting experiment' concerning a school composed of 'leading women', which points to a longstanding interest in having women educate other women:

> These students were provided with notes and when similar schools were held in other areas the most promising of the women were invited to conduct classes. Most of them did extremely well and the other women responded favourably to the experience of being helped by one of their own number. (TUC 1954: 12)

Paradoxically, in the face of the perceived obstacles to women's attendance, women-only schools continued to be relatively successful in attracting students, especially those newly involved. For example, it was noted in the 1956 CUCW report that:

> Unions are showing greater success than in the past in interesting a wider circle of their women and girl membership in educational activities. (TUC 1956)

The TUC held women's schools throughout the 1950s, although CUCW delegates were regularly reminded that the schools were intended as an introduction to trade unionism. Therefore repeated attendance by individual women was discouraged, suggesting that once women had attended a single course they should be able to cope with the male dominated context (TUC 1958). The legacy of this approach remains apparent today. There are some indications that the TUC experienced difficulties in sustaining efforts to attract newer women, but that women who did participate moved on to attend more women's courses:

> In considering the provision of educational facilities for women, it has been noted that in the last four years attendances [*sic*] have fallen by one third at the weekend schools which were intended to provide a general introduction to trade unionism, but that the two schools which had been held in each of the past two years on more specific subjects had been well attended. (TUC 1960)

The establishment of the TUC's Education Department in 1964 was another exciting and in many ways positive development which led to the mushrooming of day-release courses. However, the development also preceded and enabled a further policy shift towards prioritising the training of shop stewards (in response to the recommendations of the 1968 Donovan Report (Smith 1982). This effectively meant that the opportunity for education to stimulate interest in trade unionism prior to election or appointment as a representative had diminished. This development carried particular implications for women who were less likely to be stewards and who were therefore further excluded from the main thrust of union education. For example, CUCW reports noted in two consecutive years (1965 and 1966) that the numbers of women taking part in general TUC courses were small and had declined (TUC 1965). The TUC continued to provide women's schools throughout the 1960s and they provoked no further controversy. We cannot assume though that this was because women-only courses were now universally supported. It is equally possible that no dissent was articulated because the provision was small scale and it simply was not worth confronting the now more assertive and militant women over this minor issue.

Continuing the trend established in the immediate post-war period, the emphasis on training representatives was underscored again in 1972, when the TUC argued in response to the government Commission on Industrial Relations, for a contribution from the 'public education service' towards the cost of training union representatives in recognition of their important role in good industrial relations (Smith 1982). However, despite the TUC's fairly narrow agenda, it also established a greater variety of modes of attendance by the early 1970s, including residential weeks, summer schools, day release, weekend schools, evening classes and correspondence courses (Salmon 1983). This rendered trade union education potentially more inclusive, although in practice women continued to be underrepresented. It is not possible to be precise about the extent of women's under-representation before 1976 because the TUC only began systematically monitoring women's participation in its courses in that year. However, it is safe to assume given the greater availability of evidence, that prior to the late 1970s, women comprised only a tiny proportion of trade union students. For example, in 1976 the proportion of women TUC students was just eight per cent (Labour Research 2000). The fact that women's participation was not monitored is of course indicative of the TUC's lack of concern for developing special measures to increase women's involvement, highlighting the gender blind nature of industrial relations policy and practice of the time.

Legal reforms in 1978 conferring entitlement to paid educational leave for recognised union workplace and safety representatives had a significant impact, enabling student numbers and the number of courses provided to increase substantially, but narrowing the type of courses offered. Also, in 1978 public funds (in the form of grant aid from the Department of Education and Science) were made available for TUC-approved training courses. These developments allowed the establishment of the cornerstone of the TUC's educational provision – the Ten-day Programme, a day-release course designed to induct new workplace representatives into their role. The broad, liberal educational objectives of the early provision had now firmly given way to training courses with specific instrumental objectives (Pedler 1974).

Enter feminism – building bridges: women-only courses from the late 1970s

The third period in the history of women's trade unionism and trade union education is from the late 1970s when the demands of feminist women began to force inclusion. The twin developments of the mid- to late 1970s of paid educational leave and public funding of trade union education proved a mixed blessing and had implications for the orientation of union education. On the one hand the widespread expansion of provision and take-up was made possible; on the other hand the content of trade union education became to a greater extent circumscribed by the necessity for representatives to gain employer approval to attend. For example, a number of Industrial Tribunal cases arose from employers' refusal to grant paid time off to attend certain courses (Salmon 1983). This occurred particularly where the course syllabus was deemed to have no bearing on the employer's relations with the union, which would undoubtedly have included women-only courses.

The enabling context of the preceding period was soon to become hostile with the election in 1979 of the Thatcher government in the midst of economic and industrial decline. One outcome relevant to the discussion here was that tighter management controls rendered it more difficult for workplace representatives to take the paid educational leave which had become a central feature of collective bargaining. Further, large-scale redundancies in the unions' manufacturing and industrial heartland significantly reduced the number of trade unionists available for training. A 1982 study of shop steward training found that whilst some firms were continuing to actively encourage stewards to attend union courses (in the belief that this would improve workplace industrial relations), many others were opposed to union training (Bright and MacDermott 1982). A TUC review of its education services five years later reconfirmed that employers were becoming more obstructive in granting paid release and were also challenging attendance on grounds of irrelevance of course syllabuses (Labour Research 1988). The consequence was a substantial decline in overall provision of union education during the 1980s (Holford 1993; Salmon 1983; TUC 2001), particularly in the longer (ten) day-release courses, although short course provision increased to make it easier for trade unionists to negotiate paid leave or take unpaid leave.

Yet against this generally hostile background emerged one of the most important periods of development in women's union education attributable to the general influence of feminism, the efforts of feminist trade union women and the 'woman friendly' legal reforms[7] of the period. As stated earlier, by the 1970s feminism was a strong influence on union women, as revealed by the new demands they were making of their unions and by the way that they were using separate organizing as a strategic vehicle. Feminists now demanded inclusion on their terms: they highlighted barriers to women's participation in courses, such as childcare and called upon unions to develop responses (such as the provision of creches). Under mounting pressure from feminist trade union women, in 1978 the TUC Education Committee conducted

---

7   The Equal Pay Act (1970, 1983) and the Sex Discrimination Act (1975).

a review of education provision for women trade unionists. It examined two key areas: (i) the adequacy of existing educational provision in dealing with the issues raised by the position of women at work and in the unions; (ii) the scope for special educational provision to meet the special needs of women and to help increase their involvement and influence in unions (Elliot 1980).

The outcome was the provision of women-only 'bridging courses', which concentrated largely on basic trade union issues and on developing the skills necessary to perform in a union role. The emphasis, initially at least, was to equip women to function as activists and stewards in the male-dominated union context, i.e. to provide a bridge to participation, arguably a deficit model (Briskin 1993). This development was soon followed by the 1979 TUC charter 'Equality for Women within Trade Unions' which urged individual unions to give special encouragement to women to attend courses and promoted the establishment of women's separate organizing, although not specifically women-only courses. Individual unions also started to provide women-only courses and by 1987 nine of the eleven largest TUC unions did so (SERTUC 1987).

The historical evidence indicates that earlier incarnations of women-only courses were little more than 'remedial classes to give the ladies a chance to catch up' (Beale 1982: 104). In contrast, in the late 1970s even if the TUC aim was fairly conservative, the women tutors aimed to develop women's trade union and gender consciousness and their confidence in their personal abilities (Cunnison and Stageman 1995). The mutually supportive environment of women-only courses provided a safe place for women to develop their knowledge and skills and their own approaches as women trade unionists and, critically, encouraged women to undertake further courses (Beale 1982; Cunnison and Stageman 1995). The evidence suggests that the unions were unable to control the social processes of the courses, even if they sought to direct the educational agenda.

Women-only courses, informed by feminist practices, were usually tutored by women, on grounds that women tutors shared experiences with students and therefore could support women more effectively (Aldred 1981), therefore one of the spin-off effects of the growth of women's courses was an increase in the number of women tutors. This also impacted on the overall (mixed sex) provision, because a larger number of women began tutoring general courses and using their experiences of women-only teaching to inform their overall approach to trade union tutoring. In a 1981 article drawing on her recent experience of teaching a TUC women-only, ten-week course, one tutor described how the experience had changed her approach to trade union tutoring:

> Any doubts I had about the validity of separate educational provision for women have disappeared. Further, it has had the effect of forcing me to rethink my view on topics where I had always accepted the "correct" trade union wisdom. (Pierce 1981)

This kind of experience stimulated debate among trade union tutors about the need to address 'women's issues' within the general curriculum in order to avoid divorcing women and their concerns from mixed-sex courses. These issues were debated in the early 1980s in a number of contributions (mostly by practising trade union tutors) to the *Trade Union Studies Journal* and can be summarised as follows.

There was general support for women-only courses, but concern that they would do little to redress the male bias of general educational provision (Aldred 1981; McIlroy 1982). New course materials were needed for the general courses, dealing with the new social and economic issues, including those of specific relevance to women. For example, learning activities needed to abandon the image of the shop steward as a man working in the manufacturing industry (Holford 1993) by using language denoting both sexes to refer to stewards. Mixed-sex (or frequently *de facto, men's*) courses also needed to consider the historical and contemporary participation of women, explore sexism within unions and wider society (Beale 1982a) and confront the conflictual nature of gender relations in the labour market (Grayson 1985). For example, men needed to recognise the uncomfortable dimension of trade union history that men have not always supported women in their struggles (e.g. Beale 1982; Boston 1987). In summary it was felt that trade union courses offered potential to challenge the deep-seated sexist attitudes and assumptions prevalent in the unions, which needed to be dislodged if cultural change was to occur (Grayson 1985). A quote from one tutor captures the views expressed by many others:

> It is not just a question of educating women (like some colonised race about to be enfranchised by the colonisers) in the ways of Trade Unionism. It is a question of examining how the principles and practices of Trade Unionism can work against the interests and involvement of women, and exploring means of overcoming and changing this situation. (Elliot 1980: 4)

Despite the perceived need to rethink trade union courses altogether, women-only courses won considerable support from feminist and some male trade union tutors. They acknowledged the possible pitfalls, but believed them to be central to developing among women the confidence to challenge male norms and power within the unions. To this extent, women-only courses were positioned as a proactive form of women's separate organizing, with the aim of contributing to gendered transformation.

As trade union courses generally altered and became more 'women-friendly' (Cunnison and Stageman 1995) women's participation in mixed sex courses increased rapidly in the years following the introduction of the 'bridging' courses and the TUC charter and by 1985–6 women represented a quarter of TUC students overall (Labour Research 1988). Thus, although mixed courses were still male-dominated, women could now generally expect not to be a lone female participant, therefore the environment was less threatening to many women. In terms of the longer-term impact, Cunnison and Stageman (1995) claim that the 'feminisation' of general courses came to a halt in the late 1980s with TUC cutbacks and a generally hostile environment and relatively few unions successfully 'mainstreamed' women's equality issues into mixed-sex courses. The 1990s were a period of retrenchment and defensive union strategy generally, although women-only courses continued to be provided by the TUC and many individual unions. There is a dearth of literature on trade union education in this period, probably explained by academic researchers turning their attention to the question of whether unions could survive the harsh climate. However, the less hostile climate and feminised context of the late 1990s and early 2000s has revived interest in union education (e.g. Parker 2003; Munro and Rainbird 2000) and kindled feminist interest in the contribution women are making to the survival of the movement.

Towards inclusion: contemporary women-only courses

With regard to the contemporary empirical picture, women are now closer to proportional representation in TUC courses than formerly, making up thirty-three per cent of students (TUC 2001), against forty-one per cent of TUC members (Heery et al. 2003). Interestingly, this has produced no significant challenge to the existence of women's courses, and the debate about whether they should be temporary or permanent has not been officially revisited within the TUC since the 1960s. However, the ongoing ability of women-only courses to provoke controversy at grassroots level is shown in the later chapters of this book.

Women-only courses are now widely established and accepted as a form of separate organizing as evidenced by provision by the TUC and the majority of the largest TUC affiliated unions and many smaller unions. Many women-only courses are open to 'ordinary' members as well as to office-holders, because these courses are still seen as a device for encouraging more women to participate (Greene and Kirton 2002; Munro and Rainbird 2000; 2000a). Cook et al. (1992: 126) propose that women's courses serve four functions: induction of the inexperienced; members' exposure to female role models; their mobilisation as pressure groups for equality; and reassurance for possessive husbands. The available evidence suggests that the first three functions are critical (e.g. Greene and Kirton 2002; Munro and Rainbird 2000; 2000a) and whilst the fourth receives less attention, it can still surface as an issue (e.g. Cunnison and Stageman 1995).

Considering the centrality of union education to wider trade union objectives and the belief that women-only courses help to increase female participation, there is surprisingly little research specifically on women-only courses. Recent exceptions include Greene and Kirton 2002; Kirton and Greene 2002a; Munro and Rainbird 2000; 2000a; Kirton and Healy 2004; although some studies of women's participation touch on women's courses as part of their investigation (e.g. Cunnison and Stageman 1995; McBride 2001; Parker 2002; 2003). These studies emphasise the content, processes and outcomes of women-only courses, which give the courses a distinctive gendered character.

With regard to outcomes, one of the questions is whether women-only courses do give rise to increased female participation. Anecdotally the dominant belief is that they do, but there is only limited evidence to confirm this because research has not followed up ex-students to find out what became of them. There is also a question surrounding what counts as increased participation; i.e. moving up the union hierarchy, starting to attend meetings, doing more courses? One US study (Catlett 1986) surveyed women approximately eighteen months after attending a women-only course and found that an overwhelming majority of respondents indicated that the course had encouraged them to be more active.

Another question is whether women-only courses empower women to develop their own terms for participation (a proactive model), rather than fall in with the masculine norms and values traditionally underpinning trade union culture and practices (a deficit model). In McBride's (2001) study on women's separate organizing in UNISON, one regional women's group believed it was training women to 'run the union' through women-only courses. McBride (2001: 177) contends that the benefit of learning such skills in a women-only environment is that 'expertise' and 'democratic skills' could be conceptualised in such a way as to provide the means to challenge the male-defined 'rules of the game'. Linked to this, Greene and Kirton (2002) argue that building women's confidence is a key outcome of women-only courses. It is not always clear whether women's lack of confidence in the trade union context stems from being new or from being a woman, but their lack of confidence is seemingly enhanced by male domination of structures (Kirton 1999; Munro 1999). Participation in women-only courses appears to build women's confidence to participate in the wider union. The course activities are constructed so as to build women's confidence. For example, some women have never spoken in a public arena before and women-only courses provide a 'safe', supportive environment where they can practice.

These themes raise the question of how the processes of women-only courses differ from mixed-sex courses, i.e. why should women-only courses have these effects? Trade union courses generally employ a pedagogical model, which employs 'active learning methods' (Croucher 2004), emphasises participants' experiences; the benefits of collective organization and developing shared understandings and definitions (Walters 1996). Within this the course programme can be negotiated with participants, students are taught in small groups (up to about 20), the tutor is more of a facilitator than an expert and participant activity is central (Croucher 2004). Women-only courses also utilise this model, but the women-only environment gives it a different character, such that it is possible to argue that women learn more effectively in the women-only setting (Kirton and Healy 2004). Firstly this is because women talk about trade union issues from a women's perspective when there are no men present. This has the effect of raising gender *and* trade union consciousness (Cunnison and Stageman 1995) and secondly because modes of expression in the women-only setting are different (Greene and Kirton 2002).

The latter is worth is exploring in more detail because it is a key theme of this book. Referring to Young's (2000) notion, discussed earlier, of internal exclusion, she (2000: 56) sees the solution to the problem of internal exclusion as lying in more inclusive modes of political communication. She argues that political interactions privilege specific styles of expression, shared and favoured by members of dominant groups, for example the norm of dispassionateness and the devaluing of emotion, figurative expressions and the telling of personal stories. In contrast, Young (ibid.:

71) sees narrative as an important mode of expression for excluded groups, because the stories exchanged provide a means for group members to identify commonalities of experience, which can be part of the process of politicisation. However, storytelling is liable to be dismissed by dominant groups as pure anecdote. Thus, people's contributions to discussions are often excluded from serious consideration not because of what is said, but how it is said. The theme of modes of political communication surfaces in the analysis of the empirical data and it is also noted in Greene and Kirton (2002) that in women-only courses, participants felt at liberty to openly display emotions and tell personal stories. Other sites of women's separate organizing also provide opportunities for re-conceptualising modes of political communication, which is important for women's politicisation and indicates a link between democratic structure and process (e.g. Healy and Kirton 2000).

This chapter has shown that the development of women's separate organizing in the late nineteenth and early twentieth centuries was mainly a response to external exclusion from mainstream, male dominated trade unions (Boston 1987). Once women were more generally admitted to male trade unions, they gradually began to organise separately within them as a response to internal exclusion and hostility (Cunnison and Stageman 1995). Women's separate organizing only became a more politicised, proactive vehicle in the late 1970s under the influence of second-wave feminism. The evolution of women-only courses has to be situated within this framework of understanding. The historical analysis shows that whether women-only courses bear the hallmark of marginalization or empowerment is historically contingent upon the overall context of women's unionism in different periods.

Chapter 4

Educating Women Trade Unionists

This chapter presents an analysis of how two large male-dominated British trade unions educate women trade unionists. The unions are MSF and TGWU. The chapter briefly outlines these unions' approaches to gender equality and the various forms of women's separate organizing, within which women's courses can be located. The bulk of the chapter is dedicated to providing an overview of the unions' systems of education, a discussion of gendered patterns of attendance at mixed-sex courses and an outline of women-only education provision. Five principal data sources are utilised in this chapter: union documents; course monitoring data provided by the unions; interviews with key respondents (the unions' directors of education, education officers and tutors); observation of courses and surveys of women-only course participants.

Gender representation and gender equality strategies in MSF and TGWU

MSF section of Amicus and TGWU are both large, male dominated trade unions, with women constituting approximately 32 per cent of overall membership in MSF and 20 per cent in TGWU. MSF membership consists largely of professional and skilled workers drawn from both the private and public sectors, whilst TGWU membership is composed of manual and non-manual workers in production and services in the public and private sectors. Generally speaking the typical MSF member is more highly qualified than the typical TGWU member, but this is not an absolute rule as for example MSF has a craft section, whilst TGWU has a white-collar section.

Table 4.1 provides data on women in MSF and TGWU as members, activists and paid officers. Both unions have achieved or exceeded women's proportional representation in two senior lay structures: the executive council and TUC delegation, whereas women in both unions are under-represented amongst national and regional paid officers. In addition, little is known about the gender composition of workplace representatives and shop stewards (the former is the term used in MSF, whilst the latter is the term used in TGWU reflecting its larger 'blue collar' membership), however both unions are trying to develop strategies to recruit more women as representatives. One measure dating from around the late 1990s has been the introduction of 'women's reps', a cadre of female representatives with the special responsibility of supporting women members. It is intended that 'women's reps' will add to the existing complement of representatives and stewards, rather than act as substitutes.

Table 4.1 Women in MSF and TGWU as members, activists and paid officers

	MSF	TGWU
Total membership	416,000	832,312
Women in membership	133,141	170,384
Women as % of members	32	20
Women as % NEC members	33	33
Women as % of TUC delegation	31	29
Women as % of national paid officers	20	5
Women as % of regional paid officers	20	10

Source: Labour Research 2002, 2004

Greater advances towards gender equality in the lay decision-making structures, when compared with the paid official corps can be attributed to the pursuit of gender democracy having led to the introduction of a raft of gender equality strategies. These include women-only courses, regional and national women's committees, national women's conference and reserved seats for women on the executive committee, which over time have had the effect of increasing women's representation. This is not to say that no effort has been expended on increasing the number of female paid officers. For example, in the mid–1990s MSF established an officer training programme to increase the presence of women and other under-represented groups (see Kirton and Healy 1999). TGWU recruits paid officials from the ranks of activists and lay officers, which given male domination of the union has tended to bias selection towards men. However, the union has now recognised this as a problem and is seeking to develop strategies to tackle women's under-representation (TGWU 1999). Women's courses are for example used for the purposes of identifying women who might go further in the union and in 2001 the union held a training course for senior female activists on how to get paid employment with the union.

Thus, both unions have utilised the strategy of women's separate organizing, at the same time as providing channels for women's guaranteed representation in the 'mainstream' such as reserved seats on executive councils and commitment to a principle of women's proportionality on all union committees and delegations. Their approach and record of achievement (e.g. women are at least proportionally represented on the executive committee) compares favourably with other large unions (see Kirton and Greene 2002). However, it is clear that the gender equality project is an ongoing one in both unions with education seen as a major tool to this end.

MSF and TGWU have comprehensive in-house education programmes with broadly similar aims established by their executive bodies. These are to: provide education and training for members, representatives, activists and full-time officials; offer locally-based and national provision; provide broader social and political education; use education as a vehicle to promote the greater participation of under-represented groups and offer members the opportunity to embark on an 'educational ladder' linking with mainstream further and higher education. However, the two unions have established different systems to achieve these aims.

Educating MSF women

Education provision in MSF

Before focusing specifically on women's education, this section briefly sketches overall education provision in MSF so that it is possible to see how women's courses fit in. The union provides a range of learning opportunities for representatives and members within a centralised, national education provision including residential courses and distance learning. The education department and national courses are located at the union's residential college – Whitehall College in Bishop's Stortford, which has a capacity of about 3,500 students per year. The college can accommodate up to 55 students, although most courses are small: typically 12–13 participants (maximum 18–20), with events such as 'Women's Week' and 'Family Learning Week' offering a choice of parallel courses. In common with most other trade unions, MSF courses are free of charge to members and representatives and the cost of travel is also reimbursed. Free crèche facilities are available, although the take-up is quite minimal with the women-only 'Women's Week' and female dominated 'Family Learning Week' unsurprisingly having the highest take-up. Most participants receive paid leave from their employers and a regional official will intervene on behalf of any representative denied paid leave. In the case of 'ordinary' members, some receive paid leave others take annual leave. Anyone unable to take any form of paid leave to attend a course can claim a flat rate weekly payment in compensation for loss of wages. According to the Director of Education, this rarely occurs.

The union also provides locally based courses through its regional councils, organised by regional education officers, who are lay activists. These are usually short courses held at weekends on topics such as organizing, health and safety, legal rights, equal opportunities, women's courses and black member courses. The regional and national women's committees also regularly organise weekend schools/ workshops for women members.

Nationally, the range of courses provided by the union is broad, from introductory courses for representatives, to sector-based courses, to issue-based courses, to courses for members, examples of which are shown in Table 4.2. Overall the provision is concentrated on basic training for new representatives and for safety representatives. This is partly a response to demand, but is also seen as a priority for the education department. No courses are made compulsory for MSF representatives, although they are strongly advised to attend appropriate courses.

MSF course tutors are either paid education officers or professional freelance tutors. Freelance tutors are mostly individuals who have had a relationship with the union for some time and usually have a history of professional involvement in the union movement. For example, of the two freelance 'Women's Week' tutors in 2002, one was a full-time tutor at an Adult Education Institute (and provider of union courses), whilst another was a former TUC education officer.

The education committee steers the direction of the provision, although policy is operationalised by the education department. On occasion the education committee requests specific courses – for example in 2002 the committee asked for equality courses to be provided for the union's paid officials – however its role is more one of overseeing and advising. Generally, it is the responsibility of the team of education officers within the education department to make decisions about the offering. Provided proposals for new courses fall within the aims and objectives of the union, they are given the opportunity to develop and try out new ideas. Also, freelance tutors are free to introduce their own materials into courses provided these fit within the course programme established by education officers. The courses follow a traditional trade union pedagogic approach (Walters 1996; Croucher 2004), centred on 'active learning methods' involving participatory activities and student interaction, but involving some tutor input, although the precise mix of activities varies according to tutoring style.

Gender composition of MSF mixed-sex courses

Although overall women are proportionally represented on mixed-sex MSF courses, the education department has a number of positive action measures in place, which seek to ensure that the proportions of women attending courses are sustained if not increased. For example, the union monitors course attendance by gender and ethnicity and then uses this information to target course advertising at particular groups.

Table 4.2 provides a breakdown by gender at national MSF schools over a one-year period demonstrating that despite these measures men almost always dominate the union's mixed-sex courses. The exception is courses specifically for National Health Service (NHS) representatives, where there is a gendered reversal of domination, with women accounting for more than two-thirds of participants, almost certainly a function of the predominance of women employees in the health sector. There is also a noticeable decline, with the exception of *Economics* in the proportion of women attending intermediate and advanced courses. This is worrying because it could indicate that women are abandoning or not progressing in their union careers.

It is also interesting to note that women are more than half of participants at *Lifelong Learning* and *Family Learning Week*. These gendered patterns of attendance can be interpreted in different ways. For instance, they could simply be a function of male and female spheres of interest. However, taking the *Pensions*

Table 4.2 Gender composition of selected mixed-sex MSF national courses 2000

Course	Female %	Male %
Introductory Courses		
New Representatives	39%	61%
Health and Safety	41%	59%
Skills for Organizing	45%	55%
NHS Representatives	68%	32%
Intermediate Courses		
Representing Members at Work	22%	78%
Improving Negotiating Skills	25%	75%
Tackling Bullying and Stress	17%	83%
Advanced Courses		
Contemporary IR	15%	85%
Economics	31%	69%
Pensions	0%	100%
Other Courses		
Lifelong Learning	69%	31%
Family Learning Week	57%	43%

course as an example, MSF's National Women's Sub Committee held a well attended Women's Weekend School in 2000 on pensions, in addition to weekend events on stress and bullying. That said, it might be that certain courses do not 'speak' to women's specific concerns (*Economics* or *Contemporary Industrial Relations*, for example?), and that given gendered time constraints women select the courses they consider to be most relevant. Second, it could be inferred that (some? many?) women will opt for women-only courses wherever these are available. For example, women-only courses are available in negotiating skills (where women's attendance in mixed courses is relatively low). In contrast women-only courses for new representatives and in health and safety are not available (where women's attendance at mixed courses is higher). Third, there is some evidence from the existing literature (for example, Lawrence 1994) that women and men rank trade union issues in a different order of priority and participation in union courses may reflect these gendered divisions. For example, women's higher attendance at the *Lifelong Learning course* could be an example of this with women according higher importance to training and promotion than men (Lawrence 1994; Waddington and Whitston 1997). Fourth, *Lifelong Learning* and *Family Learning Week* are open to 'ordinary' members as well as representatives and since women are less numerous among the latter than they are the former, this could explain their greater presence at these particular courses.

On the other hand, the overall picture of male domination of MSF's courses is not surprising given that men constitute two thirds of the union's members. Using this quantitative measure, interestingly women are actually over-represented in three types of generic training courses for representatives – *New Representatives, Health and Safety, Skills for Organizing* (see Table 4.2). This suggests that the union's record in attracting women to courses is good in so far as women are more than proportionally represented in at least three core courses. Even though women are under-represented in most intermediate and advanced courses, overall they constitute 40 per cent of course participants in the period.

Publicising MSF women-only courses　　Although women are proportionally represented among course students, there is still a perceived need in the education department to sustain efforts to recruit women to courses. The director of education described advertising as 'the single biggest difficulty' for the education department, especially when it comes to attracting women. In an attempt to address this problem, courses at Whitehall College are publicised through a variety of channels in order to increase the numbers of members receiving course information. Leaflets are sent to regional paid officials, branch secretaries and workplace representatives and directly to people who have already attended a Whitehall course. Regions, branches and workplaces use a variety of more or less extensive and effective methods for disseminating course information to members and representatives, including announcements at meetings, notice boards and mailings to members' homes. That said, the 'snapshot' surveys conducted as part of this research (see Table 4.3) found that the vast majority of students heard about 'Women's Week' in 2000 and 2002 via published materials.

On the one hand, this is positive in the sense that women get to hear about courses through their own actions, i.e. reading union literature, indicating a prior or existing interest in the union. On the other hand there are worryingly low numbers of women hearing about 'Women's Week' by word of mouth, possibly suggesting low levels of sponsorship for the school or poor communication with women members at workplace/branch level, the latter unlikely to *foster* interest in the union.

Table 4.3 How course participants heard about 'Women's Week' (MSF, 2000/02)

Publicity Method	Number of Respondents (%) N = 67
Literature/publications	50 (75%)
Word of mouth	15 (22%)
Other	2 (3%)

Women-only courses in MSF

As can be seen there is a very mixed and variable pattern of women's attendance at mixed-sex courses, which is difficult to explain using monitoring data alone. However, it is certain that mixed-sex courses within MSF are mostly male-dominated and although this is not surprising, given that the union itself is male-dominated, this situation nevertheless is a cause for concern for a union hoping to pull more women members into participation. This fact alone makes a case for women's courses, which provide a 'safe space' for women's learning and a relevant curriculum. The union's director of education locates the purpose of the union's national women's school within positive action strategies:

> Women's Week is part of a programme of positive action to equip women with the knowledge, understanding, skills and confidence they need to be more effective in the union at all levels. It's about ensuring women take up their place in the union and increasing their participation rates.

'Women's Week' is the cornerstone of women-only education in MSF, although the regions also offer women-only courses from time to time as stated above. 'Women's Week' was initiated by the female director of education, supported by the women's committee, in 1982 against a background of male domination of mixed courses. It is without doubt significant that it was a woman who made the case for women's courses, which links to the debate about the importance of the characteristics of trade union leaders. The director of education believed that women's courses have a major role to play in developing women, particularly towards participation in the union's higher echelons:

> The activity rates of women as workplace reps are reasonably high, but when you get to the decision making bodies and the political administrative structure of the union, you get the phenomenon of the disappearing woman. That has changed to some extent and I think the women's courses are part of the impetus for that change. Women from the courses go on to become regional council members, to speak at annual conference. They become representatives on the executive and also full-time officers.

'Women's Week' is a five-day residential school, which attracts 35–40 students. It is publicised through the usual channels described earlier and the education officer responsible has also developed a database of women who attend in order that they can be mailed directly with course information. This approach has been taken because of concern that some (male) branch secretaries do not support women-only education and therefore do not make women members and activists aware of its availability. This is a particular problem in relation to newer women, which 'Women's Week' hopes to attract who are unfamiliar with union structures and processes and are more dependent on their branch secretaries for information. The director of education also indicated that there had originally been some opposition, especially from male paid officials, to the establishment of women's courses. Twenty years later there was still a degree of resistance, which could take the form of questioning the point of investing in this type of course, or asking why there is no men's course. Generally though there is now little opposition suggesting a greater acceptance of women's separate organizing and the important role that women have played in establishing it as legitimate.

Reflecting its aim of increasing women's participation, 'Women's Week' is open to 'ordinary' members as well as to representatives and some students will have completed a number of union courses, whilst for others it might be their first course. Since 1999 it has offered four parallel courses: Developing Women's Leadership (MSF 2000), Negotiating Skills for Women (MSF 2000a), Assertiveness for Women (MSF 2000b), Organizing Skills for Women (MSF 2000c). Women can attend 'Women's Week' as many times as they wish and it is quite common for a woman to complete all four courses.

Course content The analysis in this section is informed by course materials collected in the periods of observation and by interviews (with the director of education, education officer, tutors) and observation. 'Women's Week' courses focus on personal skills' development. This was an approach developed in the mid-late 1990s by the female education officer, partly in response to dwindling demand for 'Women's Week' courses and partly from her belief that women need certain skills in order to participate in the union on equal terms. Her own background as an activist in the union and former 'Women's Week' student had informed her belief. The underlying objective is to deliver an experience of value to participants, which it is hoped, will increase their involvement within the union.

The courses can be characterised as student-led: they emphasise active student participation based on small group discussions and feedback, and relatively little time is given over to tutor input. During the course, typically each new topic is preceded by approximately ten minutes of tutor input, after which there might be one or two student activities which could last anything from half an hour to one and a half hours. The tutor explains what the activity involves and this is also set out in the course handbook. The course handbook also contains notes to support the topics, which the tutor reads through, giving examples to explain concepts and issues surrounding practice. Students have the opportunity to make comments and ask questions, which they frequently do, highlighting the student-led nature of the courses. If the course starts to run behind schedule, then it is the tutor input, rather than the student participation that will be shortened in order to catch up. On these occasions students are advised that the course handbook contains information sheets which they can read in their own time. Following group feedback, the tutor summarises the key learning points from the activity. All of this emphasises the primary importance accorded to active student participation and the role of the tutor as facilitator, rather than expert (Croucher 2004).

The topics are often generalised and many activities are purposely not explicitly situated within the context of trade union activism in order that inactive women members might also find them beneficial. For example, on the 'Negotiating Skills for Women' course the first day is spent exploring in very general terms what negotiation is and how it is carried out (MSF 2000a). The second day considers legal rights for trade unionists in negotiations, while the rest of the day is given over to generalised principles in negotiating strategy. The third day looks at individual behaviour in negotiation situations and the fourth day has a substantial group negotiating activity. The course activities can either be situated in the trade union context or not, depending on the balance of student interest/experience. If most students are active members or interested in becoming active, the tutor will place the emphasis on the workplace/union contexts, otherwise the context will be more generalised. For example, on the negotiating skills course participants' attention was drawn to the way that people continuously negotiate in their everyday lives: this prompted women to talk about negotiations over divorce, access to children etc. Significantly, on the second or third day the tutor asks students to review the course so far and to make any suggestions for extra/alternative issues they would like to address. This indicates a degree of flexibility with regard to course content, and also highlights again the student-led and negotiable nature of the courses.

Course delivery: the role of the tutors   'Women's Week' tutors are always female. Neither of the two freelance tutors had attended women's courses as students, although they had both undertaken mixed-sex union courses. Significantly, all the 'Women's Week' tutors self-identified as feminists and expressed an ideological commitment to women's separate organizing. The question 'what makes a good tutor for women's courses?' elicited the following responses:

> You have to see the value of women and want to be part of the process of getting them to see it too. You need to be good at involving others, a good listener and interested in other women. (Ruth)

> Empathy with other women is essential and it's also essential to understand how people learn. You need to keep a very close eye on individual women so that you can help them learn. It's also important to establish relationships of trust within the group. (Gina)

A good listener. You need to be flexible enough to respond to the needs of the group and what they want to learn. You need an empathy with women and you need to create opportunities for women to admire each other to boost their self-esteem. (Jackie)

As can be seen the tutors emphasised certain qualities, which in their view facilitate women's learning. Thus, they stress the social processes of the courses, rather than their own didactic role as experts or teachers. This is congruent both with trade union pedagogy and with feminist conceptions of organizing.

Educating TGWU women

Education provision in TGWU

This section provides an overview of TGWU education provision in order to situate the subsequent discussion of women's education. TGWU provides a range of learning opportunities for stewards and members. The union operates a largely decentralised education programme with the bulk of its provision regionally rather than nationally located. In terms of student numbers, around 500 per year participate in national courses, compared with around 10,000 per year participating in regional courses. According to the director of education, this is a function of the larger size of the union – with over 800,000 members extensive regional provision is deemed essential in order to provide a cost effective education programme and to reach as many stewards as possible.

The education department is located at the union's National Office in London. National courses are held at the union's hotel and conference centre 'T&G Centre' in Eastbourne, which has a capacity of about 85 persons. Crèche facilities can be made available at both national and regional courses, but actual provision depends on a viable number of applications being made. Regional education programmes are the responsibility of paid regional education organisers (REOs) (one in each of eight regions). Until 2000, three of the eight REOs were women, but due to some internal movement in 2002 the union had only one woman REO.

All stewards are required to attend a shop stewards course and members attending courses (e.g. National Members' School) are first required to complete the first level of the union's Home Study Course. This distance learning course aims to give students 'a good idea about the history, the structure, the policies and objectives' of TGWU (TGWU 1998). It is described as the first step on the 'T&G Learning Train' (TGWU 1998). The rationale for making the course a pre-requisite is that individuals should demonstrate a commitment to the union and to union education prior to the union investing in her/his training and education. The requirement, set by the General Executive Council (GEC) is controversial, however, with some officials believing that it could deter some members (especially women and newer activists) from participating. Some members reportedly find the course quite burdensome, particularly those who left formal education many years earlier.

Importantly, TGWU operates its courses on an 'all expenses paid' basis, which includes crèche facilities and travel. TGWU expects the majority of students to take paid educational leave to attend union courses. It seems that for most stewards this will be the case, although 'ordinary' members may not be granted paid leave in some workplaces. The union compensates individuals unable to take paid educational leave with a flat rate daily payment. The director of education said that he did not believe that the issue of paid educational leave was an obstacle to greater participation in union education. However, since women are more numerous among 'ordinary members' than they are among stewards, it may be that women are less able to take advantage of paid educational leave, since only stewards are legally entitled to it. This was certainly a factor suggested by some key respondents.

Delivery of the TGWU system of education is largely decentralised, but planned and controlled from the centre. First, TGWU's national and regional provision operates within the union's '1992 Education Guidelines' and formally the general secretary has to approve all changes to existing courses and any new courses. The guidelines set out two core objectives: firstly, the training and education process should begin for all shop stewards within six months of election/appointment; secondly, equality courses should be offered to all shop stewards by all regions (TGWU 1992). Regional Education Organisers (REOs) are required to ensure that these two objectives are met. To meet the second objective, there are two types of courses: women's and black member and equalities awareness courses. REOs report quarterly to regional education committees (RECs) on their activities. In turn the RECs send these reports to the national education department, which must include gender and ethnic monitoring data. In this way the director of education is able to oversee regional education. This chapter presents data (in Table 4.4) from the union's largest region – Region 1, covering London, the South East and East Anglia.

Second, national courses utilise a mandatory set of course materials designed by national office. These are issued to tutors and must be adhered to, although tutors are able to make suggestions for changes at the tutors' 'debriefing' meeting, which follows national courses. In contrast, tutors on regional courses have some discretion as to what kinds of activities and information they use on their courses. REOs meet regularly to discuss developments in their regions and to share best practice and reports from these meetings are sent to the director of education who closely monitors the regions' activities.

Third, proposals for new courses also emanate from various TGWU committees and the education department is then responsible for ensuring that the regions provide these courses. For example, the National Women's Committee proposed a 'women's political course' and some of the industrial committees suggested women-only sector based courses. Also the education department and the equalities department work very closely together to develop new ideas – for example, the equalities department initiated a campaign on sexual harassment, which was backed up by a regional and national educational programme developed by the education department.

The tutoring system in TGWU has some unique and interesting features, which are worthy of detailed explication. Courses are tutored by education and research department staff from National Office, but mostly by 'lay' tutors from the regions. There is also a specialist national women's education tutor who is responsible for the development of course materials for national women-only courses. The large cadre of full-time 'lay' tutors located in the regions are appointed by TGWU, but technically employed by a partner college or university. The union also has a number of casual tutors, who are usually members in full-time employment who teach perhaps one or two courses per year. All tutors must have a history of 'appropriate' active involvement in the union.

'Appropriate' involvement has traditionally meant steward, branch secretary etc and given male domination of these positions this has resulted in women's under-representation amongst lay tutors. However, in recognition of this and at the behest of the (female) national secretary for equalities and the director of education, more recently women, black members and members of other under-represented groups are considered if they have been involved in, for example, women's committees, black member forums etc. Therefore there is a requirement for demonstrable commitment to the union, but each case will be judged on its own merits. This then operates as a form of positive action to redress women's and black members' under-representation. Of course the possibility that women will be less able to meet the prerequisite of prior activism still cannot be ruled out. The rationale for the lay tutor system is the belief that TGWU members are in the best position to understand the issues and problems facing other TGWU members, and they can also situate those issues and problems within the context of the union's structures, policies and objectives. This is privileged over gender or other demographic considerations.

The process to become a tutor requires considerable commitment itself, which could also produce gendered outcomes. Would-be tutors need to produce a portfolio of evidence of their own activism, which then informs the basis of the director of education's decision whether or not to accept them to a tutor-training course. They must also have completed a considerable number of TGWU courses before they are invited to attend a compulsory, tutor-training course. This is a five-day residential course taught by the director of education. It entails formal assessment and anyone who fails the course might be given the option to retake it or might be 'counselled' away from the ambition to tutor. Successful students work in partnership with an established and experienced tutor, until they are deemed ready to work alone. This is described as an 'apprenticeship' scheme. Tutors usually start working for the union on a casual basis and some are then subsequently appointed to positions in partner colleges and universities as and when vacancies occur. Some of the women interviewed for the study had ambitions to become union tutors and for a small number of activists it is a route to employment with the union.

Gender composition of TGWU mixed-sex courses

TGWU monitors course attendance by gender and ethnicity both nationally and regionally, in order that any patterns of under-representation (relative to women's

Table 4.4   Gender composition of selected mixed-sex TGWU Region 1 courses (2000)

Course	Female %	Male %
Introductory Courses		
Shop Stewards	24%	76%
Safety Reps	19%	81%
Voluntary Sector Reps	57%	43%
Pensions	21%	79%
Intermediate Courses		
Shop Stewards Part 2	22%	78%
Safety Reps Part 2	12%	88%
Advanced Courses		
Branch Secretaries	13%	87%
Shop Stewards Part 3	22%	78%
Safety Reps Part 3	13%	87%
Other Courses		
Bargaining for Equality	56%	44%
Race Equality	16%	84%
Law at the Workplace	10%	90%

share of membership) may be investigated. Table 4.4 shows that women are relatively well represented at some courses, for example, all levels of shop stewards' courses, but under-represented at others, for example, safety representatives' and branch secretaries' courses.

Monitoring information also contributes to policy developments, such as increasing the women-only provision. Women's participation in Region 1 has fluctuated since 1984 (when systematic records were first kept), but averages around twenty per cent (Batten 2000), indicating difficulty in breaking through the twenty per cent proportionality barrier irrespective of new publicity channels, more issue-based courses, etc.

Publicising TGWU courses

Although like MSF, TGWU has achieved women's proportionality overall in courses, the union perceives an ongoing need to reach newer women and to sustain efforts to recruit women students, entailing giving consideration to publicity methods. TGWU courses are publicised to stewards and members using a variety of methods, including mailings to branch secretaries, advertisements in the union's magazines (this method was particularly effective when women's courses were advertised in the women's magazine *Together)*, mailings to REOs, Regional Women's Organisers (RWOs), and Regional Industrial Officers (RIOs). REOs are responsible for producing regional course brochures, either quarterly, six-monthly or annually, depending on the scale of provision in the particular region, which are then distributed to branch secretaries, who in turn disseminate to stewards and members. According to key respondents there is a question mark around how effective the various methods are. For instance, if announcements are made at meetings about forthcoming courses, and membership attendance is low or perhaps male-dominated, there is a large risk that women members do not get to hear of courses available to them. The union's national officers are aware of this problem and seek to address it by using multiple publicity methods and continuing to monitor attendance. Table 4.5 shows how students heard about the National Women Members' School. Whilst a narrow majority heard about the course via written materials, a substantial minority did so via word of mouth, suggesting that a sizeable proportion of students are in the 'communication loop' within TGWU.

Table 4.5 How course participants hear about the National Women Members' School (TGWU 1999/2001)

Publicity Method	Number of Respondents (%) N = 99
Literature/publications	50 (51%)
Word of mouth	34 (34%)
Other	14 (14%)

Women-only courses in TGWU

Women-only courses have been provided at regional level by TGWU since 1979, when the union's conference took a policy decision to do so. This was around the time the TUC introduced 'bridging courses' for women (discussed in Chapter 3), but as the TGWU education provision had already broken away from the TUC there was a perceived need to provide its own women's courses to keep apace of women's demands. According to key respondents there has been no serious assault on the principle of women's courses, although they might meet disdain and ridicule in some union arenas. They now operate at three levels: regional and national courses for women shop stewards and the National Women Members' School open to any woman member. The establishment in 1997 of the National Women Members' School extended the women-only provision. The director of education described its aims:

> The course creates a space for women in which they can share experiences. Without a doubt it promotes greater female participation. The course puts women in touch with the union and with each other. Importantly it puts newer women in touch with successful women.

The existence of women's courses has to be situated within gendered patterns of course attendance. As seen earlier, overall women are proportionally represented at mixed-sex courses, but given small group sizes, actual numbers of women attending each course can be tiny and this constrains the likelihood of women's experiences being at the forefront of discussions.

The National Women Members' School is a biennial event. It began in 1997 following observations by union officials that women appeared very reluctant to attend mixed member schools (which are heavily male-dominated). The school attracts 50–70 students and offered four parallel courses in 1999: 'Women at Work' (TGWU 1999a), 'Women beyond the Workplace' (TGWU 1999b), 'Women in Europe' (TGWU 1999c), 'Recruitment and Organization for Women' (TGWU 1999d). In 2001 a new suite of courses was offered: 'Understanding the Union and Maximising Women's Involvement' (TGWU 2001), 'Public Speaking' (TGWU 2001a), 'Campaigning and Bargaining for Women' (TGWU 2001b), 'New Employment Rights and Organizing Women Workers' (TGWU 2001c), 'Women and Pensions' (TGWU 2001d). The new courses were developed to give a fresh look to the school to encourage previous participants to attend again; in response to new ideas from education department staff; the concern that women were very poorly represented on some mixed courses, particularly pensions.

Interestingly, there originally existed a rule, made by the General Executive Committee, that once a woman had attended the National Women Members' School, she would not be permitted to attend again for a period of five years. Instead, she would be encouraged to take advantage of other courses the union offers – either mixed-sex members' schools, or stewards' courses if appropriate. The stated aim was to ensure that the school continued to attract new women and did not become dominated by experienced stewards and activists. This rule was abandoned by the time of the 2001 school, although its introduction in the first place reflected a dominant belief in TGWU that women should not confine themselves to the comfortable space of women's groups. It also possibly pointed to an underlying suspicion of women's separate organizing as a long-term strategy, seeing it more as an interim measure.

Reflecting the centralised structure of TGWU, recruitment to women-only courses is a bureaucratically structured affair, fraught with political power struggles between different groupings in the union, mainly the RWOs and the RIOs. There are internal political problems between RWOs and RIOs (who are mostly male) with the latter group reportedly feeling threatened by the former, hindering co-operation between them. Arising from the more recent involvement of RIOs, a new development in women-only education at regional and national levels has been the provision from 2000 onwards of national, sector-based women-only schools: Women in Transport, Women in Manufacturing, Women in Food and Agriculture, Women in Services open to both active members and stewards. The intention is to provide two courses per year, rotating the sectors. The idea behind this development is to link women's education with the work of RIOs and to encourage RIOs to think of women's involvement as their 'problem'. There are signs that this strategy is having some positive impact, as the courses held in 2000 and 2001 reportedly recruited well. It is not clear whether healthy recruitment levels are a function of the recruitment channels or the fact that the courses are sector-based and therefore appeal to a narrower set of common interests, in contrast to the general women's schools, which of necessity have a broad curriculum.

Course content The analysis in this section is informed by course materials collected in the periods of observation and by interviews (with the director of education, education officer, tutors) and observation. The courses can be characterised as student-led: they emphasise active student participation based on small group discussions and feedback. However, while relatively little time is given over to tutor input when compared with, for example, certificated courses in further and higher education, there is typically more tutor input on TGWU women's courses compared with MSF. For example, the 2001 course 'Public Speaking' (TGWU 2001a) contained two lecture style presentations by TGWU national officers, each lasting approximately two hours. These sessions are not entirely passive: students can and do interject and the presentations are lively and entertaining. It is also the case that during the rest of the course tutor input is at a similar level to MSF women's courses.

The education department produces course handbooks and tutors are expected to follow the programme using materials provided, because there is a firm belief that certain areas of information and knowledge must be imparted on the courses. Therefore there is less negotiation of course content than on MSF courses. In practice though tutors do introduce alternative activities if they feel that the ones provided are too complex or uninteresting for the particular group of students, but an important observation is that tutors do adhere to union issues. Therefore course activities, unlike in MSF, whether devised by the education department or by tutors, are always explicitly situated in work/union contexts focusing on issues such as rights at work, grievance/discipline handling, bargaining, steward duties, participating in a branch. These issues are gendered by a combination of course materials (an example of a campaign of equal pay (TGWU 2001a), tutors' interpretations and students' contributions. For example, the first day of the 'Public Speaking' course is spent exploring how to run a campaign. The discussion was focused on union campaigns and in the activity students were asked to invent a union campaign that they would consider initiating at their workplaces. These included equal pay, workplace cancer screening, childcare issues and domestic violence. Similarly, the emphasis on union issues is taken forward to the second day when public speaking skills are developed and to the third day when students begin writing a press release.

Importantly, on the final day the school closes with four women from each course delivering three-minute speeches in the conference hall, which they have written and rehearsed during the week with the help of a small group of students and tutors. In this way the school provides an opportunity to enact a union conference scenario, an exercise that is regarded as particularly important for women aspiring to go further in the union.

The role of the tutors The union believes it has a 'reasonable' number of women tutors, but there are 'few' black tutors. The result is that women-only courses do not always have a woman tutor and black member-only courses do not always have a black tutor. The union is taking steps to address these imbalances. For example, one tutor-training course (in 2001) was made available only to women and black and ethnic minority members. In the meantime, the union is comfortable with the present need to occasionally use male tutors for women's courses, as are most of the women tutors. This arrangement would no doubt strike most feminist readers (and pro-feminist men) as odd, given the conceptual and ideological underpinning of women's separate organizing.

The above notwithstanding, most women's school tutors are women. However, having been drawn from the ranks of activists, tutors are inculcated in the arguably masculine culture of the union and this is reflected in their attitudes towards women's separate organizing and feminism discussed further in Chapter 5. Nevertheless, in response to the question 'what do you think makes a good tutor for women's courses?' TGWU tutors emphasised similar attributes to the MSF tutors, namely empathy with women and the ability to create a high trust, mutually supportive learning environment:

> You need to be able to relax and be able to relax them. Not an academic, but someone they can relate to, someone who has similar life experiences to them. You've got to remember that for some women, this could be their first educational experience since leaving school. They need to be supported and encouraged. (Miriam)

> You need to be able to understand their problems. The tutors shouldn't be seen as academics; we need to share our students' problems. For example, there are as many problems for women in the home as there are in the workplace and I think it's good if the tutor shares some of these problems. (Sarah)

> Someone you can trust not to gossip about them. Often they want to sound out someone as to how they can juggle union involvement with various other things going on in their

lives, so in the course of these conversations some very private stuff will come out. (Debbie)

The TGWU tutors also emphasised that tutors should share the class characteristics of students. This seemed to be of at least equal importance for them as gender, reflecting the strong working class culture of the union, when compared with the more (academically) highly qualified profile of MSF members, officers and tutors.

Summary

Using documentary sources, union data and interviews with key respondents this chapter has provided an overview and analysis of education provision in the two case study unions – MSF and TGWU – in order to depict the localised contexts in which to situate the interview findings. The main relevant points of comparison and contrast in the two unions' provision are now summarised.

First, the unions share broad aims and objectives for education generally and specifically through women's courses they hope to encourage women's participation. Women's courses though are only a small part of total provision, indicating that both unions expect women office holders at least to participate in mixed courses. In other words, women's courses complement mixed-sex representatives' training. Therefore, although women-only courses are a form of women's separate organizing, it is expected that women would participate in mixed-sex forums too.

Second, the two unions recognise that (male-dominated) branches can act as a barrier to dissemination of course publicity to women and both have developed measures to overcome this. Therefore, the unions acknowledge the masculine culture of trade unionism and accept that positive action measures are necessary as a counterbalance.

Third, both unions are overall achieving proportional participation of women in their mixed-sex courses, albeit that this is by no means achieved at all levels or on all courses. The existence of women's courses within this context points to an acceptance of the ideology of women-only courses, even when it could be argued that there is no longer a strong instrumental rationale. It is also significant that despite a weaker feminist orientation among TGWU tutors, all the women's school tutors in both unions shared a belief in the ongoing value of women's courses both to the union and to individual women. To this extent, the women-only courses in the two unions can be regarded as a proactive form of women's separate organizing.

Fourth, as a point of contrast, the TGWU's system of lay tutors has gendered consequences, one of which is that it allows for men to tutor women's courses when 'necessary'. It is 'necessary' to use male tutors when the union has decided that women need to learn about a topic for which they have no female tutor, e.g. Europe, pensions. From a feminist perspective, this dilutes the value of the women-only space and suggests that union or perhaps class issues override gender ones. In contrast, MSF engages freelance women tutors in order that women's courses are always taught by women: if the union could not provide a woman tutor, it would not offer the course. The self-defined feminist director of education thought it laughable that a man should teach women's courses. More fundamentally, this discussion over the gender of tutors also reflects an underlying tension surrounding the purposes of women-only courses and more broadly women's separate organizing.

Finally and importantly, there are significant differences in course content. TGWU's approach is more prescriptive and directed by the national education department, which has a very definite view of what the women should learn. Meanwhile, MSF sets out to be more flexible and indeed requires tutors to be flexible in their handling of the learning materials so that the women participants are able to shape the course to a greater extent. The content of MSF women's courses is de-contextualised to broaden their appeal to women who are not presently or not interested in becoming active. In contrast the content of the TGWU courses concentrates on work/union issues because the main goal is to enhance women's participation. However, it is important to emphasise that the *processes* of the courses are similar, being characterised by participative discussions and student-centred activities, which seek to validate and legitimise women's lived experiences of work, union and family and in this way reflect feminist beliefs and values. Whether the unions intend it or not, this pedagogic approach allows the students to shape the direction discussions take and therefore what is learnt from them. It is the course processes and the influences on the women that this research explores as part of its investigation into the social construction of their union participation.

In conclusion, the above discussion reveals an evolving and dynamic context of both gendered enablement and constraint where key actors (particularly female, but also supportive male officials and tutors) have played an active and central role in shaping the educational offering to render it more appealing and useful to women. It is clear that their actions and behaviours are informed by feminist beliefs and values and by an implicit or in some cases explicit acknowledgement of the patriarchal nature of union organization.

Chapter 5

Starting a Trade Union Career

This chapter discusses women's routes to union involvement, examining the people, experiences and influences that stimulate participation. Forms of participation and the structural barriers and constraints to becoming (more) active that women encounter in the family, work and trade union environment, are also examined. The analysis draws on interviews with about 30 MSF and TGWU women that were carried out shortly after completing a women-only course. Interviewees were asked to give retrospective, reflective accounts of how they first came to union participation. Quotes from the interviews are woven into the text. Generally these represent typical views and experiences, although some exceptional cases are also discussed. In addition, the book follows in more detail the illustrative stories of four women, beginning in this chapter with setting out how they began their union careers. The four women were selected because they represent a diversity of backgrounds, circumstances and experiences.

Influences on union participation

As discussed in Chapter 2, the provenance of willingness to participate in unions is the subject of much interest. This chapter draws on the ideas of Nicholson et al. (1981: 116) who contended that the origins of union participation may be explained in terms of prior needs and values, emergent goals and beliefs, and 'significant others' in the social environment. Similarly, Watson (1988) employed the concept of 'significant others' and 'significant events' to discuss how union orientations and routes to participation can be shaped by a complex interaction of previously held values and engagement with new discourses or exposure to 'unfair' conditions. These authors studied predominantly male trade unionists. However, since research has found women less willing than men to become involved especially in office holding, (e.g. Cockburn 1991; Metochi 2002), a gendered analysis of participation stimuli is critical (Kirton 2005). This chapter seeks to understand how a group of women came to attend a national trade union school and whether there were any significant influences on their union career trajectories. In order to conceptualise the nature of such influence the chapter employs Bradley's (1996) notion of passive, active and politicised identities (see Chapter 2).

Mostly, the experiences and events that influenced the women's union participation were of a cumulative, rather than one-off, nature, and were often gendered or racialised experiences in the family, work and union. The chapter also considers feminism as a possible influence, that is, whether women had a prior feminist orientation, which acted as a (contributory) stimulus[1] to participation. As discussed in Chapter 2 feminism has been influential on union women, even if it is no longer as obvious as in earlier decades (the late 1970s for example).

Family influences

The influence of family on trade union membership is a matter of interest for some commentators on the future of trade unionism (e.g. Waddington and Kerr 2002; Blanden and Machin 2003). The premise is that trade union values are 'passed down' through generations. For example, Blanden and Machin (2003) find a significant link between the union membership of young people and their fathers, with young people significantly more likely to be union members if their fathers are and particularly if their fathers are active trade unionists. However, the corollary of the decline in union membership is a decline in the number of families with trade union presence; hence the 'passing down' might be diminishing. Waddington and Kerr's findings suggest the diminishing influence of family as a means of transferring unionization (2002: 303) and Blanden and Machin suggest that the rapid decline in union membership rates over the last 25 years will have consequences for future generations as well (2003: 411).

Although family background in no way determines propensity for union activism among the interviewees in the present study, it does have an influence, although not always in the direction one would imagine. (From Tables 5.1 and 5.2 (below) the influences on participation can be connected to actual forms of participation.) In the group of interviewees there are fewer women who described their family background as union-minded (three MSF, six TGWU) compared with those who said it was non- or anti-union (11 MSF, nine TGWU). The differential class composition of the two unions probably explains the inter-union differences, suggesting that factors other than strong family influence account to a larger extent for the MSF women's membership and activism, which will be explored later.

Among the women with non- or anti-union families, several described their parents as holding conservative values, sometimes aligning themselves with the Conservative Party. This was not always related to being from a middle class background. These women typically laughed when asked if they felt there had been a family influence on their union joining and early activism. Some of this group described their background as anti-union whilst others said their parents were simply indifferent to unions and politics in general. Two MSF women, Vera and Sarah, had fathers who managed their own businesses during the 1970s period

---

1   Throughout the book I indicate the interviewees' self-defined feminist orientation as either 'feminist' or 'non-feminist', wherever it is relevant to do so. That is where it seems that feminist beliefs and values have influenced action and behaviour regardless of self-identification, or where it is important to mark a distinction between the action and behaviour of self-identified and non-feminist women.

Hilary's Story

Hilary is 32. She describes her background as non-union minded, working class. She is qualified to degree level and has worked as an administrator since leaving university ten years ago. She is married with one child aged four and lives close to her workplace. She works flexi-time enabling her to pick up her daughter from a child minder by 5pm.

Hilary joined TGWU about eight years ago when she started working at a UK airport. She has been a 'women's rep' for three years, a role she was persuaded into taking by a female shop steward (interviewee Beryl) and by the male branch secretary. She had been spotted as a woman who regularly attended and spoke up at branch meetings. She deputised for Beryl as a shop steward last year when Beryl was on long-term sick leave.

Hilary's husband is now very supportive, although initially he had been fairly sceptical about her becoming involved in the union. Hilary has attended a couple of residential union courses and her husband has taken time off to look after their daughter.

When asked whether women's involvement makes a difference, Hilary had this to say:

'Last year we renegotiated all the childcare benefits which I don't think would have come about had it been all men going and doing the negotiating, regardless of whether they've got kids of their own, it would never have occurred to them. Looking after the kids that's what the wife does, isn't it?'

Hilary said that her union priorities were at workplace level, partly because her family circumstances meant it was difficult to get more involved, but partly because that was what she felt was important.

---

of industrial unrest and they were exposed to anti-union discourse during their adolescent and young adult years. They both started work in the highly unionized public sector after university and joined their union 'because it was the thing to do', rather than from any prior belief in trade unionism. Sarah, in particular, said that even though she joined the union she thought at the time that trade unionists were 'trouble-makers', a view which was to change later as her involvement in the union increased.

Other women brought up in anti-union households described themselves as rebels. One TGWU woman, Hilary (see her story above), characterised her family as working class, but 'true blue' and said that as a 'stroppy' teenager in the early 'Thatcher years' she argued with her parents about 'social justice' issues. She felt that this had influenced her to 'stand up for herself and for others' rights' in the workplace. She did however stress that she was not interested in unions as political organizations and felt that union leaders were too involved with issues that should be left to government: perhaps the lasting grains of influence from an anti-union family.

Interestingly, but unsurprisingly given the British union movement's poor record on representing black people (Lee 1987; Phizacklea and Miles 1987; Virdee and Grint 1994), the black women in the study (four MSF, two TGWU) described their family background as non-union. However, some of these women had fathers who were politically active and for most a discourse of racial injustice was present in the family context and this had clearly influenced their view of the world as an unfair place, but one where activism could help. One MSF woman, Kamaljit, said that her father had been a community activist involved in black groups, a path, which she had followed, describing herself as 'a very political person'. Similarly, Bernadette (TGWU) a black woman, said that 'dad was a solid labour man', but it was race politics, rather than union, that were the topic of discussion in the family. Encouraged by her father, she was involved from an early age in black and ethnic minority groups. Afsana (MSF), on the other hand, also had a politically active father, but she said that coming from a traditional Pakistani Muslim family it had never occurred to her as a child or young adult that women could become involved in unions or political life generally. She had married and become a mother at sixteen and it was only after her divorce two years earlier that a 'new world' opened up to her. Therefore the influence of her father was present, but dormant until she reached her thirties because of her domestic circumstances, combined with a gendered ideology, which had influenced her in her formative years.

Women from union-minded backgrounds understandably took the family influence for granted and said that they always assumed they would join unions even if they did not become active. For example, Barbara (MSF) was brought up in a working-class community in a family with a long history of trade union membership and activism:

> At the end of the day that's where you're from, that's your roots. I mean I don't think unions are wonderful or anything. I mean I can see the negative as well as the positive, but for me personally I have to be in a union, I believe in the Labour movement.

At present she participated informally (see Table 5.1), but she could see the possibility that in the 'right' work circumstances she might become a representative – she was employed at the time in a voluntary organization, which recognised UNISON and not MSF. She had retained her MSF membership (originally from a previous job) as a tactical decision, because she did not envisage staying in that job for very long and wished to have continuity in her union membership so that she could participate in a branch structure.

All the women from union-minded backgrounds were also working class; hence the greater family influence on TGWU women, exemplified by Julie's story above. Even though some interviewees had through their education and current occupation shifted their own class status, they retained their affiliation to their working class roots and with that support for trade unionism. Most of these women emphasised their father's occupation and trade union membership, indicating that fathers had had more influence on their thinking. However two women, Deirdre (MSF) and Evelyn (TGWU), said that their mothers had been shop stewards and at 'tea time' they would talk about the problems they were dealing with. These women had strong female role models in contrast to the majority whose mothers were rather shadowy figures in their stories. Early exposure to a positive union discourse had left the women from union-minded backgrounds believing that joining a union was the 'right thing to do' irrespective of the particular work context.

The above discussion of family background shows that in a minority of cases in the study positive family influence on union joining and participation was very strong. However, the larger group from non- or anti-union backgrounds suggests that there is nothing entirely deterministic about family influences. This is brought into sharper focus by the fact that of the twenty women in the group who currently participated formally, only six were from union-minded backgrounds. Therefore factors other than family account for the participation of most of the women. Also, not all the women from union-minded backgrounds currently held union positions and some had never done so. Thus women schooled by the family in the importance of trade unionism, whilst likely to retain an affiliation to the movement, are not necessarily the ones who are its future female representatives. Thus, it is important to consider other, possibly more important sources of influence, including the work and union contexts.

Julie's Story

Julie is 39 and describes herself as from a union-minded, working-class background and a self-defined feminist. She has no children and is partner free. She is qualified to degree level and has worked as a carpenter for a local authority since 1987, when she joined TGWU. In explaining why she first joined the union Julie made reference to her family background and work experiences:

'It was my first day at work here and a steward came up to me and said 'will you join the union'? But anyway I had thought about joining a union because you know in my previous jobs on building sites there weren't any union members, but when I came here my mum said to me 'you are going to join the union aren't you?', you know it's like, what's the word, it's like it's the normal thing in my family to join a trade union.'

She also explained how she perceived the role of the union:

'We've always had regular meetings and we'd talk on the job about union things and you know I got the feeling very early on that the organization was so strong that we couldn't be pushed around, that we had a strong voice. I think unions are there to protect the rights of ordinary working-class people and I think their priorities should be terms and conditions, like pay and working hours.'

Julie has been a shop steward since 1990 and deputy convenor of the branch for one year, representing nearly 400 skilled manual workers. The deputy convenor role gives her two days per week 'facilities time'. Julie represents mostly men – there are only 11 female members among the 400 in the branch. Almost half of her members are black and minority ethnic.

Work and union influences

In Britain, branch officers are central to determining access to the structures of participation and the content of the bargaining agenda. Since women are severely under-represented among trade union leaders, it is important to consider the role of leadership style in promoting participation. Research in a number of countries has claimed that participatory, or transformational, leadership styles promote participation, whilst transactional leadership styles retain a distance between leaders and led (Cobble and Bielski Michal 2002; Dorgan and Grieco 1993; Sudano 1998; Metochi 2002). Union leaders, who adopt the more participatory approach of the transformational style by being available for members to raise issues of concern, informing members of union affairs and consulting members, encourage members to see the union as their organization. This perception then induces feelings of loyalty towards the union, which motivates members to become involved (Metochi 2002; Nicholson et al. 1981). The weakness of this theory is that studies such as Nicholson et al.'s do not gender the discussion of leadership styles, when there are clear gendered implications. For example, since there is a lack of female role models in leadership positions, even women who have a willingness to participate might be deterred unless the male hierarchy adopts a 'transformational' style (Kelly 1998). In contrast union leaders who adopt a more 'transactional' style (Kelly 1998) risk deliberately or unintentionally reproducing women's marginalisation within the structures of participation (Sudano 1997; Dorgan and Grieco 1993).

A further point to take into account is that whilst there can be no doubt that local leaders have the power either to encourage or discourage membership participation, it should not be assumed that leaders' practices reflect an either/or style. Local leaders might encourage, for example, white men's participation, but not women's or black members. Firstly, this might be because men in power want to hold onto power for its own sake as well as for the advantages it can confer, for example access to an interesting lifestyle, close relations with management, etc (e.g. Cockburn 1994). Even in the present less union-friendly context, individuals can still gain these advantages from participation in some contexts. Secondly, as Cockburn (ibid.) suggests, men might rightly fear that once in office women would use power differently. Women might want to encourage more female participation, (e.g. Cunnison and Stageman 1995; Kirton and Healy 1999) or to achieve different aims; to align the union agenda more with women's specific concerns, for example (Cobble and Bielski Michal 2002; Healy and Kirton 2000). On the second point, some authors argue that women conceptualise power differently, for example by seeing power as 'capacity' rather than 'domination' (Cockburn, 1994) and by wanting to use power to involve and empower others (Dorgan and Grieco 1993; Sudano 1997). This does not have to rest on essentialised notions of womanhood and femininity, but can be seen as a function of women's collective experiences of inequality and a desire to utilise modes of behaviour that explicitly aim to overcome inequality. This discussion highlights power as a gendered resource (e.g. Bradley 1999; Healy and Kirton 2000).

Watson's (1988) study highlights the importance of union officers who encourage and sponsor individual members to get involved. Kirton and Healy (1999) demonstrate the importance for women's participation of women officers in the context of generally low levels of female involvement, confirming the findings of earlier studies that women are more likely to 'bring on' other women (e.g. Heery and Kelly 1988; Ledwith et al. 1990).

Interviewees were asked to reflect back on whether they could identify anyone in their workplace or union who had encouraged or inspired them to become involved. Some of the women who had been positively influenced by family background, participated despite being deterred by their negative perceptions of some union activists (often men), such was the strength of their union orientation. However, exploring positive work and union influences is particularly illuminating in the case of women where there was little or negative family influence and for whom more positive embodiments of union values proved persuasive. Watson's (1988) study emphasises the importance of sponsorship from inside the union, but since the vast majority of her interviewees were men, she offers no gendered analysis of the issue of sponsorship. One question, for example, is whether women are more likely to be sponsored by other women?

Certainly Ledwith et al. (1990) and Kirton and Healy (1999) highlight the influence of 'significant others' in the workplace and union, particularly women who act as role models for other newer, less experienced female activists. It should, however, be noted that some of the interviewees in the present study worked in male dominated contexts (for example the bus drivers and those in technical jobs), whilst others described their union branches as male dominated. In these instances female role models, at local level at least, were scarce.

Some interviewees reported that there were people in the union actively on the look out for female and/or black members to bring on as activists, as suggested by Hilary's story above. Susan, a black woman from MSF with a non-union family background, attended an event hosted by the union's National Race Equality Committee (NREC) after seeing it advertised in the union magazine. She went out of interest and because working in a predominantly 'white' environment she felt that the local union did not tackle race issues. A black paid official noticed her, because although these events are publicised and open to all, in practice they mostly attract well-known black activists. The official kept in touch with her by telephone and persuaded her to attend another NREC event and 'Women's Week'. Susan acknowledged that without the official's persistence, she probably would not have gone to any other union events, because as a new woman she had felt uncomfortable. Afsana (MSF) had a similar experience when she attended a regional forum for voluntary organizations at which two black MSF activists were present: they talked to her about what the union was doing for women and black members, signed her into membership and persuaded her to attend 'Women's Week'. In this way these two black women's experiences of people in the union were both gendered and racialised. Similarly, some TGWU women had been encouraged to become more involved by a Regional Women's Officer (RWO), who acted as a female role model for some of the interviewees, including Julie (see her story below), several of whom spoke of the influence she had had on them.

Other women seemed to have benefited from the union's explicit attempts to deliver on gender equality within the union by recruiting more female activists, for example as 'women's reps'. Hilary (TGWU) reflected:

> One of the guys I work with is one of the senior stewards. So he, along with Beryl, approached me. I think I was almost coerced into it at first, but they said "We think you'd be quite good at it". I'm not quite sure whether I should be here or not. But that's how I became a women's rep.

In this sense there was a gendered dimension to some interviewees' experiences of the union. Jane and Mandy (TGWU), for example, were both bus drivers in the male-dominated transport industry. Their male branch secretaries recruited them as shop stewards following a national union-led campaign to increase the number of women activists. Similarly, Kim (MSF), had been a member for many years, but working in a non-union company she had very little contact with the union. However, following a chance meeting with her male branch secretary at a (non-union) social event, Kim joined her composite branch committee as 'women's rep' finally acting on a longstanding feeling that she should be involved.

Groups of people, especially in the same workplace, might have a less specific, but none the less important influence on individuals; union active friends, for example. Nicholson et al.'s (1981) study of union activism found that having or acquiring union-active friends, increases participation. Working in a unionized environment where it is the norm to be a member increases the likelihood of exposure to and engagement with positive union discourses and of course of making union-active friends. Some interviewees had first become union members in the period of the 'closed shop', leaving little choice but to join. However, over time they had mostly come to value their membership although in one case, Vera, this was largely for 'insurance' purposes. The effect of a critical mass of pro-union people was particularly apparent in the case of some of the women from non- or anti-union backgrounds. They spoke of how they came to see unions in a different and more positive light after working in a unionized environment among trade unionists. This was especially pronounced among, although not unique to, the MSF women, who were less likely to come from union-minded backgrounds. This then overturned the negative image of unions they had acquired through socialisation within the family. Elizabeth (below) is an example of a woman whose perceptions of trade unionism changed considerably after witnessing a union in action.

This discussion underscores the influence of both individuals and groups of people outside of the family in pulling women into participation, indicating that family background cannot accurately predict union activism, but also that some women seem to need a positive pull to actualise their willingness to participate. It is also important to note that 'significant others' often appear at a critical juncture in the woman's life. Susan, Afsana, Kim and Mandy mentioned above had recently ended long term relationships and Jane's children had grown up and left home.

They all felt that they now had spare time and energy to give, but if the same person had entered the woman's life at another time their influence might not have been the same, highlighting the inter-relationship between people, experiences and events.

Some interviewees were able to recall specific experiences, which they felt had had a major impact on their becoming actively involved in their unions primarily by stimulating a sense of general injustice. Combined and over time these experiences activated a class-based collective identity. Linda (MSF), for example, said:

> Workers need to do it for themselves. Management don't give anything away, do they? If you want something you have to be prepared to stand up and demand it, don't you?

Similarly, reflecting on the gradual heightening of her class-based awareness, Kim (MSF) said:

> As you go through your career you see a lot of injustice, you see decent people being treated like dirt and you think this isn't fair, there's got to be another way.

Elizabeth's Story

Elizabeth is 56, divorced and currently partner free. She has adult children. She comes from a non-union family background. She is qualified to 'O' level standard and her employment history is in clerical and administrative work. She has worked for a union for nine years, for the past five as the manager of a regional office. She started work there as an office 'temp', knowing very little about unions except the negative stories she had read in the press, but:

'After two or three weeks in the office here I went home and I thought 'I want to be part of that' and I've stayed ever since. Working for a union I got to see so much going on behind the scenes, so much good stuff that nobody ever hears about, so much that a union does for its members that never comes up in the media.'

Elizabeth's attachment to the union has increased considerably over time. She has been a workplace representative for seven years and branch chair for four years. Recently, she has also begun to participate beyond the workplace as a delegate to the union's national women's committee and a regional TUC women's committee. She has attended several courses for union representatives and has been to Women's Week twice before.

Reflecting on how she now perceived the purpose of trade unionism, she said,

'I suppose it's a bit like asking why you have fire insurance in your home. Yeah, it's a bit like an insurance policy. But I believe that if you have problems at work, it is very unlikely that you can pursue them as an individual person. There is definitely strength in unity. There are cases I've seen where people wouldn't have stood a chance if they had taken them individually.'

If willingness to participate is to be translated into actual participation it is important that there is a belief in the effectiveness of collective methods of representation and action (Kelly 1998; Metochi 2002). Some of the interviewees' significant experiences had occurred in a unionized context, where they were able to see how the union handled the situation and if it had been successful, this had a positive influence on their perception of the union. Judy (TGWU) is an interesting example. A bus driver, Judy had informally participated by attending workplace union meetings for many years, largely because it was the norm at her workplace to go to union meetings, but had not formalised her involvement through a position or committee participation, for example. In 1996 Judy suffered an industrial accident which left her permanently disabled and a wheelchair user. Until that point she felt that she had been treated fairly well as an employee and had had no grievances, but she felt that her employer handled the accident poorly. This profoundly changed her view of management, triggering a stronger sense of 'them' and 'us' (Kelly and Kelly 1994), and a class-based identity. The union supported her personal injury claim and she retained her membership despite being unable to work: she was subsequently encouraged by her branch to become involved in the union's disability and race committees, since which time she had developed more politicised race and disability based identities.

However, just as there is nothing deterministic about family influences, a unionized work environment does not necessarily improve perceptions of unions, as survey data and case studies such as Waddington and Kerr's (2002) and Walters' (2002) respectively show. Neither is there any necessary relationship between strong union presence and the collectivisation of all employees. One MSF woman, Vera, had worked in the unionized NHS all her working life and her local union branch was very active, holding regular membership meetings, distributing literature and encouraging members to go on courses. Vera came from an anti-union background and despite being exposed to the more pro-union work environment she remained ambivalent about the purpose of trade unionism:

> I must admit that in more recent times I have questioned my membership, the point of it, I mean. On balance I still think it's a safeguard, but I'm not really sure that I believe in unions as such.

What is interesting is not so much that this attitude exists in the membership, but that someone who has chosen to participate in a course should display it. This suggests that various motivations, including individualist and/or instrumental, could lead people to participate in a union's educational activities aside from a desire to become union active. This theme is explored in Chapter 6. It is quite obvious that those who have become active for the most part will have come to believe one way or another in trade unionism, whilst the more ambivalent members are likely to be inactive.

The interviews also sought to uncover gendered experiences that might activate a gender identity; that is experiences of sex discrimination rather than simply of general unfairness. When asked about this some women said that they had no personal experiences, but had witnessed instances and this seemed enough to have engendered a sense of anger about the way women in general are treated, especially by employers. However, when asking people about personal experiences of discrimination it is always worth treating their answers with caution because recognition of discrimination requires a prior awareness or gender consciousness, which not all women have (Kelly and Breinlinger 1996). For example, Mandy, a lesbian from TGWU, reflected on the way that discrimination is not always recognised as such by the 'victims'. She said that after attending the women's school she was able to identify many instances of discrimination on grounds of sex and sexuality from her own work life, but she said that as they had occurred she had simply accepted them and had not seen them as discrimination. Thus Mandy had made sense of discriminatory experiences retrospectively, and a previously passive gender identity was activated. She was visibly excited about this process of illumination and was eager to raise other women's consciousness.

Kamaljit (MSF) had active gender, lesbian and race identities. She said that as a black lesbian she had experienced a lot of racism and homophobia in her working life and felt that working in a unionized organization provided the opportunity to try to tackle these issues at workplace policy level. Similarly, Fiona and Helen (MSF) worked in an organization, where many women had experiences of sexual harassment, including Helen, and where women were badly paid. Management's ineptitude and complacency at dealing with these 'women's issues' eventually led a group of women to leave the staff association and join MSF, with Fiona and Helen emerging as 'natural' leaders. As Fiona said, 'I've always been bolshy', but it was gendered workplace experiences that had activated a collective gender identity and pushed her into investing her personal abilities in collective organization.

Even the ambivalent Vera talked about sexism and discrimination in employment and she displayed an active gender identity, albeit an individualistically oriented one, in the sense that she was acutely aware of the problems her gender had caused her in her own career. But unlike other women, she was vague in the attribution of blame and was not convinced that the problem could be tackled through collective organization. She felt it was a 'reflection of society in general' and could not see what unions could do on gender inequalities and therefore could not see the point of participating. In contrast most other women felt that collective organization could help, in that there was practical work for unions to do at local and national levels on representing women and their concerns. In addition their own shifting class and gender identities meant that they wanted to participate in collective organization.

Kelly's (1998) work on mobilisation theory provides a framework for understanding the importance of a sense of injustice combined with attribution, which is relevant to the discussion of significant others and experiences and links with the concept of shifting identities between passive, active and politicised. Kelly suggests that grievances are necessary for employees to become collectivised, however it is also essential that workers blame the employer for their problems (1998:45). Some interviewees clearly had grievances with their present employer and they very clearly placed the blame on management as in the case of Judy, Fiona and Helen, for example (See Helen's story below). For these women there was a direct relationship between the grievances and previously passive identities becoming activated or politicised and their getting (more) involved in the union. Similarly, Sarah became active when MSF first took up an equal pay claim on behalf of speech therapists. She was already a member, but for her, the equal pay issue was a turning point when it struck her that, as a woman, she was being treated unfairly and that the union might make a difference.

Helen's Story

Helen is 35, Irish and she left school at 16 with a couple of 'O' levels and has since been employed in secretarial work. She describes her background as working class, non-union. She is recently divorced and currently partner free, with three young children. Her ex-husband was abusive and she lived in a women's refuge for a time.

Helen has been an MSF member for about two years. MSF is one of five recognised unions in the factory where she works, with 54 out of 74 clerical workers in membership. She, along with interviewee Fiona, was one of a small group of women who led an exodus from the company's reportedly weak and ineffective staff association to form a branch of MSF. She had no previous experiences of unions, but felt that the female administration workers had received a raw deal from the company in comparison to the unionized male factory workers. One of the most significant issues for the female workforce was sexual harassment that many women workers had experienced and which management had failed to deal with.

Helen is one of four workplace representatives. She became a representative 'because no one else would do it' and her close friend Fiona who is branch chair, talked her into it.

Helen describes her union role as involving arranging meetings, communicating with members, liaising with the company, typing minutes, intervening in disputes, in addition to carrying out her 'real' job as a personal secretary.

Helen enjoys her union work enormously and talked at length about the personal gains from being involved, but she regards her family circumstances as a constraint on taking on any more union roles. She gets very little financial support from her ex-husband and a restraining order against him means that he has very little involvement with her children.

However, there were other interviewees who had no specific grievances at their workplace, but they still became involved and still had a clear sense of (gendered) social injustice. Susan and Linda (MSF) are good examples. Both women worked in large unionized organizations, Susan in the private sector and Linda in the public. Both women considered their employers to be 'good' and could think of no particular problems that either they or co-workers had experienced, but their lived experiences beyond the workplace had caused them to identify racism (in Susan's case) and sexism (in Linda's case) as societal problems. Kelly (1998) largely confines his analysis of how employees are mobilised to the level of the workplace, therefore identifying grievances and blaming the employer or management are essential preconditions of collectivisation. Shifting the analysis to the more general labour market context, it is possible to see how individuals who perceive very few problems in their own workplace can identify wider social injustices and place the blame variously on the capitalist-labour relation, patriarchal relations or racism. For some women then, the existence of a sense of injustice combined with attribution at a macro level was sufficient to stimulate a desire to be involved, or to activate class, gender and/or race identities, as in the case of Susan and Linda.

The discussion of experiences of discrimination reveals that both a general sense of workplace/social injustices and a range of gender specific workplace/social injustices activated identities which engendered in many of the interviewees a willingness to be involved, especially where there was a sense of attribution. Importantly, the diversity of the interviewees allows for a consideration of crosscutting identity-based experiences of injustice including race, disability and sexuality as being influential.

The influence of feminism

An active, even politicised feminist identity is an important, although not necessary, component of transformative strategies towards (emancipatory) social change because it provides a first step to resistance and stops women believing that their sufferings are natural (as in the 'other women's movement') or merely personal (Young 1997). This is not to say that women, who do not self-identify as feminists, will not share a common agenda for change with women who are comfortable with the feminist label. Many women in the trade union context, where there is a long history of feminist influence (Boston 1987), are uncomfortable with feminism. It is often felt to undermine the movement's solidarity and unity, to constitute (inappropriately) a single cause and to reflect largely the concerns of white, middle-class women (Cockburn 1991; Colgan and Ledwith 1996; Kirton and Healy 1999; Humphrey 2002). It is also the case that in many social arenas there is now an anti-feminist discourse, which is bound to deter some women from publicly adopting the label.

Yet it is clear feminist beliefs and values inform much of trade union women's strategies and practice and some trade union women display feminist beliefs and values, even when they do not self-identify as feminists (e.g. Healy and Kirton 2000; Kirton and Healy 1999; Colgan and Ledwith, 1996, 2000, 2002; Cunnison and Stageman 1995; McBride 2001). Such women might not engage intellectually with the ideology of feminism, or they might have dismissed feminism as an explicit identity but might be committed to its goals as a project for gendered social change.

As discussed in Chapter 1, feminism provides the conceptual tools for explaining patterns of women's trade union participation and at the same time an analytical framework for interpreting the voices of women trade unionists. Further, consideration of the influence of feminism on trade union women is relevant to understanding the *nature* of women's participation; for example, do women speak *as* and *for* women or as individuals in a sex category (Cockburn 1991)? Indeed, many of the strategies aimed at increasing women's participation, especially those based on women's separate organizing (Briskin 1993), are rooted in feminist beliefs and values. However, feminism has suffered an ideological assault by a range of social actors in the 1980s and 1990s, so that fewer women are now comfortable with the label.

Table 5.1 Influences on and forms of participation of MSF women

Name	Influences on Participation	Form(s) of Participation on Attendance at Women's School (2000)
Fiona, Age 34, White, Partnered, 2 children, clerical worker	Non-union family background; experiences at the workplace; self-defined feminist	Formal participation: workplace rep; branch chair
Deirdre, Age 47, White, Disability, Partnered, voluntary worker	Union minded family background; experiences at the workplace	Formal participation: branch chair; regional council member
Elizabeth, Age 56, White, Partner free, office manager	Non-union family background; experiences at the workplace	Formal participation: workplace rep; branch chair; SERTUC Women's Committee member
Kim, Age 38, White, Partner free, sales manager	Non-union family background; others in the union; self-defined feminist	Formal participation: branch women's rep; branch committee member
Helen, Age 35, White, Partner free, 3 children, clerical worker	Non-union family background; others in the union; experiences at the workplace	Formal participation: workplace rep; branch committee member
Linda, Age 48, White, Partnered, one child, technician	Union-minded family background; others in the union; self-defined feminist	Formal participation: 'women's rep'
Kate, Age 30, White, Partnered, technician	Anti-union family background; experiences at the workplace	Formal participation: workplace rep; health and safety rep; branch committee member
Kamaljit, Age 29, Asian, Partnered, health worker	Non-union family background; others in the union; experiences at the workplace; self-defined feminist	Formal participation: workplace rep, branch committee member

Vera, Age 46, White, Partner free, senior medical officer	Anti-union family background	Inactive member
Susan, Age 36, African-Caribbean, Partner free, clerical worker	Non-union family background; others in the union	Informal participation at workplace level; informal participation in national race committee
Sarah, Age 43, White, Partner free, speech therapist	Anti-union family background; experiences at the workplace; self-defined feminist	Informal participation at workplace level
Barbara, Age 35, White, Partner free, advice worker	Union minded family background; self-defined feminist	Informal participation at branch level
Afsana, Age 35, Asian, Partner free, 3 children, community worker	Non-union family background; others in the union	Inactive member
Christine, Age 38, African-Caribbean, Partner free, one child, day centre manager	Non-union family background; experiences at the workplace	Formal participation: workplace rep, branch committee member

Table 5.2 Influences on and forms of participation of TGWU women

Name/Details	Influences on Participation	Form(s) of Participation on Attendance at Women's School (1999)
Sally, Age 44, White, Partnered, Clerical worker	Non-union family background; experiences at workplace; others in the union	Formal participation: shop steward; branch committee member
Melanie, Age 30, White, Partner free, Clerical worker	Union minded family background	Formal participation: shop steward; branch committee member
Jane, Age 47, White, Partnered, Bus driver	Non-union family background; others in the union	Formal participation: shop steward; 'women's rep'; branch committee member; regional and national trade group and women's committee member
Delia, Age 32, White, Partner free, Clerical worker	Union minded family background; others in the union	Informal participation: at workplace and branch levels
Judy, Age 36, African-Caribbean, Disability, Partner free, Bus driver	Non-union family background; experiences at the workplace	Informal participation: at branch level; plus formal participation: regional disability committee member
Evelyn, Age 45, White, Partner free, One child, Advice worker	Union minded family background; experiences at the workplace; others in the union	Inactive member
Beryl, Age 47, White, Partnered, Clerical worker	Non-union family background; experiences at the workplace; self-defined feminist	Formal participation: shop steward; 'Women's rep'; branch committee member

Hilary, Age 32, White, Partnered, One child, Clerical worker	Non-union family background; others in the union	Formal participation: 'women's rep'
Mary, Age 53, White, Partnered, One child, Clerical worker	Non-union family background; experiences at the workplace; self-defined feminist	Formal participation: shop steward; branch chair
Julie, Age 39, White, Partner free, Carpenter	Union minded family background; experiences at the workplace; others in the union; self-defined feminist	Formal participation: shop steward; branch committee member; deputy convenor
Suzanne, Age 40, White, Partnered, 2 children Technician	Union minded family background; experiences at the workplace	Formal participation: shop steward; branch committee member; regional and national trade group committee and women's committee member
Bernadette, Age 37, African-Caribbean, Partnered 2 children, Policy officer	Non-union family background; experiences at the workplace	Informal participation: at branch level
Mandy, Age 40, White, Partner free, Bus driver	Non-union family background; experiences at the workplace; others in the union	Formal participation: shop steward
Molly, Age 48, White, Partnered, 3 children, Secretary	Non-union family background; experiences at the workplace	Formal participation: shop steward
Diane. Age 32, White, Partnered, 2 children, Kitchen supervisor	Union minded family background; self-defined feminist	Inactive member

Nevertheless, because of its aim of gendered social transformation, there is considerable interest in whether feminism still informs the practices of union women (for example, Cockburn 1991; Colgan and Ledwith 1996; Cunnison and Stageman 1995; Kirton and Healy, 1999; Healy and Kirton 2000). Put simply, this is crucial to answering the questions 'do women make a difference?' and 'does it matter who gets elected?' or is the pursuit of women's equal participation in unions, simply borne of a concern for the liberal democratic principle of proportional representation?

Colgan and Ledwith (1996), for example, developed a typology of trade union women's consciousness derived from types of feminism (e.g. Walby 1986; 1992). Their research found that regardless of self-perception, trade union women's primary attitudes seemed to be in agreement with what can be termed feminist principles and strategies (1996:176). Thus, it has to be recognised that not all women who display feminist beliefs and values will now (if ever they did) self-identify with feminism, although those prepared to adopt the label are probably likely to be most committed to and comfortable with feminist practices.

Bearing this in mind it is not particularly useful conceptually to classify women as either self-identified feminists or non-feminists, because this binary divide will not reveal very much about women's beliefs and values. However, there are conceptual and methodological difficulties surrounding the researcher attaching labels, which interviewees themselves dissociate from, i.e. some women are feminists, but do not know it; invoking connotations of false consciousness. To avoid this quagmire, an alternative approach is to explore *orientations* to feminism, rather than simply describe women as either feminist or not. This captures a spectrum of beliefs and values, without requiring unequivocal self-identification.[2] For example, women who support women's separate organizing in theory and/or practice, in doing so arguably display a relatively strong feminist orientation, whilst women who do not support women's separate organizing, yet show a concern to tackle women's inequality using liberal measures show a weaker feminist orientation.

As a starting point for the discussion with interviewees, they were asked whether or not they considered themselves to be a feminist. Only a minority (six MSF, three TGWU) self-identified as feminists. This resonates with Colgan and Ledwith's (1996) study of predominantly branch level activists, whereas Kirton and Healy (1999) found that the majority of senior women in MSF self-identified as feminists. The latter perhaps a function of their seniority, possibly indicating that feminist women are more likely to seek upward union careers or that as they move upwards, women begin to adopt a stronger feminist orientation. The other women revealed

---

2   Nevertheless, for the sake of clarity and simplicity in order to distinguish women who self-identify as feminists from those who do not, in subsequent chapters 'non-feminist' is used to describe the latter group. It is then possible to see whether those who are ambivalent or reluctant to adopt the label are equally equivocal with regard to feminist practices.

differing degrees of feminist beliefs and values,[3] that is, weaker or stronger feminist orientations.

The self-identified feminists in the study were far more likely to be highly qualified women (seven) and white (eight), possibly reflecting the argument and criticism that feminism has most appeal to white middle-class educated women (e.g. hooks 1989). This was recognised by one MSF woman, Barbara, a self-identified feminist, with a politicised class identity:

> Feminism has been very white and very middle class and has ignored a lot of groups that are under-represented. I mean you can talk all you like about women being strong, about getting out of oppressive relationships, but it's not that easy for some women. We haven't all been brought up in this privileged position that a lot of feminists have.

The larger number of self-identified feminists in the MSF group than in the TGWU is probably a reflection of the class and occupational composition of the group, but possibly also indicative of the prevalent discourses in the unions. This will be explored in Chapter 6 in the context of the content of women's courses.

Diane (TGWU) typical of the self-identified feminists spoke as and for women using a feminist vocabulary:

> If women can get together and develop an agenda then it will bring out women's issues, because there are still barriers. So at least if we can get our agenda clear, then we can get through the barriers that are set up by men.

Diane, like the other self-identified feminists, indicates support for women's separate organization as a strategy for overcoming the barriers associated with male domination.

In contrast, the majority of interviewees who were reluctant to self-identify as feminists expressed concerns about what the concept meant. As Hilary (TGWU) understood it, feminism demanded 'preferential treatment' for women, which she was uncomfortable with. However, she did display an active gender identity:

> Whilst I agree that some women have a really rough time just because they're women, not for any other reason, then yes, I'm very against that. On the other hand I don't think that women should have any preferential treatment just because they're women.

Some of the women reluctant to label themselves as feminists used phrases such as 'man hating' and 'bra burning' to describe their doubts about feminism, suggesting they had been influenced by prevalent anti-feminist discourses, as with Christine (MSF):

---

3   These can be defined as embracing 'strategies of challenge and change towards the transformation of patriarchal structures and obstructions in women's attempts to participate and progress' (Colgan and Ledwith, 1994: 14).

Feminist? I just see someone, like, burn your bra kind of thing. I believe in justice, in equal rights for women, but feminist? No, *I don't think so*. [said with emphasis]

Similarly, Melanie (TGWU):

Feminist? Not in a bra burning sense, but I do think women should have equal rights with men.

There were also some allusions to the perceived incompatibility of femininity with feminism, as suggested by Elizabeth (MSF):

No I'm not [a feminist], but I very much feel that if women are doing a job equal to a man's they should be paid the same. But at the same time I quite like it if a man opens a door for me and the courtesies that go with being female: I enjoy that. But women can do just as good a job as men, so if that makes me a feminist, then I'm a feminist.

However, all the interviewees were clear that the struggle for women's equality was far from won and they were agreed that 'something had to be done', but they did not all associate the gender equality project with feminism.

Nevertheless, it can be argued that feminism influences the beliefs and values of trade union women, and that an understanding of feminist orientations is useful to thinking about women's trade union orientations. However, only a minority of women in the study self-identified as feminists and therefore had a prior feminist consciousness. Most women who did not self-identify as feminists were eager to stress their commitment to 'equality for all' or social justice generally, seeming to view feminism as a 'single issue' project and indicating that they privileged their trade union identity, as with Deirdre (MSF):

You what love? Me, a feminist? No, I think of myself as an individual person, not as a category. Everyone should be equal, not the same, but equal, but it is true that men often look down at women.

The interviewees' feminist orientations are returned to in subsequent chapters.

Forms of participation and involvement

Having explored how and why the interviewees in the study first came to join a union or, where applicable, to participate, this section examines where they were in terms of their union careers when they were interviewed for the first time shortly after attending the women's school. As discussed in Chapter 2, there are different definitions of participation: the one employed here is multi-dimensional and includes a range of activities from office holding to attending union meetings, voting in elections or taking part in industrial action (Fosh 1993; Flood et al. 1996). This approach fits with the objectives of this study, which are to explore the varied ways in which women participate. However, it is important to distinguish different forms of participation so that the gendered triggers can be more effectively unpacked. Thus, a distinction is made between informal and formal participation.[4]

The women in the study were at different stages of their union careers when they attended the women's school as shown in Tables 5.1 and 5.2. Only four women (two from each union) were inactive, whilst five (three MSF, two TGWU) participated informally in their workplace/branch. The majority of women, however, were office holders (nine MSF and 11 TGWU) of workplace and/or branch positions and one TGWU woman participated in a regional disability committee, although their levels of experience in and training for their roles were more varied than their office holder titles might suggest.

Significantly, particularly for the discussion in Chapter 7, but also for the discussion below of barriers and constraints, only five interviewees (two MSF, three TGWU) participated in structures beyond the workplace/branch. The workplace context of women's activism has been the subject of research interest (e.g. Cunnison and Stageman 1995; Munro 1999). Some research (e.g. Lawrence 1994; Cully et al. 1999) has found that women are more likely to hold office when women constitute the majority of the members. Interestingly, this is not entirely reflected in the present study. Nine of the office-holders represented mainly or exclusively women, three had gender balanced constituencies, whilst seven represented predominantly men. However, of the latter group three were 'women's reps' and it seemed that none of these women had any meaningful roles in that capacity, aside from taking the minutes at branch meetings, which they all did and providing a female presence, in an otherwise all-male branch committee. This contextual discussion will be returned to in Chapter 7.

Barriers and constraints to participation

The majority of interviewees did not participate beyond the workplace/branch; thus even with a relatively active group of women it is worth considering the factors that 'confined' them to the lower levels of the union hierarchy. This section explores what at this point in their union careers the women perceived as barriers and constraints to participation,[5] focusing on home and family, work and union and personal confidence issues.

---

4   This is discussed in Chapter 2. However, to reiterate, informal participation means active engagement with the democratic processes and structures of the union, for example, interacting with union representatives, actively seeking information, voting in elections, attending union meetings: in short, taking an active interest in the union, rather than simply paying membership dues for 'insurance' purposes. Meanwhile, formal participation involves participating in the union's committee structures or holding a workplace union position.

5   Chapter 6 follows this up two years after the women's schools.

Home and family

In the absence of a revolutionary re-negotiation of the gendered division of labour in the home, it is inevitable that some women will perceive their domestic responsibilities as impeding their union participation. That said a substantial minority of twelve interviewees had dependent children and eight of these were office-holders, denoting a high level of formal participation among the mothers in the sample. This is interesting and could either indicate that the sample in the study is itself atypical in this respect, or that childcare responsibilities are perceived by women as less of a barrier to participation in political life than formerly.[6] Rees' (1990) earlier study, for example, of women in NALGO found that female activists had fewer domestic commitments than the female membership. In contrast in the present study, even of the four lone parents who one would expect to be most 'time poor', two held union positions, although the other two felt that time constraints would prevent them from getting involved beyond attending workplace meetings. One single parent though, Afsana (MSF), said that if she could take her younger children to union forums, she would get involved. She had taken two of her children to residential schools, including the women's course, but there was no childcare available at her local branch meetings. This highlights the utility of union interventions (e.g. provision of childcare) for encouraging greater participation among at least some women.

However, it is not possible to read from the high level involvement of mothers in this study that fundamental social change has occurred, such that women no longer experience motherhood as constraint. It must be remembered that overall mothers of dependent children are among a minority of women involved in political life (Walby 1997). Nevertheless women have always made individual decisions about how to juggle their different roles and there have always been exceptions to the norm. However, the high level of involvement of mothers in this study does indicate that gender relations are never cast in stone and that there is scope for negotiation within households over childcare and other domestic duties. Mirroring other research (e.g. Lawrence 1994) some mothers emphasised the importance of a supportive partner prepared to take on practical tasks such as collecting children from school/day care and cooking the family meal. Just as important though was that the partner had sympathy for the union movement, so that there was a shared understanding that what the woman was doing in the union was important and worthwhile and therefore her time and effort were well spent. In this regard some of the interviewees mentioned that their partners were also union members.

---

6   It is difficult to answer this question based on a qualitative study, but it is nevertheless worth flagging up as noteworthy. A quantitative survey could usefully address this issue.

However, as a caveat to the above optimistic picture of women successfully combining motherhood, paid work and union participation, it should be noted that there was only one mother-office holder in the study whose activism extended beyond the workplace. Typically mother-officer holders said that time constraints would not allow them to get involved at regional or national level. When asked to explain their union roles and activities, they appeared to perform the bulk of their union duties during normal working hours, rarely taking union work home. They had sufficiently generous 'facilities time' (paid time off for union duties) to render this unnecessary and most emphasised that weekends and evenings were family time. The exception was Helen (MSF), a divorced mother of three small children who would often spend the evenings on union business: she liked to keep busy, she said. Generally it was clear from interviews that the mothers' union roles rarely intruded into the domestic domain, typically only one week per year when they attended a residential course and it became necessary for partners to 'help out' with domestic duties. In this regard a couple of women mentioned that they had spent the weekend before the school cooking meals for the freezer which their husbands could reheat for the family during the week.

The one notable exception to this general pattern was Suzanne (TGWU). She had been a shop steward for twelve years and was a delegate on a range of regional and national committees, which entailed using her three days' per month facilities time, seven days per year annual leave entitlement and many evenings and weekends. This level of participation had been arrived at over a period of years, with initially a reluctant and then later a supportive husband. She described herself as 'lucky' to have a supportive husband and compared her own domestic situation with that of one of her female union colleagues, whose husband had not 'let her' attend the women's school in Eastbourne. Suzanne's aim now was to become a paid official therefore it was important to 'be seen'. The above indicates that despite increasing involvement of women with dependent children at the lower levels of the union hierarchy, women union leaders outside of the workplace are still likely to display 'atypical' characteristics. Equally it is possible that some women active at workplace level only when children are young, will expand their activism later and that they will take with them the store of knowledge and experience they accumulate from juggling three roles.

As noted above active women trade unionists are generally atypical. There is no doubt that managing a family and household is a time consuming task if added to the demands of paid work. Nevertheless, some interviewees did manage to successfully juggle three careers: work, family and union. On the other hand other women perceived their family circumstances as incompatible with union activism, indicating that traditional ideology continues to influence some women. Walton (1991), in her study of union women, found that women who said children were the main reason keeping them from being involved, did not have very young children. She concluded that their reluctance was more to do with how they *saw* their role in the family than the practical constraints of finding and paying for a babysitter, for example. In the present study some women became active fairly soon after the breakdown of a long-term relationship, whilst others became active once their children were older, both groups saying that they would not have had time to become involved before. This is perhaps reinforced by the fact that a narrow majority of interviewees were partner-free, including a minority of the office holders. The partner-free women typically emphasised that *their* time was their own and that they were not answerable to anyone in the domestic setting, implying that they clearly thought some women were.

Work and union

In addition to the domestic context, the work context could stand in the way of women's involvement in unions. Generally speaking women are less likely to work in unionized settings.[7] However, the vast majority of interviewees worked in union recognised organizations. Those who did and who held workplace union positions were all in receipt of what they regarded as fairly reasonable and flexible facilities time. Although asked explicitly, the interviewees rarely reported practical problems around getting paid time off for union activities such as attending courses. Interestingly, in the overall context of diminished union presence and influence, this indicates that there was no overt employer hostility to union organization in the contexts concerned.

Those who did not work in unionized organizations were involved to different extents, but perceived the fact that they did not belong to a workplace union to be a barrier to further involvement. Most people's first point of contact with a union is through their workplace (Waddington and Kerr 2002). Given the arcane nature of unions as organizations it is hardly surprising to find that the workplace is the primary route to activism. The workplace is also probably the place where individual activism is sustained, with people who change jobs to non-unionized employment likely to give up their union membership (Woodland and Cully 1997). Delia (TGWU), for example, was now employed in a non-unionized organization, having recently left the transport industry. Although she was determined to remain involved, she was beginning to question the point of being a member in her present work circumstances. Afsana (MSF) and Diane (TGWU) knew very little about the union's structures and the opportunities for participation for someone not employed in a unionized workplace, although they both expressed an interest in finding out more. Meanwhile for Judy (TGWU), disability intersected with unemployment as a dual constraint. First, she was unable to work and felt this would limit her involvement to participation in committees outside of the industrial structures. Second, she faced transportation difficulties. She described how on one occasion

---

7   This is partly because of women's propensity for part-time work, which has lower union density rates than full-time work (Waddington and Kerr, 2002).

she arrived at a union meeting, which was on the top floor of a building with no lift. Determined to get there, she climbed the stairs 'on her bottom' and was then carried into the meeting by another participant. She reflected on how humiliated and exhausted she felt. Third, she was not in good health, her accident having triggered a degenerative condition requiring constant medication. For someone like Judy the pull to participate would need to be strong enough to overcome these enormous barriers.

On the other hand, the absence of a union organised workplace did not have the same impact on the more experienced activists in the study such as Bernadette (TGWU) and Deirdre (MSF). Bernadette had stood down from her position as senior shop steward in a local authority when she became a local councillor. Deirdre was now unable to work because of disability and ill health. She no longer had a workplace union position, but she was chair of her local voluntary sector branch. Because of their former union roles, they both had extensive contact networks within their unions and whilst the nature of Bernadette's involvement was now less formal than Deirdre's, they sustained participation in structures outside of the workplace.

The other major work-related barrier to involvement mentioned by MSF women was heavy workloads and long hours. Three women, Christine, Barbara and Sarah, were managers and professionals in the public sector, working with vulnerable people. Christine, for example, was a senior workplace representative and manager of a day care centre for older people. She said that her professional commitment to her clients would prevent her from getting involved beyond the workplace because unforeseen work crises could occur at any time and she needed to be able to respond by staying late, going in at weekends and so on. Interestingly, although Christine was a single mother, it was her work that she emphasised as constraining. Kim's job entailed extensive travel and she was often away from home, so she felt that she would not have the necessary commitment to take on further union roles, than her position as branch women's representative. There is a gendered dimension to these women's experiences to the extent that although men typically work longer hours than do women, this is not generally reported as a major barrier to male union participation (e.g. Lawrence 1994), because men are more likely to have partners taking care of the home and family (e.g. Watson 1988). When women work long hours, a union position can be one burden too many.

The literature on women in unions often identifies the internal union context as a barrier standing in the way of women's participation (e.g. Cockburn 1991; Cunnison and Stageman 1995; Franzway 2000). This is a theme returned to in Chapter 7, but it is also relevant to the discussion of how and why women came to be active. The main thrust of the arguments concerns the conceptualisation of unions as patriarchal organizations (Cockburn 1991) with masculine cultures adapted to the needs and norms of male trade unionists.

Some interviewees worked in female dominated occupations or organizations and it was women who dominated the local branch. Other women accepted that men ran the local union and they did not problematise this because they had not experienced male domination as disempowering. Kate (MSF) was the only female representative in her branch. Her occupation (laboratory technician in a university) and work environment were male dominated. As a consequence she said she had never identified with other women or with feminism. She got on with men and could not understand the need for separate women's forums within the union. Kate's story will be revisited in subsequent chapters because after attending the women's course she had changed her views on feminism and on male domination of unions, suggesting that the dominant masculine discourse of the local union had obscured her gender identity and its salience. Jane (TGWU) on the other hand was among a number of women who felt constrained by the attitudes and behaviour of a male-dominated branch. Although Jane was recruited as a 'women's rep', in practice the male-led branch had no role they were prepared to give her. Jane was very frustrated by this:

> It's always been male-dominated. I mean I don't do any disciplines or grievances or anything like that, even though I've been going to the education programmes to try to improve my understanding. But no matter how much I learn I'm not going to get anywhere because it's always been male dominated and always will be.

When asked what her union duties were, Jane said that she kept an eye on the ladies' toilets because there were lots of complaints from the few women members about vandalism. Her job was to report these problems to management. Jane's story suggests that although male branch officials might comply with national union edicts, they are able to actively limit the impact that gender equality strategies have in practice, thus consolidating the position of the male-gendered oligarchy (Healy and Kirton 2000). Beryl's story bore similarities to Jane's in that she was originally recruited as a 'women's rep' and given very little to actually do by her male-led branch. However, she recruited other women representatives so that they could stand together to ensure the culture of the branch changed. Beryl thus consolidated and strengthened her position using a gendered strategy. Although now very active at workplace and regional levels, Beryl's time for the union was constrained by multiple domestic responsibilities, as she is a grandmother of four (and helps her daughter with childcare) and part-time carer of an elderly mother and elderly father-in-law. Despite these family circumstances, Beryl spends a lot of time on union business, including participating in some regional committees, and she is also active in the Labour Party, however, she noted:

> I wouldn't have thought I'll take on any more at the moment because I've got a lot of family commitments. I think if you're going to go further in the union you've got to … I mean you can have commitments, but not the sort that I've got at the moment.

Personal confidence issues

The other major issue, which arose as a barrier was lack of confidence in personal skills and abilities, which had various dimensions and clearly intersected with other barriers in the home and family and work and union contexts. For example, when talking about their pasts many women qualified their work histories with the word 'only', i.e. 'for years I was *only* a cleaner', or 'when the kids were young I *only* worked part-time', etc. This was particularly the case with the women who had left school with no or few qualifications, indicating that their gendered work experiences and class positioning had taught them to think of themselves as low achievers.

Privileging the roles of wife and mother can often result in a devaluing of self and low self-esteem in women, but there are also more sinister threats in the domestic situation. Deirdre and Helen talked about low self-esteem when they had lived in the shadow of violent domestic abuse. In addition to domestic violence, Helen had also experienced sexual harassment at her workplace, feeling that she had become marked as a 'victim'. After leaving their husbands both women described how getting involved in the union had represented a turning point when they gradually came to value themselves. As their gender identities shifted to become more active, the women realised that they were not to blame for their predicaments. Both women said that they would never again allow a man to treat them the way their ex-husbands had done, neither in a verbal or physical sense, indicating that union involvement can teach women to construct images of themselves as powerful agents, rather than victims.

Lack of confidence was also often related to interviewees' unfamiliarity with the workings of trade union organization mirroring earlier research (e.g. Cockburn 1991; Rees 1992). Some women felt that they had to learn more before they could become more active or even consider taking a position, whilst other women felt they lacked the confidence to go further in the union: hence their participation in the courses. Interestingly this dimension of lack of confidence was less related to class in so far as many highly qualified women also talked about feeling unconfident to take on a union role. In common with other women, Hilary a TGWU steward situated her own lack of confidence firmly in the context of male-domination of the union. She commented:

> You tend to think you can't compete with them [the men] because they've been involved in the union for years and years and years.

Susan (MSF), a black woman in a work context with few other black people and no black or female union representatives, made similar remarks, for example:

> All the reps in work are quite outspoken and basically I just think I need to have the confidence to do that, which I don't have at the moment.

The discussion of barriers and constraints underscores how women's material circumstances in the home, work, and union contexts have an influence on union participation. Nevertheless, the analysis also reveals instances in which individual women successfully overcome or simply live with the barriers. There are also indications that gendered ideologies continue to have some influence on women, especially on how they perceive and interpret their familial roles. Further, some women's life experiences incline them towards a devaluing of self, which for the purposes of the discussion of union participation engenders the self-perception that they do not have the skills and experience to usefully contribute. The confidence-building capacity of women's courses is one of the primary motivations and outcomes, underlying women's participation as will be discussed in Chapter 6 (see also Greene and Kirton 2002).

Summary

This chapter has explored women's routes to participation and involvement in their unions. The chapter has identified the various influences and orientations the interviewees in the study took with them to the women's schools and outlined where they were in their union careers at that time. It is clear that union participation and union careers are gendered from beginning to end. There are gendered stimuli to participation in the first place, which are reinforced by gendered experiences and roles over the life course, which combine to shape women's relationship with trade unionism. However, as a caveat and reflecting the theoretical underpinning of the research discussed in Chapter 1, this does not mean that women have an entirely common and uniquely female experience. They also share experiences with men in their families, communities, unions and workplaces, such that there is a large class-based element to their social identities. They are also divided by other identity characteristics such as race, sexuality and disability.

Significantly, the analysis shows that union involvement for women is possible irrespective of domestic circumstances (mirroring other recent research, e.g. Munro 1999). However, the consideration of barriers and constraints highlights the importance for a woman-centred gender analysis of exploring both the public and private domains, without which women's problematic relationship to trade union participation cannot be properly understood. In particular, Afsana reminds us that the social organization of trade unionism has not evolved with carers in mind:

> Barriers? Children and time. It's all very well for me to go away for the odd week; that can be arranged. But for lone parents like me, it's very difficult to get more involved. I need to think about the children. If I could take the children with me to meetings I would get more involved. (Afsana, MSF)

The next chapter explores women's experiences of women-only trade union courses.

Chapter 6

The Shaping of Women's Trade Union Careers

The aim of this chapter is to explore experiences of women-only courses and to discuss how the courses influence women's union orientations. The analysis draws on interviews with MSF and TGWU course participants, interviews with tutors and surveys of participants.

As background to the discussions in this chapter it is relevant to note that most interviewees in the study (10 of each union) received paid leave to attend the women's school. Those who did not were, with two exceptions, either currently self-employed, unemployed or in non-unionised employment contexts. Regarding the two exceptions, Sarah (MSF) felt it inappropriate as a part-time worker and non-office holder to ask for paid time off. Mandy (TGWU) was the only representative denied paid leave. She had recently attended a shop stewards course and her employer said that the women's school was not relevant to her union duties, as there were only two women in her branch consisting of male bus drivers. She took annual leave. The other office holders reported no problems in getting 'reasonable' paid time off for union courses. What was 'reasonable' was determined by a combination of the woman's perception of job constraints and management's willingness to endorse paid leave. In this respect the findings mirror those of other studies in well-organised contexts, where there is often little sign of major detrimental changes in union-management relations (e.g. Bradley 1999: 194) despite an overall context in Britain of union decline.

It is also worth noting that many of the women interviewed (eight MSF, 11 TGWU) had prior experience of at least one union course. Some of these had also previously attended at least one women's course (four MSF, five TGWU). From Table 6.1 it is possible to see that the interviewee sample's prior union education experience closely resembles that of the larger group of survey respondents.

Table 6.1 Previous MSF/TGWU courses (last 2 years)

	MSF 2000 and 2002 (N = 67)	TGWU 1999 and 2001(N = 98)
Yes	38 (57%)	67 (68%)
No	29 (43%)	31 (32%)

Therefore, overall a majority of interviewees (and women's school participants) in both unions were not newcomers to union education, suggesting that the aim of attracting less experienced women is not being fully met in either union.

Why attend a women's school?

This section considers interviewees' motivations for attending the women's schools. As explained in Chapter 4 the national women's schools of both unions are open to 'ordinary' members as well as activists and office holders, therefore it is likely that women attend for a variety of different reasons. We cannot fully understand how their union careers develop after the school without knowing why they attended in the first place.

Although some interviewees had multiple motivations that emerged during the course of interviews, most were able to articulate their primary reason when asked explicitly. Three broad reasons were identified, which related to the woman's perceptions of her learning needs and her expectations of the content of the course: union reasons, work reasons and personal reasons. The interviews addressed the women-only dimension of the course as a motivator, but most women had to be prompted to talk about this. Therefore the simple fact of it being a women's school was not in itself articulated as a motivator, although it was often bound up with other motivators to the extent that it was difficult to disentangle as discussed below.

Union reasons

It should come as no surprise that the majority of interviewees (eight MSF, 13 TGWU) expressed 'union reasons'; although there was a greater variety of motivations among the MSF interviewees and a more explicit prior union orientation or commitment among the TGWU women. The women who cited 'union reasons' expressed an explicit desire to gain/improve skills and knowledge related to office holding or to developing a union career (including contacts and networking). About half were (relatively) new workplace representatives or inexperienced members. These women typically emphasised their need to gain skills and confidence to carry out their present union roles and/or their desire to learn more about the union and the types of involvement and paid careers possible. Linda as a new MSF workplace women's representative was typical. This was her first course, suggested by her male branch secretary: she felt that before she could begin to participate in workplace negotiations and representation she needed some training so that her skills would 'match' those of management.

The more experienced women who gave 'union reasons' for attending the women's schools typically stressed the importance of the opportunity to network with women in the union and the importance of keeping abreast of changes in the employment relationship, particularly legal aspects. For example, Bernadette and Mary (TGWU) commented:

You get to meet your sisters basically and there's a sense of solidarity and a sense of support. There's an element of networking involved as well. If you've got a problem you can talk with other people and try to resolve it. Plus, it's also about keeping up to date with current issues, the law etc.

It helps a lot you know because you get to know where to go for help. I mean you've got all the handbooks, so you know where to look, but you also need something more. Once you've met people that you can relate to and contact, it's so much easier.

Work reasons

Only two MSF women (and no TGWU women) emphasised their wish to gain/ improve skills related to their present paid work or to developing their paid work careers. Kim was seeking promotion in her paid work:

It [negotiating skills] was something I knew was on my training plan. I've wanted to go on a negotiating course for ages because that's part of what I do. I also thought it would be useful for my personal life.

The perception that a union course might provide an opportunity to learn skills relevant to paid work was partly attributable to the broad appeal of MSF courses noted in Chapter 4. Nevertheless, Kim was also actively involved in her union branch as women's officer, although as this was a composite branch and her workplace was not unionised, her role did not involve negotiating. Her case does, however, highlight that union activism and wishing to move upward in a paid work career are not mutually exclusive (see Healy and Kirton 2002). She indicated that she preferred to do the union's negotiating course, rather than a management course selected by her company. Susan was in a similar situation, in that she had recently begun to participate in union affairs and expressed a desire to increase her involvement, but she was not an office-holder. Her primary reason for attending the women's course was that promotions were coming up at her workplace and she thought a negotiating skills course might equip her with the necessary skills for the higher level job. Strangely perhaps, Kim and Susan both received paid release from work. This does not necessarily indicate a generous or pro-union employer, but perhaps a cost-conscious, astute one. Union courses are after all free of charge and the union reimburses travel expenses. If work skills are developed, the employer's costs are minimal compared to the prices charged by staff/management training organizations, which could be one reason why they received paid leave.

Personal reasons

Six interviewees (four MSF, two TGWU) cited 'personal reasons', expressing a general interest/curiosity in the women's school and sometimes indicating that they were bored with their lives/work, or that they had a desire to socialise with like-minded people. With one exception these were hitherto inactive members or they participated informally. The exception was Kate (MSF) who held two local positions, which she was about to resign because of impending redundancy. She attended 'Women's Week' because after a long period of high union involvement she felt quite negative about the union and under stress. She thought that a 'quiet week' would help her reflect and make sense of her present situation. Here, it is important to note the pleasant environment the MSF college offers. Similarly, three other women were in need of a retreat for reflection. Barbara (MSF) and Delia (TGWU) were informally active and had, supported by their unions, recently been through stressful Employment Tribunal cases of sexual harassment. Evelyn, an inactive member of TGWU had recently suffered the death of her young son and was persuaded to go to Eastbourne by her branch secretary as a temporary distraction from her grief.[1]

The significance of the women-only setting

In context of a discussion about the role of women-only trade union education in the making of women's trade union careers, it is relevant to explore why women opt for women's courses when there are a plethora of mixed-sex courses available (especially to activists and office-holders), some with ostensibly similar content. In many cases, as stated above, the fact that the courses were women-only events intersected with the interviewees' primary motivation to attend. Over half the interviewees (nine MSF and nine TGWU) admitted, sometimes reluctantly, that part of the reason they had chosen the course was because it was women only.

Half (six MSF and three TGWU) of these women had no previous experiences of women-only courses, but their prior belief, in some cases (six) based on their experiences of mixed-sex courses, was that it would be a more comfortable environment. These women had active gender identities: they were conscious of the male-dominated nature of their unions and believed that they would escape the 'macho' context by attending a women's school. It is undoubtedly significant that most (seven) were also self-defined feminists,[2] therefore it seemed that feminist values, which see the importance of women-only spaces had underpinned their motivation or in Briskin's terms (1993) that they had ideologically bought into the 'politic of separate organizing' (see Chapter 2). Diane (TGWU), for example, had recently completed a degree in women's studies and had no experience of trade union courses. Even so, as a self-defined feminist her prior belief was that a women's course would be 'less macho' than a mixed-sex one and that consequently as a complete novice she would feel more comfortable. One black woman from MSF, Kamaljit, a self-defined feminist, was a firm believer in separate spaces for women. She argued that some Asian women had a preference for women-only forums, but equally she thought they were important for lesbians. She said that from her experience heterosexual

---

1   The tutors had been made fully aware of this woman's situation and the compassion they showed her was very touching and served as a reminder of the broader role that a union can play in the lives of its members. She was immensely grateful for the support and kindness she received during the week.

2   See broader discussion of feminism in Chapter 1 and 2.

women were 'more tolerant' of lesbians than were heterosexual men and therefore she had anticipated that she would feel more comfortable at a women's school. When asked whether she had thought instead about attending a black member school, she remarked:

> When I was 18 I went to this black only group and I was told I wasn't black. I know the definition of black has changed in ten years, but that was my starting-point, so that wasn't very positive. I think there are different issues for black women than for black men and I would be more interested in black women-only.

Another black woman, Afsana (MSF), who was not a self-defined feminist, but who had an active gender identity, also felt that as an Asian woman she would be more comfortable in a women-only environment on religious and cultural grounds:

> Speaking from an Asian background, when women get together they sort of come out of their shells and they can talk about anything. But when you're with males you tend to be a bit quieter.

Other interviewees had been influenced by previous positive experiences of women-only union courses (three MSF and five TGWU). Two of the MSF women in this category had no experience of mixed-sex courses (see Helen's story below).

Helen's Story

Helen was not a self-defined feminist and had no prior value commitment to women-only spaces, and in 1999 when she first attended 'Women's Week' she had been indifferent to the women-only dimension of the school; the dates had been convenient and the content was relevant. In 2000, however she consciously chose a women-only course, indicating a shifting gender identity:

'The first time I just liked the idea of a negotiating skills course. I felt that was what I needed and it just happened that Women's Week was offering the course at the right time for me. But I got so much out of it. It was so great that I wanted to go back this year and never really considered doing any other course than Women's Week. I think that we're representing nearly all women and we have no men on our negotiating committee, so it just seemed appropriate that I would do a women's course.'

Helen explained what she had gained from Women's Week:

'I found the whole learning experience invaluable, from a personal and union perspective. We learned that individually and as a group we are all strong and capable individuals. What emerged was that, as women, we can break through the glass ceiling and draw on each other and support each other and not make excuses or apologise if we're not perfect.'

Her comments are suggestive of a growing union and gender identity.

Fiona, a self-identified feminist, felt strongly that there is a place for women-only courses, but that mixed-sex courses also needed to appeal to women. When asked whether she was so enthusiastic about 'Women's Week' because it was so enjoyable or because the women-only dimension was important for the learning, she said emphatically that the two could not be separated. She stated that 'Women's Week changes people's lives.'

Judy (TGWU) on the other hand, in common with other TGWU women influenced by previous experiences of both mixed-sex and women-only courses commented:

> It did appeal to me that it was women only because then you get no sort of macho business coming through. It was really good seeing them enjoying themselves, you know like you're let off the leash. You get that comradeship that you don't seem to have when you're on mixed courses.

Judy's remark about 'macho business' was typical of these women's perceptions and experiences of mixed-sex courses, which undoubtedly coloured their decision to opt for the women's school. The case of a small group of TGWU women contradicts Walton's (1991: 168) finding that women who have been on several courses are less supportive of women-only courses because they are less sympathetic to the forms of women's oppression that less successful women experience. It suggests that some 'successful' union women continue to see the relevance of women's groups for themselves and other women. It is also worth noting that two of these women did not self-identify as feminists, indicating support from some non-feminist women for feminist practices. Thus, a gender identity can become a base for action without an espousedly feminist identification.

As a motivating factor some interviewees had not attached any significance to the women-only aspect of the course. They generally said that they had not given any thought at all to the fact that all students would be women. These women typically said that the school was on convenient dates, that the content appealed, or that someone else (a paid officer or a branch official) had 'put their name down for it'. For example, in Evelyn's case (above), her branch secretary felt that the women's school would be less threatening in view of her recent bereavement, whilst Evelyn herself had not thought about it in advance of the course. Some of these women were quite surprised to be asked whether the fact that the school was women-only figured at all in their decision to attend, but usually they did go on to describe their course *experiences* in gender aware terms, as will be discussed later. The comments below reflect this view of the insignificance (as a motivator) attached to the women-only status of the courses. The first is a woman from a female-dominated workplace and the second from a male-dominated:

> It's no different from what I normally come across, because the majority of office workers are women anyway, so that's normal for me. It wasn't an issue for me as long as I get on well with everyone. (Susan, MSF)

I don't care what the course is, as long as it helps me, whether it's with male, male and female. It doesn't matter, it's totally irrelevant; I don't just go on women's courses. (Jane, TGWU)

Susan displays an active, but not politicised gender identity, whilst Jane displays a passive gender identity. There was one other group of women who expressed in principle opposition to women-only courses. None of these women were self-identified feminists even though later in the interview they talked in gender-conscious terms and demonstrated at least partial and contingent support for women-only courses. For example:

I wasn't interested in feminist issues. I felt that just because I'm female it doesn't mean that I'm going to go on a female in the union course. I really thought they were going to be men bashing, slagging men off the whole week and I thought that it wasn't right. I went down there absolutely determined that if anyone started slagging men off in general, then I would object, because I felt that that is anti-union and just because we get together with women, we shouldn't use that as an opportunity to start insulting our brothers in the union. (Kate, MSF)

Kate displayed a politicised class identity and her fear seemed to be that feminism, by "blaming" men, stood in opposition to class politics.

Elizabeth's Story

Elizabeth had attended numerous mixed-sex and women-only trade union courses and she displayed an ambivalent attitude towards women's separate organizing. She appeared concerned that it undermined the commonality of purpose on which trade unionism is built:

'I can see why some women would like it to be women-only, but I think it is actually very discriminatory, because we don't have a men-only course. The workforce is made up of women and men and men have similar problems to women. Men have sexual harassment, men suffer from bullying, men have career problems and I don't see why that should all be women's issues.'

Elizabeth was prepared to be pragmatic: she found 'Women's Week' useful and enjoyable, plus it was convenient for her to attend. In the course of her union career, she had also participated in other women's forums within the union movement. She did not entirely approve of their existence at an ideological level, yet she believed them to be doing valuable work in pursuit of women's equality. She explains why she is a delegate to a TUC regional women's committee:

'Partly because no one else wanted to go on it, so I did. There are certain issues which I think are women-related. One that I've been working on lately with the committee is advertising – the way they use women in advertising. There's no need for a woman in a bikini to lie across the bonnet of a Fiesta, for example. So as far as I'm concerned I'm very much on women's side. There are a few other issues too. I think that women are still working under a glass ceiling. There's definitely discrimination at the top level of management and I think that needs to be addressed, so that's why I'm interested in it [the women's committee].'

Like Elizabeth Mandy (TGWU) was also uncertain about the rationale for women-only forums:

> I always said that I don't want preferential treatment, so I didn't want to get involved (in women-only forums). I wanted equality not preferential treatment. But then coming here I realised it's not about asking for preferential treatment, it's equality we're after and that is all they want to give us.

Mandy had found talking and listening to 'role model women' encouraging and inspiring:

> I would say I've got a lot more from this one. There's more inclusion certainly from all women and you see other women who started where I am now and you see that you've a chance to do it yourself.

Nevertheless, she felt that it was important for women to attend mixed-sex courses, because they could learn a lot from men too:

> I mean men have been at it a lot longer than we have and they've been through a lot more. They're just letting us in, but only letting us peep round the door at the minute. We're just sticking our heads into the room; that's how I see it, we're not in the room yet. They know the rule-book back to front and you get valuable experience from that. They do it with their heads and we do it with our hearts, I think.

Christine's concerns stemmed not from a politicised position, but reflected a belief held by some (generally non-feminist) women that women-only environments were 'unnatural' and therefore threatening:

> I'm not used to being in a women-only environment for longer than a couple of hours. I had kind of a little anxiety about it, but the fact that Jane (a work colleague) was going to be there helped me calm down about it. I'm not used to being with a crowd of women, it makes me freak, I just don't like it, because you know the bitchiness will start.

In summary, whilst there are three broad reasons which drove the interviewees to attend the courses, the majority of the TGWU women were primarily motivated by 'union reasons', whilst there was greater variety of motivators among the MSF women. The reasons for this can only be conjectured. It is possible for example that the publicity material influences members' perceptions of the relevance of courses. MSF highlights the 'life skills', which 'Women's Week' seeks to develop and therefore its relevance to *all* women members and activists. TGWU places more emphasis on union skills and therefore attempts to appeal more to women, who are or who wish to become active/office holders. Most women pointed to both the form and content of the courses as being important: that is getting together as women and/ or trade unionists to learn from each other, but also the desire or perceived necessity to acquire knowledge/skills generally underpinned the motivation to attend. Some women ended up on a women-only course more by accident than by design. If by accident, it was only afterwards when reflecting back during interviews on their experiences that they attached any significance to the women-only dimension, as we shall see later. If by design, there were a variety of reasons primarily related to gender, but at times intersecting with race and sexuality.

The chapter now turns to the participants' experiences of the women's schools. First, there is a brief discussion of the confidence and knowledge building capacity of the courses. Following this there is a more detailed examination of perceptions and experiences. This is organised around the key elements and processes, which emerged from the data analysis: 'safe space', shared learning, and the privileging of 'women's issues' (see also Kirton and Healy 2004).

Perceptions and experiences of women-only schools

Building confidence and knowledge

It cannot be emphasised enough that according to participants increased confidence was the most significant personal outcome from the women's courses. As Table 6.2 demonstrates, an overwhelming majority of the survey respondents said that the school built their confidence, whilst the gendered knowledge gained and the opportunity to network with other union women were also hugely important for the majority of students, especially in TGWU.

Table 6.2 Purposes of women's school

Purpose	MSF: Number of Respondents 2000/02 (%) N = 66	TGWU: Number of Respondents 1999/2001 (%) N = 99
Built my confidence	55 (83%)	71 (72%)
Provided an opportunity to network	43 (65%)	57 (58%)
Deepened my understanding of women's position in society	34 (52%)	63 (64%)
Given me practical suggestions for improving things for women at work	35 (53%)	82 (83%)
Other	8 (12%)	26 (26%)

These findings were mirrored in the interviews, where women talked about confidence levels, but also about the specificities of the knowledge and skills they had gained from the particular course they had attended. Even more experienced women perceived that they had gained confidence and some from male-dominated workplaces and/or branches felt that they needed to regularly attend women's events in order to remain confident in their roles or at articulating their opinions. The tutors also concurred that to build women's confidence was the primary aim of women's courses as well as the main outcome:

> Confidence. That's the main difference between women's courses and men's courses. Men dominate in mixed courses. Women have the space to be more vocal and assertive on women's courses and that's good for your confidence. (Sarah, TGWU)

> Women's courses give women a voice. They show women they have the right to a voice. They break women's silence. (Ruth, MSF)

Of course it is recognised that confidence cannot be built or put to good use in a vacuum, as Elizabeth (MSF) suggested when reflecting on what she had gained from 'Women's Week':

> Confidence really, apart from the knowledge that I wanted anyway. But the confidence and the backing-up of my own gut feelings, if you like. But the confidence has got to be backed up by the knowledge in the long run. But then if you've got the knowledge and not the confidence, then you can't put it over anyway, not matter how much knowledge you've got.

Thus, the knowledge building capacity of union courses is almost taken for granted – after all one expects to acquire information and knowledge from a course. However, the fact that an overwhelming majority of women (see Table 6.2) felt that they had learnt about how women's working lives could be improved is obviously significant from the point of view of achieving gendered transformation of the workplace.

Whilst the more experienced women expected to get a little more confident with each course they did, some of the newer women were quite amazed by how different they felt about themselves at the end of the course. Some were very animated and quite emotional as they recalled their feelings at the end of the women's school and described the impact the week had had on their confidence, self-esteem and sense of personal efficacy. The following quotations are cited in an attempt to capture this:

> The women's week was excellent, it really was. I learnt on the course how long women have been trying to be heard in unions and it's given me strength, I'm proud to be a woman, a black woman, I'm proud to be one. It gave me that inner strength and confidence that I think I needed to be able to say "just because you're a man and I'm a woman, I can do this thing just as good as you". It gave me inner strength and confidence. (Christine, MSF)

> What did I gain? Oh my God, I just gained so many things – self-confidence and regained my belief in myself, and the things I stand for really, which was wavering. Meeting so many people in different situations and some of them in more difficult situations than myself, and they're still fighting on. I think it enabled me to really tap into my own resources. God yeah. It's been huge, massive for me, in terms of my self-esteem and what I think I can do now. (Kamaljit, MSF)

This was my second "Women's Week" course at Whitehall and the high and the sense of empowerment I felt at the end of the week are very special. It is impossible to explain to anyone else just how special "Women's Week" is. All I can say is I am a better person for having attended and I strive to become a better organiser! (Helen, MSF – taken from her written assignment for credit with Leeds University)

I had a wonderful time I really did. It was great, it was very enlightening and I thought the tutors were wonderful. I couldn't believe it at the end of it there was me giving a three-minute speech in front of all those people. It just seemed like everybody was like one big family there. (Sally, TGWU)

It gave me this enormous confidence. I don't think I'd have been able to go on last week's [mixed-sex] course this time last year. You get a much greater camaraderie and I think the change in people, not in their personality, but in their confidence – it grows tremendously when there are other women. (Delia, TGWU)

The interviewees talked about the women-only setting being empowering for women, but the concept of empowerment is slippery, so it is necessary to interpret what precisely this means. Young (1997: 89) states that empowerment can be defined either as the 'development of individual autonomy, self-control and confidence' or as the 'development of a sense of collective influence over the social conditions of one's life'. Young prefers the latter because she believes it has the greatest potential for social change, but from this study, elements of the former could be seen as necessary preconditions of the latter, so that the two definitions are not mutually exclusive. Chapter 7 addresses the question of how the empowered group of women sought to develop influence over their work/union lives.

The next three sections examine the main features of women-only courses that together create this empowering setting. The main elements of this discussion are also represented schematically in Figure 6.1 (Kirton and Healy 2004). The three concepts in the left-hand column provide a way of conceptualising the women's course experiences in a way congruent with the feminist paradigm of the research outlined in Chapter 1.

'Safe space'

Feminist writers have argued that the position women occupy in contemporary societies is one that discourages them from participating equally in mixed-sex meetings (e.g. Phillips 1991). Accordingly, forms of women's separate organizing emerged as a response in order to create a space for women free of the constraints of patriarchal gender relations (see Chapter 2). The tutors in the study all agreed that women's courses created a 'safe space' for women to learn the craft of activism, but they revealed different orientations to the concept of women's separate organizing, the principle of which was more likely to be accepted by the self-defined feminist MSF tutors.

The three MSF 'Women's Week' tutors all self-identified as feminists and although they recognised that not all women identify with feminism, feminist values nevertheless underpinned their own practice. They all used the feminist concept of 'safe space' to describe the purpose and rationale of women-only courses and talked about what they felt this meant for women, for example:

> Women-only courses are about recognising that women have specific needs in terms of confidence building. Women are more comfortable in a women-only environment, they are forced to take on dominant roles, rather than leave them to the men. They also need a safe space to concentrate on women's perspectives and issues. (Ruth, MSF)

Figure 6.1   Map of concepts, process and outcomes of women-only trade union courses

Concept	Processes	Outcomes
'Safe Space'	Women talk more openly, free from the constraints of patriarchal relations.	Women develop a language in which to voice their experiences and perceptions.
	Less formal arrangements (i.e. free flowing contributions, rather than ordered through the chair/tutor.)	Women develop the confidence to participate.
	Women take risks and make mistakes (in their contributions), but encourage and support each other. Emotions are displayed.	Women practice the art of public speaking and develop the skills of articulating opinions.
Privileging of 'women's issues'	In classroom activities women are placed at the centre of the trade union 'stage' and in the 'dramas' enacted.	Women become visible as women to themselves. Gender identity is built/enhanced/affirmed, alongside trade union identity.
	Personal stories of harassment, discrimination and oppression are told.	The trade union agenda is 'gendered' to include sexual harassment, domestic violence, women's health, etc. Women become sensitised to the heterogeneity of female experiences and 'realities'.
Shared Learning	Camaraderie develops, especially in the residential context.	Friendship groups and informal networks emerge.
	Students 'talk union'.	
	The more able/more experienced support and encourage the less able/less experienced.	Participants become more interested in the union. Women's confidence and self-esteem grow.

They were aware of the controversy surrounding forms of women's separate organizing, but this did not alter their firmly held support for women-only courses. They were asked to explain the rationale for women's courses when women are proportionally represented among students of mixed-sex courses and the following response typifies the views expressed:

> Consciously making space for different interest groups is now recognised within the trade union movement. The evidence that specific interest groups are more likely to participate within their own spaces is very compelling. There can be barriers to women's learning opportunities in the male-dominated environment. Also, women often spend their time talking to the men, but not to each other – they need the space to talk to each other without the distraction of men's presence. Plus, the fact that women are there doesn't mean that they are learning as well as they can, or about the same things as in women-only courses. (Gina, MSF)

The above signals support for a politic of separate organizing (Briskin 1993). In contrast with the MSF tutors, none of the four TGWU tutors self-identified as feminists. As a possible consequence, the TGWU tutors revealed more ambivalent views about women's courses. They did show at least partial and contingent support, but this was viewed much more as a temporary strategy and only necessary as long as women continued to be heavily outnumbered on mixed-sex courses. The following quotation typifies the views expressed:

> Sometimes when women introduce themselves on mixed courses, you can tell they feel intimidated, that's reality, that's how women are around men. It's not the way I think it should be. Ideally we shouldn't need separate courses for women, but that's the way a lot of women feel when they're around men, so women-only courses are essential. (Miriam, TGWU)

The above is reminiscent of Briskin's (1993) 'deficit model' of women's separate organizing: the idea that women are lacking in attributes necessary for trade union participation, which women's groups can correct. This might be expressed as women needing more confidence, but the emphasis is on empowering women to *cope with* rather than *challenge* the male-defined status quo. However, it could be argued that 'coping' and 'challenging' are not 'either/or' scenarios, rather the first is a prerequisite of the second, as many of the women in this study appeared to recognise, as we see below.

This clear ideological division between the MSF and TGWU tutors might be explained by a combination of two factors. First, the three MSF tutors are all highly educated professional workers and middle class (although two are from working class backgrounds). In contrast, the TGWU tutors comprise one current and one former factory worker (now a full-time TGWU tutor), a school cook and a former nurse (now with TGWU Education Department). This reflects the argument in the literature that feminism has most appealed to middle class women (e.g. hooks 1989). Second, the internal culture of the two unions is different. To begin with MSF's director of education is a self-identified feminist herself and her position has undoubtedly influenced the longstanding existence of 'Women's Week' and has legitimated feminism as an ideological standpoint within the education department. In contrast TGWU has a very strong unitarist working class culture, which informs discourse and practice within the education department. This is perhaps most evidenced by the fact that men occasionally tutor on women-only courses, a practice, which would not be countenanced by MSF but which was opposed by only one of the TGWU tutors.

Interviews with the women participants indicated that the tutors' assessment of the value of the 'safe space' were correct. This emerged strongly in the context of both unions, with many women articulating a critical appraisal of mixed-sex courses. Sarah, for example, a seemingly confident, highly educated, professional woman, concurred with the MSF tutors that a masculine culture pervades mixed-sex courses and this inhibits women's learning.

Hilary's Story

Hilary had previously attended women's and mixed-sex courses. She was able to compare these experiences:

'I think in the women-only ones [courses] you tend to be more honest, more open; perhaps because women are less judgmental. You're with your peers and some of the experiences that people talk about, you know you can recognise the things they're saying, you associate with them. I mean I know when I've done a week on the shop stewards courses [mixed-sex], after a couple of days, yes you do get more relaxed, but it seems to happen much quicker with the women-only courses.'

Hilary felt that being able to relax and feel empathy for the stories women told was very important for the learning, but she was also uncomfortable with the idea that women-only might mean feminism which might mean 'man-hating':

'I think although it's women-only and women are running the course, I think that the tutors have to make sure that they give both sides of the story, if you like, or both sides of the argument so that you don't end up with a room full of men haters or staunch feminists that weren't when they went into the course. Obviously the idea is to educate, but not to sway people's minds like that.'

As a mother of a pre-school daughter, Hilary could have used the T&G Centre crèche, but she said that she preferred to have the week away to concentrate on herself and the course. However, she had to negotiate time away from home with her husband:

'I mean I think if it was too regular he'd [her husband] probably complain, but as long as I don't drop it on him and say 'oh by the way I'm not going to be here next week', he's fine about it. There's give and take on both sides, so he's very supportive.'

If as Briskin (1993) argues, male power is socially constituted it is bound to be reflected in and reinforced by patterns of behaviour in arenas such as trade union courses. Hilary (TGWU, above) talked about her contrasting experiences and perceptions of mixed-sex and women-only courses. Several women across the two unions alluded to the different atmosphere of mixed-sex courses, particularly the competitive nature of masculine behaviour, indicating that the women-only setting provides an escape or a shelter. Some women indicated that it was not simply that men intimidated them; it was more that they did not want to play out traditional gendered social relations, which would cast them in the subordinate position. For example:

> The mixed course I went to, I felt that some of the men tried to show off and it was a bit embarrassing, whereas if I wasn't there they probably would have acted differently or if it had been equal men to women. At the women's school you didn't even have to think about any of that. I was in no way intimidated; I just thought they were showing off. (Melanie, TGWU)

Similarly, Kim (MSF) also expressed a widely held view:

> There wasn't this competitive element; you didn't have to constantly have your guard up like you do with men. Because if you're not careful they will take advantage in all sorts of subtle, psychological ways. They do like to think they're better than everybody else and it gets very wearing after a while.

Kim and Melanie's remarks demonstrate that the concept of 'safe space' is not simply about protecting timid, unassertive women from competitive or aggressive masculine behaviour, although it can be. It is also an acknowledgement that women do not always want to 'play by men's rules' as Linda (MSF) put it. For some women then, the 'safe space' was less of a protective zone or shelter; rather it was a space for the expression of women's oppression. Further, as suggested by Cunnison and Stageman's (1995) work it was a space where women felt 'safe' to negotiate their own 'rules' of behaviour, rather than adopt male-defined rules (Bradley 1999). Thus on women's courses, women's gender identity is not being questioned. The female-defined rules included 'allowing' the expression of emotion, openly supporting each other (rather than competing) something according to tutors and more experienced interviewees, rarely seen on mixed-sex courses (see also Greene and Kirton 2002), where as Gottfried (1998) asserts 'gender displays' are regarded as unruly practices. This analysis also fits with Young's (2000) assertion that emotions and storytelling are examples of more inclusive modes of political communication. This is highlighted by Sally (TGWU), where we see the significance of female-defined modes of expression:

> I just felt that everyone was so supportive of one another. I really felt the emotion, like when somebody went up to do their little speech in front of the class and they were struggling, you know, and they got stuck and you could see the look on people's faces. It was so emotional where they were just going like "come on, come on". The real encouragement was there.

Shared learning

In addition to being integral to trade union education generally the sharing of and learning from each other's experiences is embedded in feminist approaches to women's collective organization. This was one of the aims of the small feminist groups spawned by the women's movement of the 1970s, which sought to create an atmosphere of mutual support to enable women to contribute to meetings, often for the first time (Phillips 1991). Thus the women-only setting, the 'safe space', is intended to be developmental and empowering (Reinelt 1994) for women individually and collectively (helping them to develop the intellectual and practical resources to contribute on their own terms), rather than simply remedial (equipping them to cope with the male-dominated status quo). This legacy is reflected in women's structures in trade unions generally (e.g. Colgan and Ledwith 2000) and therefore in women's courses.

Women's residential schools have a special character. To begin with, for many women, especially mothers, it was clear that the course represented a rare opportunity to 'escape' domestic responsibilities for a few days, which many relished, as in Hilary's story above. Many interviewees commented on how refreshing they found the experience and how being away from home meant that they did not have to think about picking up children, cooking dinner and so on.

Of course the extent to which the mere fact of being away from home shapes the learning experience is debatable. But from observation and interviews it is clear that the experience of residential courses is a very intense one and that this does impact on the learning. Living for six days in an enclosed environment with a small group of women, undisturbed by the outside world is inevitably a different experience from day release courses: union talk goes on well into the evening. Also, some interviewees reported sharing personal things about themselves that they had not thought of in a long time or that they had never talked to others about. For example some women revealed experiences of domestic violence, of poverty, of disability and of single motherhood. Such issues only got onto the agenda because the women were together for several days building up trust between them. Thus the concept of 'shared learning' needs to be interpreted broadly in the context of women's schools, for it extends beyond the taught 'curriculum' and beyond the traditional trade union agenda. Most of the interviewees believed that this kind of personal 'opening up' and the mutually supportive environment were crucial for their learning and had a role to play in the confidence building or empowering processes of the courses. Christine (MSF) voices an opinion shared by many of the interviewees:

> I think that women don't have to wear masks then, I think that women think that in that situation [a women-only setting] they will be understood, no matter what issues they come out with, other women will understand.

It was also clear that the telling of personal stories helped the course participants construct an understanding of their lives as socially conditioned and constrained by wider social dynamics, as suggested by Young (1997: 91). For example, Mary (TGWU) commented:

> Because you're not inhibited in any way you can really entirely speak freely and only other women can really understand because for so long women's contribution hasn't been recognised, but now that's changing.

Related to this, the argument has been made that women-only courses are designed to reverse 'internalised oppression' where women react to their low status by undervaluing themselves (Brew and Garavan 1995). This was either implicitly or explicitly acknowledged on the women's courses. The MSF education officer responsible for 'Women's Week' explicitly articulated this goal in interview and has designed an exercise for the end of the second day of the course which seeks to foster a sense of self-worth in the women. This involves each woman in turn saying something she does well and something she is proud of in her life. On the courses observed women frequently mentioned their children as a source of pride, but also other (gendered?) positive personal characteristics, such as 'being a good friend' or a 'good listener'. Each woman is applauded and in interview many participants commented on how touching and uplifting they had found the exercise.

A similar scenario occurs at the TGWU women's school, when women in senior union positions form a panel to talk to the students in a highly personalised way about how they got where they are as women in a male-dominated union, often balancing work and family at the same time. Many interviewees talked about how inspired they were by these role model women. These types of exercise signal that women's courses are not simply about getting women to behave like men. Therefore the findings indicate that the emphasis on building women's confidence through shared learning on women's courses is not simply about 'changing women' as Briskin (1993: 96) suggests. Rather, it is about valuing women as women and developing among the women a positive collective gender identity.

Another dimension of shared learning is that the tutors in the study did not position themselves as experts. It was evident from interviews and from observation that they saw themselves more as facilitators of other women's learning than as teachers. This is in keeping with trade union pedagogy (Croucher 2004) and the feminist egalitarian ideal that as women we can all learn from each other by sharing our life experiences. Many women spoke with obvious surprise about how the tutors were 'just normal' or 'like one of us'. This occurred in both unions despite the possible greater class distance between MSF tutors and some students.

The mix of 'successful' experienced union women and newer women also provided important opportunities for shared learning in both unions. The more experienced union women represented role models to the less experienced, as Sally (TGWU) suggested:

> It was very enlightening to see what other people are having to deal with and I must admit when it came to some of the stories – I thought my company was bad, but … I just felt that also you learn that if you, if something is not going right, I think women sometimes

don't want to stand up and say anything and I just felt it was nice to see women there that actually really wanted to make a difference.

However, the more experienced women also felt they had a lot to learn from the less experienced:

I didn't feel that I was up there because I'm Chair here. I thought that if anything they were slightly better than I was and in a way I felt slightly humbled. (Elizabeth, MSF)

Without doubt for many participants the women's schools are important opportunities for personal growth. Beyond that though, how does the shared learning that occurs, contribute to the shaping of women's trade union and/or gender identities? Earlier research has highlighted the role of residential union courses in nurturing a spirit of comradeship (e.g. Miller 1983), which from interviews and observation certainly occurred at the women's schools: interviewees talked about the feeling of 'bonding', 'solidarity' and 'camaraderie' that the courses fostered. It was also the case that the sharing of gender specific life experiences appeared to heighten women's gender consciousness and thereby in many shifted a previously passive gender identity towards an active or politicised one. This gendered knowledge base has the potential to become a powerful resource, which could contribute towards advancing women's equality in the workplace and in the unions.

Privileging 'women's issues'

The concept of privileging 'women's issues' concerns the opportunity, rarely afforded by mainstream union democratic processes and structures (e.g. Munro 2001), for women to emphasise the issues that are particularly pertinent to them and to explore the gender dimensions of the traditional trade union agenda. These discussions might not take an explicitly feminist character, but they do seek to cultivate gender consciousness, as indicated by the following tutor remarks:

If we want to recruit women, then the union must deal with the issues that affect women and this school is pivotal for this. (Charlene, TGWU)

There's a focus on gender and gender relations, although a different language is being used to describe these things, probably with less of an explicit emphasis on feminism now. But the courses still start from the point of women's personal issues and personal problems, then move to gender relations, i.e. they are still situating the personal within a political context. (Gina, MSF)

That said, the TGWU tutors placed less emphasis on the content of the women's school (i.e. the opportunity to privilege 'women's issues') and more on the form (the women-only setting), as Michelle indicated:

I don't think the courses should just be about women – there should be something for everyone, even on women's courses. We're not trying to develop militant feminists. After all, they have to go back to their workplaces and bargain for everyone and they need to be able to appeal to everyone, not just women.

Nevertheless from observation and interviews with students it is clear that the women-only setting tends to trigger discussion of trade union issues that are especially pertinent for women, in other words 'women's issues'. An alternative way of seeing this is that as women the participants address the gender dimension ever present, but rarely recognised, in the traditional trade union agenda (Munro 2001). The latter does not necessarily occur in a self-conscious manner, although it can. Alternatively, it might be argued that in the women-only setting women talk from their gendered position because this is what they know and understand. Arguably, men also do this, except they often claim to be speaking for everyone (Cockburn 1991). This type of gender neutral or masculine discourse can shut down debate about gender issues in mixed settings and activate a class-based union identity, but not a gender identity, which then carries the risk of reproducing the masculine culture. This is without doubt one of the most significant features of women-only courses in the making of women's trade union careers.

One example from observation of MSF 'Women's Week' was an exercise on the 'Skills for Organizing' course. Students were presented with a model for encouraging membership activity – 'Anger – Hope – Action' – and had to identify issues that made them or their members angry, around which collective action might be mobilised. This activity could potentially head in a number of directions including the traditional trade union agenda and in fact it is an exercise used on mixed-sex courses for new workplace representatives.[3] One group's discussion centred on sexual harassment that without doubt many women will have experienced in one form or another. Helen and Fiona talked about how sexual harassment had for a number of years been a widespread problem at their workplace and Helen herself had been a 'victim'. The problem had not been openly acknowledged by management or by employees and individual victims had been left to suffer in silence. The group discussed strategies for mobilising members on this issue. Although it is not impossible that this issue would have arisen on a mixed-sex course, if we accept that men typically dominate the discussions, then it is far less likely, as suggested in interview by the very experienced tutors.

An example from observation of the TGWU school was an exercise on the 'Women at Work' course, where students were asked to draw up an agenda for a branch meeting, in which they could include anything they considered relevant. The groups produced posters containing agenda items which can be characterised as 'women's issues', such as domestic violence, childcare, flexible work hours, cancer screening, as well as more traditional items such as pay. When the tutor asked if they had actually seen the 'women's issues' on their local union agendas, the reply from the experienced union women was overwhelmingly no, but they agreed they should

---

3   This was ascertained from an examination of course materials for a 'New Reps' course.

try to do something about that in the future. Table 6.2 also demonstrates the gendered nature of the course learning.

Women-only courses might be a woman's first engagement with feminist or gender-conscious discourse and this can be a revelatory experience, in which women's eyes are opened, sometimes for the first time to what Briskin (1993: 97) has called the 'gender specific character of experience'. This is reflected in Mandy's (TGWU) comments on what she had learnt from the women's course:

> You don't think you're discriminated against any more. Until it hits you, you don't realise it's there, but it is and we're not aware of the issues until they're put forward to us.

Kate (MSF) in her years of union involvement had always distanced herself from separate women's forums; however following her first 'Women's Week' she had this to say:

> Afterwards I began to identify some of the things I was experiencing as a woman with things other women were experiencing. Before I didn't think these were things I had in common with other women, I thought I felt that way or that had happened to me because I'm me not because I'm female.

Kate went on to declare that she now considered herself a feminist and could now see the purpose of women's structures, which she had previously opposed. Her engagement with a gender conscious discourse caused her to begin to explain her own life in gender conscious terms. Kate's personal transformation underscores the capacity of women's groups to engender new orientations to feminism and more politicised gender identities, mirroring other research situated in women's groups (e.g. Reinelt 1994).

Through listening to other women's 'stories' and participating in activities which place 'women's issues' at the centre of the trade union agenda, a consciousness of women's collective disadvantage can evolve, irrespective of personal experiences of discrimination or disadvantage. This was particularly noticeable in the case of interviewees who had forged 'successful' paid and/or union careers in male dominated contexts, such as Kate above. Some of these women were adamant that they had not personally experienced sex discrimination, but still engagement with the gender conscious debates of the women's schools had led them to recognise women's collective inequality.

Women's diversity and the women-only setting

The interviews with participants attempted to gauge the extent of inclusiveness of the women's schools. In general terms this was important if women were to be conceptualised as occupying multiple social locations and in order to consider the impact of these on women's experiences. More specifically it was important to be able to consider the widespread criticism of women's groups in unions as dominated by white, middle-class women and their concerns (see for example, Colgan and

Ledwith 2000a; Humphrey 2002; Kirton and Greene 2002; McBride 2001). In Colgan and Ledwith's (2000) study of UNISON black, lesbian and disabled women felt marginalised by women's self-organised groups in their union. In contrast, in the present study there was very little evidence of perceptions of marginalisation at the women's schools.

The six black women interviewees were very positive about their experiences. The MSF black women were all inexperienced activists and first-timers at a union course. The two TGWU women were experienced activists, who had both been on a range of mixed, women-only and black member courses. There were no reports of marginalisation, isolation or discomfort. Earlier in the chapter Christine and Kamaljit (MSF) indicated that they had drawn considerable personal strength from the experience. In the quotation below Kamaljit sees the diversity of women at the school as a resource from which valuable knowledge could be gained as well as personal friendships:

> At that point in my life women's week was almost life saving for me, it came at just the right time. I made friends with women I wouldn't even have imagined in my circle of friends before. They worked in different areas to me. They were regionally different. They live such different lives to me. I would never have imagined that we could have anything in common, but in fact we had so much in common.

Afsana (MSF) highlighted religious and cultural reasons for her preference for women-only courses. All the black interviewees were supportive of black member-only groups as well as women-only. Bernadette (TGWU), a black Caribbean woman had been an activist in black and women's voluntary organizations. She commented:

> The T&G have quite a lot of ethnic minority members and I do think they need to be encouraged to take more of an interest. I don't know what the answer is, but I think for some people going to a place and seeing people like you has to be part of the answer. For me, I'm quite open minded – you see my husband's Indian, so maybe I've broken away from that cultural dependency, but I do understand why some people would find it important.

Interviewees were not asked about their sexuality. However, two women revealed their lesbian identity, allowing for more probing questions into this dimension of diversity. As stated above, Kamaljit found the women-only setting more inclusive and less threatening. Mandy was more critical of the content of the women's course, even though she had enjoyed it and learnt a lot. She felt that there had been too great a focus on traditional women's issues, such as maternity leave and that the curriculum could have been more progressive and inclusive. Her comments also hint at a degree of discomfort:

> I'm not that brave yet [to "come out"]. I mean I never deny that I am. I'll tell anyone, but to stand up in a forum and say "what are you doing for us?" The programme should initiate it. Not everybody's happy to know that you are anyway. You don't wish to offend or throw

it down anybody's throat, but that's what I am and I'm too old to hide it now. We're not only discriminated against in the workplace, we're discriminated against throughout life and I think it would be a good idea for them to initiate something for us, rather than for us to have to raise it.

There were also comments from some heterosexual women who felt that lesbian women in their group had been marginalised or isolated, suggesting that some lesbian women might have encountered some hostility, even though this was not evident from the interviews with self-identified lesbian women. Similarly a couple of non-disabled women felt that the courses had not addressed disability issues, although again this was not remarked upon by the disabled women. However, it is likely that the presence of women with disabilities brought the issue of disability to the forefront of the non-disabled women's minds.

Another dimension of diversity evident in the union context is class. There is greater objective class diversity in MSF than in TGWU because of the industries and occupations the unions are largely based in. However, the majority of interviewees in both unions were highly qualified women, who mostly self-identified as working class. Their qualification level suggests though that women who opt to attend the women's schools might not be entirely representative of the unions' membership composition. A couple of MSF women reported feeling intimidated by one or two of the more overtly 'middle-class' students and a couple of the TGWU women talked about the 'airport women' (white-collar workers) in a similar fashion. However, as the groups got to know each other over the first couple of days, these feelings seemed to disappear. From observation 'middle-class' women were sometimes quicker to contribute to discussions, but this was also dependent on union experience, because there were some very experienced and dominant working class women in the groups. In some cases their experience mitigated the traditional disadvantages of class, suggesting that the union education setting is something of a level playing field in class terms, where union experience counts for more than academic qualifications or occupational status. The general consensus was that the variety of backgrounds was a resource the groups could draw upon, rather than a problem.

Overall the interviewees in the study talked very positively of their experiences of the women's schools and most women felt that they 'fitted in', even if some dimensions of diversity were not explicitly addressed by the course content. However, in order to rebut charges of naivety, which perhaps could be inferred from this rather upbeat 'melting pot' picture, it is important to add some caveats which perhaps in part explain the overwhelmingly positive experiences of a diversity of women's school students.

First, it is important to acknowledge that new activists often feel intimidated by union meetings where everyone seems to know each other and where everyone seems to be at ease with the jargon (see for example, Cockburn 1991; Kirton and Healy 1999). This can lead to new women activists feeling uncomfortable. For example, Susan, a black woman of MSF, had had a somewhat negative experience of a predominantly black forum, a meeting of the union's national race committee:

I went down to Whitehall College for a weekend and they were all reps and they were all on the National Race Equality thing and mostly knew each other. I smiled at this particular person and they didn't smile back and I was thinking "ooh that's a bit cold".

Julie's Story

Working in a highly male-dominated environment meant that Julie was rarely in the company of women exclusively. She had been encouraged to go to the women's school by a regional women's officer. Although a self-identified feminist Julie had not actively participated in women's groups. She was asked how she felt about the course being women-only:

'It sounded like a challenge – working with all men, you almost forget you're female. I mean you don't forget you're female, but women's issues seem to take a bit of a back seat. And, you don't notice sexism in the same way – you get so used to it. It was such a pleasure for me and a challenge to be with all women.

Julie went on to explain that part of the 'pleasure' for her was to do with the way women behave differently when there are no men around. She described men's presence as a 'distraction' to women's learning and she also felt that women were conditioned to place their attention on men's needs rather than their own.

As well as displaying an active gender identity, Julie was also highly conscious of class and as a highly educated woman, conscious of the privileges of her own class position. She explained why she did not volunteer to present one of the speeches on the last day of the school:

'I'm always conscious that I've been university educated and I've had opportunities to do stuff like that and I'm always consciously thinking of people who it would be a massive thing for, to stand up and speak. It's not to say that I wouldn't be scared out of my wits too, but I always think that it wouldn't be such a big thing for me.'

Susan was in favour of black member groups, but as a new activist she found the women's school a far more supportive setting:

People felt more comfortable because we were all women, you didn't feel intimidated, even if you were a quiet mouse you would speak up and say something, because it was more supportive.

The perception of the women-only setting as more supportive and welcoming might not be a function of it being women-only *per se*; equally it is possible that the feminist values underpinning the organization of the courses render them more welcoming to inexperienced members. Susan's experience is indicative of the difficulties of feeling comfortable in taking the first step into activism and finding the appropriate forum for oneself. Women's schools are intended to assist with this process, but it is also likely that other union forums could usefully learn from the experiences. Naturally courses are learning environments where new and experienced activists come together to share knowledge. At women's schools there is no stigma attached to admitting ignorance and asking questions because so many women are in the same position and the more experienced women seem to enjoy 'helping' the newer. The tutors also play a role in rendering the environment a mutually supportive one and it was clear from observation and interviews that they were highly conscious of the need to give extra encouragement to newer women.

Second, although the students spend a week together, they need never see each other again. There is no expectation of an ongoing relationship between group participants as there is in other women's groups, such as the self-organised groups in UNISON or the women's committees of MSF and TGWU. Although students might jostle for attention and 'talking space' on courses, there is not the kind of intense power struggle between individuals and interest groups at play that is often seen inside union decision-making structures, where the allocation of resources to campaigns or other such activities is at stake. Therefore to attend a women's school does not involve making the same kind of choices as involved in deciding whether to give over time and commitment to an ongoing women's group, a black member group or a lesbian or disabled group. Therefore we cannot necessarily assume that women in this study prioritised their gender identity over other identities. It seems unlikely that the interviewees faced the same kind of dilemmas as those reported in other studies (such as McBride 2001; Humphrey 2002) where the research focus was on other forms of separate organizing and where women had to decide which identity to privilege.

Finally, at women's schools everyone is away from their habitual environment, most participants do not know many, if any, other women and they are generally 'on their best behaviour'. The tutors are also there to manage difficult situations should they arise and as part of this they establish with the students ground rules at the beginning of courses which dictate mutual respect and tolerance. Thus, it would not be possible to conclude from a study of women's schools that some women do not or would not feel marginalised within women's groups in unions more generally.

Women's schools – a women-only ghetto?

It could be argued that by virtue of their attendance, the interviewees in the study supported the existence of women's schools. However, as the earlier discussion of their motivations for attending shows, support for a politic of women's separate organizing cannot be assumed, although it is more likely that feminist women will support it. One of the controversial questions surrounding women's separate organizing is whether it empowers women or confines them and their concerns to a powerless ghetto (see Briskin 1993). The interviews sought to ascertain how women positioned women's courses within this debate having completed the course.

Women who were concerned about the 'women-only ghetto' charge emphasised the importance of women 'progressing' from women-only courses to mixed-sex ones to avoid ghettoisation, thus they positioned women's courses within the deficit model of women's separate organizing (Briskin 1993). For example, Deirdre

(MSF), a non-feminist expressed this view, held more widely in TGWU than in her union. She said that she would have been intimidated by the thought of a national residential mixed-sex school, but that she now felt she could 'handle' a mixed course because 'Women's Week' had given her lots of confidence and strategies for dealing with men. In common with some women in MSF and most in TGWU, she felt quite strongly that individually and collectively women should not confine themselves to women's groups. The reality of the unions is male-domination and women needed to learn how to function in that environment if they were to take up positions. Also some interviewees felt women individually and collectively had a lot to learn from men. Beryl (TGWU), a self-identified feminist, concurred with this view that women's courses were 'stepping stones' to mixed courses, although her own repeated attendance at women's schools was not entirely congruent with this since she had considerable experience in the union.

Some women therefore did not buy into the ideology of a politic of separate organizing, which would stress the importance of women organizing collectively with the goal of effecting institutional change (Briskin 1993). Contrary to what might be expected their views on this were not clearly related to their self-identification with feminism, although as might be expected self-identified feminists were more likely to reveal unequivocal support for women's courses.

Beryl was also concerned that not just women, but *'women's issues'* might be ghettoised by separate courses and she shared with other women a belief that men also needed to be educated in equality issues:

> I think it would benefit the men [to attend equalities courses] because the men would actually hear the women's views on what they think of the men and the things that concern them and they might understand that sometimes it's not what they say, it's the way they say it. I think you need the two [women's and mixed courses].

Other women were more comfortable with the concept of a politic of separate organizing. For these women, it was not a question of facilitating women's 'progression' to mixed-sex courses. Rather, women's courses for them served a separate and specific function. Kamaljit and Diane, both self-identified feminists, commented:

> I would do a women-only course again and yes, it was important. I think a lot of women, myself included, need space without men, because generally men do dominate, I mean they're conditioned to, and they do. (Kamaljit, MSF)

> Certainly I think women-only courses are important, particularly as there are things like equal opportunities and sexual harassment, which are basically specifically women's issues, so I think it's important and it's nice that women are now being recognised and having their own separate agendas. (Diane, TGWU)

Kate (MSF) was a new advocate of women-only groups having undergone something of a conversion to feminism following 'Women's Week':

I always thought that we shouldn't be sisters in solidarity and we shouldn't exclude men, but now I think it's important to have these groups. You only have to look round the world to see how women are treated. It's valid for women to look at these issues together.

Thus, some women recognised the need for the union to change, rather than for women to do so and to this end women's courses represented a vehicle for the positive appropriation of women's experiences. Generally the TGWU women were less comfortable with a politic of separate organizing than the MSF women, although this was not an absolute rule as can be seen from the discussion above. The TGWU women typically saw women's courses as an interim strategy to empower individual women to operate effectively within the union, resonating with Briskin's (1993) deficit model. In other words, it is implied that gender can be *made* irrelevant by working on women's skills, even if it is recognised as relevant presently. During interview the more experienced TGWU women tended to take an objective position on the discussion, saying such things as 'it doesn't matter to me who's there', but at the same time recognising that some (newer, less confident) women might be more attracted by a women-only setting. This obviously stood in contradiction to their (possibly repeated) attendance at women's courses, but underlined their view that gender-neutral integration was the ultimate aim.

The MSF women's orientations, on the other hand, inclined more towards a politic of separate organizing (Briskin 1993). They typically saw women's spaces as necessary to the ongoing development of individual women and women as a group and even the more experienced women were happy to talk about what they had gained personally, rather than what women in general gain. Whilst the psychology behind these differential views is beyond the scope of this study, it is possible to posit a socio-cultural explanation. The different cultures of the two unions play a role in socialising women into these attitudinal positions, with class-based identities much stronger in TGWU than in MSF. The tutors' position (discussed earlier) and their representation of this debate no doubt has a role in reproducing or reinforcing a 'deficit' orientation to women's separate organizing and downplaying (politicised) gender identities. Whilst it was the case that the tutors of both unions supported women's groups and women's courses, the TGWU tutors' support was more qualified: they were much keener to emphasise that women should 'progress' to mixed courses. In contrast the MSF tutors were comfortable with the concept of separate women's spaces, which women could participate in if they chose. The fact that more MSF than TGWU women students and tutors identified with feminism also seems reflected in these orientations to women's separate organizing.

Summary

This chapter has examined women's motivations for attending women's schools, together with their perceptions and experiences. Most women interviewed expressed 'union reasons' for attending, whilst a minority attended for 'work' or 'personal reasons', indicating a prior union orientation or commitment among the majority.

The corollary of the variety of reasons for attending is that it is unlikely that all the women will increase their participation following the course and this would be an unrealistic expectation. Nevertheless, the fact that all the women clearly valued the course would point to a strengthening of their attitudinal attachment to the union. Whatever their previous experiences of trade union education, over half of the interviewees had consciously chosen a women's course, while for others the significance of the women-only setting only dawned on them afterwards, indicating different levels of prior gender consciousness. However, following the course most of the women talked in feminist or gender conscious terms about their work and union experiences and it therefore appeared that the course had for many women shaped a stronger gender identity.

Increased confidence was reported as the most important personal outcome of the course and this was built in the context of the 'safe space' of the women-only setting through the processes of 'shared learning' and 'privileging women's issues'. From the perspective of participants the courses seemed able to accommodate a diversity of women, even if it was felt that a fairly narrow interpretation of 'women's issues' pervaded the curriculum. Following the schools, the participants all expressed at least partial and contingent support for women-only courses, with some women positioning women's courses more within the 'deficit model' of separate organizing than within an ideology of separate organizing.

Chapter 5 highlighted the importance of significant experiences, others and influences for stimulating women's participation. From the analysis it is clear that the courses could be characterised as a significant experience for most of the women, which exposed them to significant others and influences, which could be expected to impact on the trajectory of their union careers. The next chapter moves to explore whether and how having undergone women-only union education, women develop their participation and involvement in the democratic processes and structures of their unions. This chapter closes with Delia's thoughts on what would happen if more women started to take up educational opportunities and then participated more in the union:

> I think the shop stewards would be challenged in their positions. So I think it could be a good thing for the union. But you've got to get through that barrier. It becomes an exclusive club, doesn't it? (Delia, TGWU)

Chapter 7

The Making of Women's Trade Union Careers

As we saw in Chapter 6, women feel more confident and empowered after completing a women-only course, but does this help them develop and sustain their union careers over time? This chapter continues to follow the MSF and TGWU interviewees by investigating the trajectories of their union careers approximately two years after attending the women's schools using data from second interviews. There is no attempt to establish a causal relationship between attendance of women's schools and particular union career outcomes. However, the chapter does attempt to unravel the longer-term influence of the social processes women engage with during women-only courses. In particular, whether there is any perceived lasting impact from the sense of empowerment or increased confidence that the vast majority of interviewees clearly feel directly after the courses. Chapter 5 discussed the women's orientations to feminism, finding that only a minority of interviewees self-identified unequivocally as feminists. That said all the women were supportive of the feminist goal of women's equality, but some were more ambivalent about feminist practices such as women's separate organizing. This chapter explores whether and how having engaged with a gender conscious (if not overtly feminist) discourse within the 'safe space' of the women's schools, this then seemed to shape women's subsequent and developing gender identity, feminist orientation, behaviour, and contribution to trade union work. The discussion is situated within the work, union and personal contexts in which the interviewees' participation takes place so as to show the interconnections between these three 'worlds' and to explore how the women navigated them. The chapter first considers the circumstances of women who ceased or did not begin to participate and it then turns to women who went on to develop a union career.

First there is a discussion of women's intentions, ambitions and aspirations for a union career that were first explored shortly after completion of a women-only course. This allows for a comparison between what women envisaged as a career trajectory and what actually transpired during the intervening two-year period.

Intentions, ambitions and aspirations for a union career

A small number of women with no previous history of union involvement (two from each union) were asked whether they now intended to participate and if so in what ways. Of these, three women expressed an interest in participating informally, for example, attending workplace/branch meetings and/or in finding out more about opportunities to participate more formally later on. Vera (MSF) was the exception: she was one of the women motivated to attend the women-only course for 'personal reasons' and she remained resolute that she was not interested in participating, even informally.

Turning to a small group of women (MSF three, TGWU two), who were informally involved prior to the course, most were interested in formalising their participation by becoming representatives or participating in committee structures, or in one case in becoming a lay tutor. Most of these women felt that they needed to know more about what was involved before they could participate more formally. Significantly then, these women lacked knowledge about how to move forward, for example how to set about becoming a representative or non workplace routes to participation in branch, regional or women's structures. This was surprising considering they had recently attended a union course, where one of the aims is to encourage greater women's participation in democratic processes and structures. It appeared then that the information they had received on the opportunities via course materials, discussions, tutors and other students, had not been fully digested. This might be significant for the unions as they could risk losing potential activists by not 'capturing' them whilst they are still enthusiastic immediately following courses.

Women who held workplace/branch/committee positions had varying levels of experience in the unions and they were asked if/how they envisaged moving forward. Some were relatively new workplace representatives who felt they still had much to learn for their present roles. Helen and Fiona, two relatively new MSF representatives, were mothers of young children and they anticipated that lack of time would prevent them from becoming involved beyond the workplace, although Fiona said that she would 'love to work for the union full-time' in the future.

The more experienced women were asked whether they would be interested in moving up the lay hierarchy, perhaps to the NEC/GEC. There was a resounding 'no' in answer to this question, with most women from both unions declaring a firm commitment to workplace activism. Hilary's (TGWU) comments were typical:

> I've got no desire to be a high flyer in the union, I'm quite happy at the level I'm at now because I see my role as a workplace rep, dealing with the people that I work with on a day to day basis. That's what I want to carry on doing. My priorities are at the workplace, because they're the people that elected me, so they're the people I owe most to. I think even if I was single I would still prioritise the people I work with.

Some of the MSF women were dismissive of the idea of participating at NEC level. Deirdre described the NEC unflatteringly as a 'bunch of hypocrites' a view shared by others if expressed in more circumspect language, for example Kate:

The more you find out about what goes on at regional council and in the NEC, the more involved you get at that level the more unhappy you feel about the union, because you just think of people stabbing each other in the back, factions. All these people in high positions, they've either got some personal agenda or a political agenda. I couldn't possibly go that way, I just couldn't stand it.

These negative views on the higher echelons of the union were confined to MSF and are possibly explained by the negative press coverage of MSF senior officials during 1999 and 2000,[1] and perhaps reinforced by personal experiences, as in Kate's case. Some women did, however, express an interest in paid officer positions. This was especially the case in TGWU where there is such a strong tradition of paid officials having a history of lay activism in the union that it is almost unheard of for an 'outsider' to be employed other than in research positions. There are therefore possibilities for employment for a small number of activists, usually with a long history of lay office holding in a variety of roles. Suzanne had already been rejected for three paid officer positions. She said that there was an 'informal queue' and that an applicant stood a greater chance if they were asked to apply; she was hopeful that it would not be too long before it would be 'her turn'. Other women were possibly less realistic and more naïve about the opportunities for paid employment in the union and although they expressed an interest they did not appear to be laying the foundations to make this become a reality.

In summary, congruent with their principal reason for attending the women's schools (i.e. union reasons), most of the inactive or informally participating women intended to increase their involvement, mostly to formal participation within workplace or other committee structures. Whilst those participating formally were not generally aspiring to the higher levels of the lay hierarchy, they hoped to become more effective and confident in their current workplace/branch/committee roles. In other words the latter group did see their trade union careers developing, but not necessarily in an upward, hierarchical sense. (The concept of union careers is discussed later.)

For the present analysis this is unproblematic because it is not the intention of this chapter to attempt to establish a causal relationship between attendance of women's schools and increased participation in the union. However, it is nevertheless worth mapping any objective changes that had occurred in each interviewee's involvement by the time of the second phase of fieldwork. This is set out in Tables 7.1–7.4 from which it can be seen that the majority either developed further or sustained their participation. The text below moves on to explore the circumstances underlying these patterns of participation and also to unpack more qualitative changes in the women's involvement. First there is some discussion in the next section of the women who ceased to be or did not become active.

---

1   In 1999 the MSF General Secretary was accused by an Assistant General Secretary of misuse of union funds. The story was leaked to the press and triggered an internal enquiry and an investigation by the Certification Officer. Although neither investigation proved Lyons' guilt, the negative press coverage was very damaging for the union.

Stunted union careers

Tables 7.1 and 7.2 map the influences on and forms of participation at two points
in time of interviewees who ceased to be or did not become union active. From this
there are indications that family background was less important for the women's
union careers than the work, union and present family contexts, indicating that
women's orientations to trade union participation are fluid and emergent, rather than
fixed by prior beliefs and values.

There were two women who had no previous involvement (prior to attending
the women's schools) with their unions, whose stories raise a number of interesting
issues. One remained an inactive member and the other took a first step towards
informal participation, but then retreated. During the two years the first woman,
Vera (MSF), had not participated actively in the democratic processes and structures:
for example, she had not attended any meetings, nor voted in any elections. She
had, however, returned to 'Women's Week' for a second time in 2001, seeing the
school as an 'excellent' personal development opportunity and time out from a busy
professional job, especially as her daughter was now grown up, she was divorced,
had time to spare and the course was free. Vera still had no wish to become involved
in the union either at workplace or any other level, but she did confess to taking an
interest in the union magazine and she was now no longer questioning the point
of being a union member. Vera is perhaps the exception that proves the rule that
a previously weak collectivist orientation (as indicated by her anti-union family
background and non-feminist identity) is unlikely to translate into strong union
commitment by simply attending a union school.

The second woman, Evelyn (TGWU), was a single parent, who felt time
constrained by the combination of domestic circumstances and paid full-time work.
Since the course she had nevertheless taken a first tentative step towards informal
participation by attending a couple of branch meetings, but she had been deterred by
male domination – 'it's quite a male thing, isn't it', she remarked. The branch met
above a local pub and went down to the pub afterwards. She felt that as a woman:

> It's not your style, not how you choose to do things. You don't feel included, even though
> you're not actually excluded.

Her comments point to a masculine union culture, which symbolically, although not
literally, excludes women. Congruent with her union minded family background
she had not been completely deterred. She said that she would remain a member
and she was interested in the work of unions, but her initial reactions were that
neither informal or formal participation were for her, particularly in view of the
timing (evenings) and location (the pub) and nature (male domination) of meetings.
Her case suggests that efforts to change the way the unions operate could render
participation more appealing to some women.

Although only concerning two women, their cases are indicative. First, unions
cannot hope to win over all course participants even to informal activism: even after
two residential courses, Vera remained uninterested in participating. In other words,

the experience of 'talking union' or even 'talking women' for a week will not shape or shift the union/gender identities of all participants. However, it is important that even members, not ideologically committed or politicised trade unionists, perceive that they derive some benefit from membership and in this sense the provision of courses could be seen as an important individual membership benefit (Munro and Rainbird 2000). Second, Evelyn's experiences suggest that even where initial enthusiasm or interest is generated by course attendance, it is the local context that is likely to have to sustain and develop that interest, which in Evelyn's case was very fragile and weakened by her actual experiences of attempts to participate. Equally, with encouragement and support, particularly in view of her pro-union family background, Evelyn might have gone in a different direction, something she herself conceded. In the event it appeared that Evelyn was 'lost' as a potential activist. Her case ties in with the literature arguing that women's experiences of unions must be positive if they are to attempt to juggle work, home and union roles (e.g. Walton 1991).

The analysis now turns to consider interviewees (see Tables 7.1 and 7.2; three MSF and four TGWU) whose union careers came to a halt during the two years following the women's schools. A change in work circumstances was generally responsible, although for two women circumstances in their personal lives led to less union involvement. Susan (MSF) and Judy (TGWU) both spoke about constraining health problems. Susan had been interested in becoming a workplace representative, but had become pregnant and had a late miscarriage, which had led to several months of sick leave. She said that in theory she was still interested in the union, but she now seemed to feel vulnerable and unsure about committing to extra activities, since she wanted to become pregnant again. Judy had participated in the regional disability committee and had wanted to get involved in the women's and race committees. However, as a result of an industrial accident in 1996, which left her a wheelchair user, her health had deteriorated further and she now had memory lapses and concentration difficulties, which meant that she found participating in the union too strenuous. For both these women the cessation of union involvement in no way signalled disaffection with the union or a weakened attitudinal commitment to the union, rather it was a case of personal circumstances intervening to force a rethinking of priorities. Therefore, there was the possibility in theory at least of future participation, should personal circumstances become more favourable once more.

Some women left unionized employment during the two years and because their participation had been largely concentrated at workplace level this led to the cessation of their involvement in all cases and also to resigning membership in two cases. Kate (MSF) became a full-time PhD student after completing an Open University degree; she felt trade unionism was about the workplace (rather than political or policy issues more broadly) and she now felt disengaged from the activities of the union and was therefore no longer involved. Kate's reluctance to embrace a more political union orientation suggests that the influence of her anti-union family background had not entirely disappeared even if diluted by positive experiences of workplace activism and the gender conscious trade union politics implicit in the women's course. Another three (one MSF, two TGWU) women moved on to what they considered to be better jobs. It is significant that they all attributed their work 'success', in part at least, to the increased self-esteem they felt following the women's schools, suggesting that some women might use the schools for their own social mobility. They all made comments such as 'I wouldn't be where I am today if it wasn't for the courses/the union.' Jane (TGWU), for example, had been expelled from school with no qualifications and had previously been a cleaner and then a bus driver for five years. She said that her experiences of union education, in particular women's courses and her involvement in the union had made her believe she was capable of something more. She now had an administrative job in a non-unionized insurance company. She gave up her union membership partly because her company was 'anti-union' and partly because her initial request to be transferred to a composite white-collar branch had not been acted on quickly enough in her view. Jane had participated in committee structures beyond the workplace and in this sense was quite a loss for the union. However, her priority was her workplace, and in the absence of any connection to a unionized environment, her motivation to continue in her committee roles was very low.

Similarly, attending the women's schools had led Kamaljit (MSF) to reflect on her life and what she wanted to do. She decided to become more involved with the Asian women's community and took a job setting up and managing a new voluntary sector organization. She reflected back on the impact of 'Women's Week':

> The course, in terms of empowering women, is really important. I've now moved on to manage a project and that's not something I would have thought myself capable of before. It's been huge, massive for me, in terms of my self-esteem and what I think I can do now.

She was still a union member, but working in a small non-unionized voluntary sector group, she had not remained active.

It is of course paradoxical that in the case of some women, their union education and involvement experiences empowered them in the sense of the development of individual autonomy and confidence (Young 1997). They reassessed and acted to change their work lives, which resulted in most cases in their moving away from union involvement, rather than increasing their participation. These cases also underline the fragile nature of women's participation in a context where much of women's employment remains non-unionized and where their participation is concentrated at the lower levels of the union hierarchy. If they leave unionized employment there is often no obvious (to them) arena for their activism and they might lack knowledge as to other possible arenas for activism or lack the experience to be effective union organizers in non-unionized contexts. Some women had made a conscious decision to privilege workplace activism and when this connection was severed they lost a sense of purpose and no longer felt psychologically attached, despite a previously politicised union identity. All of these women perceived however that for them participating in union education had represented a turning point in their lives. They all felt strongly that should they find themselves working in unionized contexts in the future, they could imagine becoming active again, underscoring the fluid nature of union identities.

Table 7.1 Stunted union careers – MSF women

Name	Influences on Participation	Form(s) of Participation on Attendance at Women's School in 2000	Form(s) of Participation at 2nd Interview in 2002
Kate	Anti–union family background; significant experiences at the workplace	Workplace rep; health and safety rep; branch committee member	Inactive member
Kamaljit	Non–union family background; significant other in the union; significant experiences at the workplace; self–defined feminist	Workplace rep, branch committee member	Inactive member
Vera	Anti–union family background; significant others in the union	Inactive member	Inactive member
Susan	Non–union family background; significant others in the union	Informal participation at workplace level; informal participation in national race committee	Inactive member

Table 7.2 Stunted union careers – TGWU women

Name	Influences on Participation	Form(s) of Participation on Attendance at Women's School in 1999	Form(s) of Participation at 2nd Interview in 2001
Sally	Non–union family background; significant experiences at workplace; significant other in the union	Shop steward; branch committee member	Inactive member
Jane	Non–union family background; significant other in the union	Shop steward; 'women's rep'; branch committee member; regional and national trade group and women's committee member	No longer a member
Delia	Union minded family background; significant other in the union	Informal participation at workplace and branch levels	No longer a member
Judy	Non–union family background; significant experiences at workplace	Informal branch level participation; regional disability committee member	Inactive member
Evelyn	Union minded family background; significant experiences at the workplace; significant other in the union	Inactive member	Informal participation at branch level for a period; now inactive member

Sally (TGWU) was a separate case as she ceased to be involved because of changes in union behaviour at her workplace. She was a relatively new representative when she attended the women's school and was very positive about the activities and contribution of her local branch. Since then the company she worked for had instituted a number of changes at the workplace, which had given rise to 'infighting' among the senior stewards about how to respond. This combined with the long-term sick leave of the branch chair had rendered the branch dysfunctional and she had ceased to participate. It was clear that after initially being highly enthusiastic about the union, Sally was now very disillusioned. She had remained a member as an 'insurance policy', but the possibility of her becoming involved again seemed doubtful. This underscores the significance of the local industrial relations context for sustaining activism, a theme returned to below.

What we see from the above analysis is that despite an almost universal intention to sustain or develop participation, personal, work or union circumstances sometimes interfered with the realisation of that intention, some of which were gendered, whilst others were not. These stories of stunted union careers raise several issues. First, union participation involves individuals giving time, commitment and energy on top of other paid work and domestic roles; it is by nature then fragile, but particularly so when it is at an embryonic stage. It is therefore important that unions continue to have mechanisms (such as courses) for drawing in potential new activists and therefore they should not be concerned if some course participants show no subsequent interest, because undoubtedly some will do so. Second, it is important to give women positive reasons for participating at all levels, rather than simply removing barriers to their participation. However, the workplace/branch is usually the site for activism, especially for newcomers and if the culture of local branches remains unappealing to women, then the valued work of women's schools will be diminished, if not lost as a union resource. The questions of how to change local union cultures or how to organize non-unionised workplaces are of course topics for debate/analysis in themselves. Third, circumstances relating to the workplace were by far the dominant cause of cessation of union participation. This is perhaps surprising in view of the emphasis in the literature on women's domestic roles as standing as a major barrier to participation. However, it has to be noted that of the above nine women, eight were childfree and five were partner free; therefore domestic constraints were less pronounced than for many women. Fourth, the analysis highlights the fluid and dynamic nature of union identities and the importance of exploring identities in context. The chapter now turns to the stories of the fifteen women who went on to develop their union careers.

Developing a union career

The various experiences and influences that contributed to developing a union career are similarly complex. For example, most of the self-defined feminist interviewees (four MSF, three TGWU) developed participation, while only five (two MSF, three TGWU) came from union-minded backgrounds, indicating once more the fluid and emergent nature of the women's orientations to participation.

For an analysis of how women's union careers developed over time, it is first necessary to consider the meaning of the concept of 'career', in particular what a 'lay' union career looks like. Ledwith et al. (1990: 116) define a union career as a vertical progression consisting of four positions: activist, local union leader, quasi-elite branch level officer and elite national level officer. Arguably, this definition with its implicit emphasis on continuity and explicit emphasis on linearity is a masculine construct (i.e. a model of a male career, e.g. Healy 1999) that tends to conceal women's contribution to unions as they are less likely to rise through 'the ranks'.

Here a broader and more horizontal (Healy 1999) view of the lay union career and of union career progression is taken, reflecting a more gender sensitive analysis and interpretation. Within this, individuals can hold simultaneously several careers, for example a union career, a paid work career, a home/family-based career, to which they affiliate and commit (as suggested by Layder 1993). These careers interconnect and overlap, sometimes complementing and at other times competing with one another. The second point is that women's union careers often develop in qualitative ways, which a linear model does not allow for or recognise; in other words career 'progression' might not have any objective manifestation, such as higher status or title. Indeed some women might not seek higher status, but still invest in their careers. For example, a local union leader might develop in her role gaining greater expertise through experience and education, but not seek further upward progression. It should not be assumed that her role has remained the same; that she has not progressed; that she is 'stuck' or barred from progression, (although she might be). She might have made an informed choice, possibly in view of her other careers, to remain where she is, but still grow (the role and personally). A broader concept of career allows union careers to take different shapes and allows women to emerge as active agents in the making of their own career histories, as the stories of the group of women in this study show.

The above discussion notwithstanding, it is worth mapping the objective changes in women's trade union careers over time. This is shown in Tables 7.3 – 7.4 together with the influences, discussed in Chapter 5, on their participation. From this it can be seen that most women's union careers did not follow a linear path.

This section also examines the structural contexts of women's union career development; it then moves on to consider how women navigated these contexts, often at the same time as balancing other careers, in particular motherhood, i.e. how their careers unfolded over the two years of the fieldwork. It considers one of the union roles created especially for women – 'women's reps', exploring how a small group of women interpreted and behaved in that role and whether the concept of 'women's reps' represents a step towards incremental gendered transformation of local union cultures. It also examines women as representatives and explores

---

Hilary's Story

Hilary (from a non-union background) did not envisage a vertical union career. The reasons she gave for this were twofold, first relating to her family circumstances, but also to her union priorities and values. She reflected on her commitment to workplace activism:

'I suppose if people asked me 'why did you become a shop steward?' it would be to defend those people at work who can't necessarily do it themselves.'

Hilary believed that it was at the local level that she could make the most difference and therefore this was where she wanted to concentrate her efforts. However, this did not mean that her union career did not develop over the two years of the study. During the period Hilary had completed her shop stewards' training and become a shop steward and was now participating in local negotiations. She had also taken on the role of branch education officer with a remit to encourage increased take-up locally of TGWU courses. One of her intentions over the next two years was to publicise and promote the courses open to 'ordinary' members that she felt very few members knew about. She said that she was going to set a target for every shop steward to identify a small number of members interested in participating in TGWU member courses. She felt that the educational opportunities were a particularly good way of attracting women into the union:

'I think it would be very positive to get more women members onto courses, even if they're not shop stewards. You know they could be talking to friends at a playgroup or something and they might say 'I went on this really good course' and that's something that eventually will attract more women into the union. It's not something that's going to happen overnight, but I'm sure it will work.'

Participating in women's union courses was also a vehicle for altering perceptions of trade union women:

'I'm sure there's an awful lot of women that think there's no place for you in the union unless you're a real tough nut. But you know I'm certainly not the dungaree wearing, Doc Martin type and I'd like to think that I can show other women what we're really like.'

Hilary's story illustrates the agency of union women and their gendered perspective on union practices.

---

whether there was any evidence of feminist or gender-conscious strategies or priorities, which could also be incrementally transformative. Before concluding the chapter offers the women's final reflections on women's courses.

First, there is a brief discussion of how the interviewees saw a union career. After the women's schools all the women talked about feeling more self-confident, yet it was notable that most of the women stated that their primary commitment was to the workplace or branch, even if they were involved beyond that level. There was little sense that increased confidence would push most of the women to move upwards in their union careers. This could be a function of a weak prior ideological union commitment, as indicated by the fact that only five women were from union minded backgrounds. However, there are other, less deterministic, ways of looking at this.

Within a masculine construct of career, the women might appear modest in their aspirations or not ambitious, stereotypically feminine characteristics. Alternatively, from a gender perspective each woman takes the decision whether or not to move upwards, in the light of the work, union and personal/domestic circumstances she faces suggesting a dialectical and dynamic relationship between the subjective career of the self and the objective circumstances of career (discussed below).

This decision, however, is not necessarily purely a time rational one rather it is also influenced by the degree of commitment to workplace/branch activism that women feel, compared with commitment to trade unionism more broadly. This ties in with debates about the nature of union commitment generally; that is do people join and participate for instrumental collectivist reasons (for support and protection at work) or for solidaristic collectivist reasons (a belief in the broad principles of trade unionism) (Healy, 1997)? Those with the former orientation are arguably most likely to achieve their union goals through local level participation where it is possible for representatives to influence bargaining outcomes. In contrast, those with the latter orientation might seek to influence the union's broader social, political and economic policies at regional and national levels.

Workplace participation then seems congruent with Hilary's (above) goal to represent effectively her members. Similarly, Sarah and Kim (MSF) (anti-union and non-union backgrounds) were ploughing most of their time and energy into the concerns of their professions because they felt that the union should be pushing forward a professional agenda with local management. Congruent with this Sarah had become a workplace 'learning rep', whilst Kim chose to confine her participation to her branch and organised various professional activities for branch members. However, Sarah, as a NHS employee, had also become involved in the national NHS committee, indicating the overlapping nature of instrumental and solidaristic orientations to collectivism.

Linked to the widely held belief that unions should focus their efforts on workplace bargaining and representation, there was a strong view that unions are too political, as expressed by Elizabeth (MSF) (non-union background) below.

Most women felt that engagement with national structures inevitably entailed wider politics, which was a distraction from the 'real' (instrumental) purpose of trade unionism, as Kim (MSF) relates:

> When you go to annual conference – some of them are there because they really do care and they do want to change things, but a lot of them, you think they're just there because of their egos and they want to be important. The politics become the point of it and I can't really be bothered with all that stuff. To be honest I think that's how a lot of women feel. I think we're less interested in politics as an end in itself.

The dominant orientation of commitment to workplace/branch participation, in one sense symbolises an instrumental, rather than solidaristic collectivism, but equally it is difficult to disentangle instrumental from solidaristic commitment, because the two are bound together, as Suzanne's remark suggests:

Elizabeth's Story

'I think they [unions] should have a political influence, but by virtue of being able to negotiate and discuss, through dialogue, rather than forcing issues because they're paying so much towards the Labour Party. I'm thinking more and more that although unions are a good idea, they should stay out of the political scene, out of party politics. What we're here to do is wage negotiations and to help people when someone has kicked them and they're down.'

As can be seen from Table 7.3, despite a somewhat ambivalent attitude towards unions, Elizabeth had sustained all her union roles over the two year period of the study. She also talked about how her confidence had grown and how this made her more effective in her position as Chair of the branch, such that she now seemed to feel as though she acted as a kind of role model for other women:

'I mean partly you get more confident as you get older and wiser, but also when you have a couple of successes under your belt. And then you find that people actually come to you more often for help, because they see you as someone who can get things done. I've also managed to get a couple of new people [women] onto the national negotiating committee and so you pass that confidence on to others. A couple of years ago I didn't feel that confident. I didn't feel capable of winning an argument, but now I can make my points and stand by them.'

Despite feeling more confident Elizabeth was feeling under pressure from her union roles and had considered giving up, but said that no one else want to do it and that the members had persuaded her to stay on.

Elizabeth also remained ambivalent about women's separate organizing even though she continued to participate in various forums. She compared this with her views on special measures for disabled people:

'People who are disabled have a different kind of need. I mean as a woman I can talk, I can see, I can walk. I can do whatever I want to, I can fend for myself. I can go and be educated, I can travel – it's all down to me. If you're disabled you haven't got those choices and therefore you're limited, so I think, yes, they have special needs that women don't have.'

People often ask me, why do you still want to be involved, but I still think things can be improved for people at work and through the union, that's the way to do it, I think.

However, Suzanne's clarity of purpose is possibly a function of her union-minded background and solidaristic commitment in comparison to Elizabeth's seemingly instrumental collectivism. Whether borne of instrumental or solidaristic collectivism it is important to note that most of the women were interested in changing things and they thought they could make most difference at workplace or branch level. The next section examines the contexts of formal activism.

Table 7.3 Developing union careers – MSF women

Name	Influences on Participation	Form(s) of Participation on Attendance at Women's School in 2000	Form(s) of Participation at 2nd Interview in 2002
Sarah	Anti–union family background; significant experiences at the workplace; self–defined feminist	Informal participation at workplace level	'Learning rep'; branch committee member; national NHS committee member
Fiona	Non–union family background; significant experiences at the workplace; self–defined feminist	Workplace rep; branch chair	Workplace rep; branch chair
Deirdre	Union minded family background; significant experiences at the workplace	Branch chair; regional council member	Branch chair; regional council member
Elizabeth	Non–union family background; significant experiences at the workplace	Workplace rep; branch chair; SERTUC Women's Committee member	Workplace rep; branch chair; SERTUC Women's Committee member
Kim	Non–union family background; significant other in the union; self–defined feminist	Branch women's rep; branch committee member	Branch women's rep; branch committee member
Helen	Non–union family background; significant other in the union; significant experiences at the workplace	Workplace rep; branch committee member	Workplace rep; branch committee member
Linda	Union–minded family background; significant other in the union; self–defined feminist	'Women's rep'	'Women's rep'; branch committee member

The contexts of formal activism

The context in which participation occurs is important because it structures the opportunities, barriers and constraints for activism. Most of the women in the study (12 of 15) who had sustained or developed formal participation over the two years of the fieldwork worked in unionized workplaces. This is clearly significant and indicates that a pro-union or at least non-hostile employer helps to create conditions conducive to participation for example time off for courses and union duties. Only one formally active woman, Kim (MSF), reported an overtly union hostile employer. Ironically though her immediate manager, seeing the courses as useful to professional development, was prepared to authorise her repeated attendance of 'Women's Week' during paid working time, provided it was kept secret between them.

It is worth noting that Kim's commitment to participation had weakened over the two years, attributable in part at least to the structural conditions within which her participation occurred. Participation in a composite branch can be problematic with the absence of a common workplace and the shared problems that go with it. Further, Kim was still the only active woman in her branch and had become disillusioned by what she saw as membership apathy, although she could see that social changes in the home and work were at least partly responsible:

> Getting them [members] involved is the problem. They turn up when there's something of interest to them, but they just don't want to go to committee meetings and get involved in actually running the branch. It's not just us, it's not just the PSA, it's not just MSF, it's everywhere. I asked one or two people, especially the younger ones, why they don't come along and most of them said once you've got a home and family and you know my wife works full-time too, the weekend is the only time you have with the children and there's always so much to do. Once you get involved with the union, because not enough people get involved, once you do one thing, you get caught up doing lots of things. Whereas in the old days the wife stayed at home and did all the housework, it's not like that anymore, men have to do things in the home and help with the kids too.

Kim's comments reflect a broader political policy debate concerning 'work-life balance' and the problems of reconciling work, family and participation in public life (see Bradley et al. 2005). As a freelance worker, Bernadette (TGWU) was also a member of a composite branch. At the first interview it had been three years since she had been a senior shop steward in a local authority, but she was regularly attending branch meetings and union courses. By the second interview, now five years since she had participated at workplace level, she no longer attended branch meetings, although she had trained to be a lay tutor. She too seemed to be lacking a sense of purpose in terms of composite branch-level activism. Nevertheless, in the face of a weakened behavioural commitment, she declared that she was 'T&G through and through' and 'wouldn't dream of going anywhere else or not being a member', this despite being from a non-union minded background. These women's stories point to the challenge which unions have in organizing unorganised workers.

Kim's and Bernadette's weakening commitment to participation stood in contrast to those who worked in unionized contexts, whose commitment and enthusiasm seemed to have strengthened over the two years, indicating that for union identities to become politicised is at least in part contextually contingent. It is probably self-evident that unionized contexts are bound to fuel a greater sense of solidarity borne of common conditions and a common 'enemy' (the employer) and that for many activists this will be a necessary pre-condition for participation (Kelly 1998). This is of course problematic for unions in an era when the number of unionized workplaces has declined and raises questions about how unions become meaningful as democratic participatory organizations to (women) workers in non-unionized settings or how women can be encouraged to take the lead in attempting to organise a non-unionized workplace. Conversely, it also suggests that there is potential to activate union identities in more members in unionized organizations than presently.

As suggested earlier, it is probably the case that a stronger solidaristic commitment is necessary for participation beyond the workplace, especially for those employed in non-unionized settings. In fact three of the five women in the study from union minded family backgrounds participated at regional and national levels and Melanie was now a paid organiser with another union, in contrast to only three of the nine women from a non-union background. For example, Deirdre, not in paid employment because of disability, had thrown herself into more or less full-time union and community activism. She confessed to feeling demoralised after attending MSF annual conference because she had 'heard the same motions year after year and still nothing changes', but nevertheless she battled on, always looking for new ways of generating interest in the union movement. Instead of blaming member/worker apathy, she firmly believed that the onus was on the unions to make greater efforts to render the movement more tangible to members and that trade union education was one of the ways of achieving this. She had a strong belief that unions need to be more active in the community and on behalf of her branch and regional council she was playing her part in taking the union to the community. One of her initiatives had been the provision of a course for young prostitutes organised through her MSF region. She was also in negotiations with an MSF education officer to hold a course for young, single mothers at Whitehall College to be jointly funded through a lottery grant and the regional union, highlighting the creative and active ways that women are engaging in critical appraisal of their unions.

Turning to the interviewees employed in unionized settings, the local union context of both MSF and TGWU was generally vibrant, with examples of regular, well-attended member, as well as committee meetings. There were also examples of industrial action, including strikes, indicating a willingness and ability to mobilise members. In some cases, women had played a key role in building support for action, challenging the traditional assumption of women as less militant (e.g. Purcell 1979).

Workplaces/branches were reportedly mostly 'self-servicing', that is there was little evidence of being 'serviced' by paid officers, indicating that the workplace/branch consisted of highly skilled lay trade unionists, able to handle negotiations and individual case work. This contradicted the picture often portrayed in the literature of the predominance of a 'servicing' culture in British unions (Carter 1997; 2000). There were, however, a couple of examples where union life was rather dormant, but one where a newly enthusiastic activist succeeded in re-invigorating participation. After participating in further courses and her branch committee, Sarah felt that members should be more involved in the unions' activities and she instigated the re-convening of workplace member meetings that had been abandoned because of low attendance. This initiative was successful because she tagged union meetings onto the end of departmental meetings that all staff had to attend, so she had a captive audience.

In terms of union-management relations, most representatives in the study reported receiving respect from local management, albeit sometimes grudging, although some reported poor relationships with HR departments. The changing role of HR was significant in a number of contexts and some women reported a changing approach to industrial relations with HR getting more involved in day-to-day matters, for example sick leave, discretionary time off, time off for trade union duties. This was problematic because the good relationships established over time with local managers were now of lesser importance. Asked whether this concerned them in any way, for example whether they felt that job security or promotion prospects were in jeopardy for union representatives, most women were unperturbed. This could suggest that their paid work careers were either of low importance to them, or that experience had taught them not to expect promotion. In fact most women were in jobs where they felt that 'realistically' there were no promotion prospects, so they were prepared to invest their energies elsewhere (see also Bradley et al. 2002).

In some environments a changing and more hostile industrial relations climate has led to reluctance on the part of members to get involved or stand for election. Some interviewees talked about members not wanting 'to put their heads above the parapets'. Ironically the tougher environment had created opportunities for women who often stood uncontested for the all too familiar reason that 'no one else would do it' (see for example, Bradley 1999). Julie (TGWU), for example, laughed when asked if her election to the deputy convenor post had been contested. This climate also meant that some women, like Julie employed as a carpenter in a local authority, were representing predominantly or all men, which according to the literature has been resisted at times and in contexts when standing for union office was more competitive (e.g. Ledwith et al. 1990: 120).

In exploring the contexts for activism, it is also important to examine local union culture, which research has found to be a barrier to women's participation (e.g. Cunnison and Stageman 1995). In some instances interviewees did not interpret certain practices as sexist, although some examples were clearly open to that charge. For example, Linda (MSF) was the only active woman in her branch. Instead of filling one of the vacant workplace representative seats, she was 'appointed' as 'women's rep', which meant that she could only observe (i.e. not vote) at branch committee meetings and could not get involved in negotiations. This arrangement circumscribed, whether consciously or unconsciously, women's contribution to the union. Mandy (TGWU) also reported how obstacles can be deliberately erected by the masculine hierarchy, resonating with other research (e.g. Cockburn 1994). Mandy had wanted to be nominated as a branch delegate to the regional women's committee, but this had been blocked by the male branch secretary. Instead she went through national office to get onto the regional and national lesbian and gay committees, a route only possible because of the difficulty unions have in locating lesbian and gay activists. There were clear efforts by the male branch secretary to hold back Mandy's union career and her story suggests a reluctance to renegotiate the gendered distribution of power within the local union context:

> It's my branch secretary. I'm the only woman driver in my depot now – just one woman out of all that lot, which has its good points and bad points. I have to work a lot harder to be accepted, but in saying that because I'm a woman they really respect me for the things I've won for them, which they don't expect from the other one [the male branch secretary]. But every time I try to get involved beyond the branch, I meet barriers.

Beryl (TGWU) felt that her workplace union had made great strides towards gender equality within the local context, but had now taken a retrograde step:

> I feel that a lot of the men have gone backwards. Because there are a number of women around now, they feel OK about saying "can you make the coffee" or "can you wash up" to a woman and this sort of thing.

According to Beryl, women's increased presence meant that men no longer felt they had to be cautious about lapsing into gender stereotypical roles and relationships, as though believing that the battle for women's equality had been won.

In summary, the analysis of the contexts of the interviewees' activism suggests that a well-organised workplace is the most enabling context and that the enabling mechanisms that propel women into activism are likely to be weaker for those employed in non-unionized environments. It is also likely that those from union- minded family backgrounds with an associated stronger ideological commitment to trade unionism are more motivated to participate beyond the workplace. Importantly, a changed and changing industrial relations climate has given rise to the lesser willingness of members generally to get involved in unions, and this rather ironically in turn has created openings for some women. However, once there the culture of the local union is not always conducive to developing women as activists or to developing women's participation more generally.

Balancing the double or triple load

Balancing work and union is something that all union activists must do, whether male or female. However, the literature (for example, Lawrence 1994) has established that women's domestic roles and relationships place extra strain on the work-home-union balance, often creating a triple load and leaving women 'time poor'.

The double load of work and union commitments can prove arduous for some women, even before family commitments are added in. Kim (MSF), for example, was partner free and childfree and therefore without the typical gender constraints cast by the domestic patriarchal order. However, she was now seeking further job promotion and she was in a new relationship, and consequently feeling time pressures weighing on her. She was now beginning to question the purpose of participation in her composite branch (discussed above), which she had been so enthusiastic about in the first interview shortly after she had completed a women-only course:

> I really don't know why I've carried on. I mean I've just been put up for promotion at work, so I've got that coming up and then there's my involvement in the industry association and I'm trying to have a life as well. You begin to think, "what am I doing?" I think I'll keep it going as long as possible and see how it turns out.

Of course professional men also face competing demands on their time and they too might be faced with a choice between privileging work or union careers. However, given the gendered nature of the 'glass ceiling', women who wish to progress their paid work careers face more obstacles and to overcome them involves considerable time and energy investment. Therefore, even the double load of work and union can prove a gendered constraint.

Paradoxically perhaps, of the interviewees who sustained or developed formal participation, most were partnered (ten, eight married) and a minority (six) had dependent children, seemingly defying the contention that women who lead a more traditional domestic life are less likely to participate in their unions (e.g. Lawrence 1994). However, these women did emphasise the importance of a supportive partner (e.g. Hilary's story above).

Beryl (TGWU) had no dependent children, but had a number of other significant caring responsibilities that left her time poor. At the first interview Beryl did not envisage taking on any more union roles as she felt her domestic circumstances would not permit her giving over any more time to the union. Despite an even more burdensome domestic situation, two years after the women's school, Beryl had additionally become a health and safety representative, delegate to the regional trades council and regional women's committee. Beryl describes her domestic situation:

> My daughter, who's 24, her boyfriend was killed in a road accident and she's got four little ones under seven, so that's been very traumatic. My other half's got a bad back and that's deteriorated, he's only 42 and he doesn't think he'll be able to work till 50 now. My mother's got dementia now and my father-in-law's bedridden now, so I've had quite a lot on my plate the last couple of years. So a lot's happened since I've seen you [laughs] – nothing good at all [laughs].

Table 7.4 Developing union careers – TGWU women

Name	Influences on Participation	Form(s) of Participation on Attendance at Women's School in 1999	Form(s) of Participation at 2nd Interview in 2001
Beryl	Non–union family background; significant experiences at the workplace; self–defined feminist	Shop steward; 'Women's rep'; branch committee member	Shop steward; 'Women's rep'; branch committee member; health and safety rep; trades council delegate; regional women's committee member
Hilary	Non–union family background; significant other in the union	'Women's rep'	'Women's rep; shop steward; branch committee member; education officer
Mary	Non–union family background; significant experiences at the workplace; self–defined feminist	Shop steward; branch chair	Shop steward; branch chair
Julie	Union minded family background; significant experiences at the workplace; significant other in the union; self–defined feminist	Shop steward; branch committee member; deputy convenor	Shop steward; branch committee member; deputy convenor; national women's committee member
Melanie	Union minded family background	Shop steward; branch committee member	Inactive TGWU member; USDAW organiser (paid position)

Suzanne	Union minded family background; significant experiences at the workplace	Shop steward; branch committee member; regional and national trade group committee and women's committee member	Shop steward; branch committee member; regional and national trade group committee and women's committee member

Suzanne	Union minded family background; significant experiences at the workplace	Shop steward; branch committee member; regional and national trade group committee and women's committee member	Shop steward; branch committee member; regional and national trade group committee and women's committee member
Bernadette	Non–union family background; significant experiences at the workplace	Informal participation at branch level	Lay tutor
Mandy	Non–union family background; significant experiences at the workplace; significant other in the union	Shop steward	Shop steward; branch committee member; Regional and national lesbian and gay committee member

Beryl clearly derived immense satisfaction from her union work, which seemed like an outlet for her energy and intellectual capabilities, which were not utilised in her fairly low-level paid work. She showed a remarkable capacity to battle on against the odds, even taking on more union duties, against a heavy domestic workload. Whilst on the one hand this might appear counterintuitive, on the other hand her commitment to the union, her union and gender identities had strengthened over time. She had become more confident and able to define and pursue a gendered union agenda of her own design, from which she could see results, such as her success in negotiating a new non-see-through uniform for female reception staff. Therefore stronger perceptions of personal and political efficacy (or agency) combined with continuing industrial relations problems meant that Beryl felt unable and unwilling to retreat from participation.

Helen's Story

Helen, still separated from her husband, faced a difficult family life, yet she took most of her union work home, she explained:

'I enjoy it. I find it [union work] a challenge. It's the one thing at work that keeps me going, I have to say, because there are a lot of interesting things going on and we've done so much that you really feel you've achieved something. If it wasn't for the union work I might have left [the company] by now, I really do think that.'

However, while Helen felt she had become more competent and effective as a workplace representative, she was reluctant to take on any additional union roles because of family commitments. During the two year period she had attended Women's Week for a third time, which she had found extremely useful. She had also attended her first mixed-sex union course, which she said she was unimpressed by:

'There were 12 of us and we hadn't met the tutor before. We walked into this room at 12 and he started with this lecture – at 3pm we left and no one knew anyone's name. We had dinner together and we [the students] sat together and they [the tutors] sat together. When we came in the next day, it was the same thing. We did one or two exercises but that was all and we were expected to do role-play with people we hadn't even been introduced to. It was the most uncomfortable feeling I've ever had in my life. I just felt like I didn't get anything out of it at all. It wasn't a safe environment at all.'

Helen's case also illustrates how it is not necessary for women to have an espousedly feminist identity in order to identify and pursue a women's trade union agenda. Nevertheless, her gender identity did appear to have shifted towards a more politicised position:

'Well the way men are behaving at the moment at work, I'm rapidly becoming one [a feminist]. I'm thinking maybe I should take a more principled stand on the way women are treated there. But it's nearly all females we have in our group and I do identify with them, but male or female, I'm interested in people's rights'.

Hilary (TGWU) (see her story above), a mother of a young child, had also developed her role by becoming a fully-fledged shop steward as well as 'women's rep', and completing the three stages of shop stewards training. She managed to juggle work, union and home demands, by limiting her union roles and ambitions and importantly she also had a supportive partner. She said she had been encouraged by others in the branch to stand for a senior representative position, but she had decided not to, largely because it would entail regional meetings:

> Working full-time and being a mum, I mean if you're involved outside the airport you have to go off to London and here, there and everywhere and with a five year old that I don't see during the day anyway and then if I didn't see her at all during the evenings, I don't think that would go down too well at home. So it's juggling the time – if you're going to do it, you have to do it well, you can't do it half-heartedly because people are depending on you.

Among the women who were mothers, the motivation to balance the 'triple load' appeared to reside in a combination of commitment to the union and in the immense personal satisfaction that they drew from their union work. The intrinsic satisfaction derived from union participation was emphasised by Helen's story (MSF).

'Women's Reps'

The creation of 'women's reps' is one of the positive action initiatives that workplace unions/branches in MSF and TGWU are encouraged to adopt, according to the unions, for three reasons. First the role is intended to facilitate recruitment of more female representatives, especially in male dominated union contexts. Second, it is intended to enable the union to provide better support to women members in cases of sexual harassment or on other 'women's issues'. Third, 'women's reps' should be able to contribute a gender perspective to the union's activities generally. These three reasons could be taken as indicative of an ideological commitment to increasing women's representation in order to deliver on gender democracy. Alternatively, the initiative could constitute an effort to appropriate 'women's knowledge' towards unions goals at a time when unions need female members, out of a belief that women's presence will help to plug a kind of cultural deficit.

The establishment of 'women's reps' could be an important development, which could represent one step towards gendered transformation in local union contexts. However, evidence from this research suggests that 'women's reps' was a less of a revolutionary concept in practice than in theory. The feminist orientation of the women in these roles is relevant in so far as feminist women are more likely to display politicised gender identities and be prepared to use the position of 'women's rep' to advance a women's agenda. Feminist women, critical of male dominated structures, are also more likely to recognise the limitation of the role of 'women's rep'.

As shown in Tables 7.1–7.4, a small number of interviewees (two MSF, three TGWU) were 'women's reps' at the first interview, three of which were self-identified feminists (two MSF, one TGWU). Four women still held the position by the time of the second interviews, whilst the fifth was no longer a trade union member. In the case of the two MSF women, this was and remained their only union position. One of the remaining TGWU 'women's reps' was also a shop steward and the other TGWU woman went on to additionally become a fully-fledged shop steward by the second interview. Two years after attending the women's schools it was interesting to explore how the remaining four women had developed in their roles as 'women's reps'. Although only a small group, their stories reveal some important insights into the lived experiences of 'women's reps'.

One of the problems of creating additional positions especially for women is that there is no challenge to male authority and power, because there is no risk of unseating (possibly longstanding) male office holders. This argument is well rehearsed in the literature (e.g. Healy and Kirton 2000; Cockburn 1995). However, Beryl (TGWU), a self-identified feminist, was the only 'women's rep' who actually complained of this. She had started her union career as a 'women's rep', but quickly recognised the limitations of the role and that the way to make a difference was to become a shop steward, which she did at the earliest opportunity. She then used this position to identify and recruit other women as 'women's reps', as she had Hilary, who also went on to become a shop steward after the women's school. In their workplace union 'women's reps' were not part of the negotiating committee and therefore wielded little power or 'say' in what bargaining agendas should be pursued, something which had frustrated Beryl. Hilary, meanwhile, (a non-feminist) had a more conciliatory stance and was less critical of arrangements and practices in the local branch. She felt that the 'women's rep' position afforded her time to 'learn the ropes', for example she attended various meetings and hearings as an observer. When, after the women's school, she felt more confident, she stood uncontested for a shop steward position and was now representing an all male manual work group. Thus, these two women interpreted the role of 'women's rep' differently: Beryl experienced it as constraining, whilst Hilary experienced it as enabling, at least in the initial stages of her union career. Despite different personal experiences and perspectives, both women were in agreement that the position of 'women's rep' helped to draw in some more hesitant women.

An issue that emerges from the experiences of Beryl and Hilary is that the impact, which individual women can have as 'women's reps' is severely circumscribed by the masculine hierarchy because the more experienced men define the parameters of the role. There may not necessarily be a conscious strategy of internal exclusion to keep women on the margins, but without doubt the male oligarchy has an interest in controlling women's roles, whilst appropriating their knowledge. In practice this means that a lone and inexperienced woman activist can find herself taking her cue from a man, who does not have a clear sense of the purpose of 'women's reps' or any ideas on how to be proactive in the role. This was the MSF women's experience of being 'women's reps'. Linda, for example, was the only woman active in her branch and had been encouraged to attend 'Women's Week' by the male branch secretary. She found the course very useful saying that she had learnt a lot about the union. Two years later, however, she had done little in her role, other than publicise her existence to women members via a newsletter and a leaflet. Linda was, however, unconcerned about her lack of power and influence, saying she was happy 'to do her bit'. Ironically she was a self-identified feminist with, in one sense, a politicised active gender identity, but she did not marshal this to develop a critical appraisal of her local male dominated branch. Linda said she had little time to give to the union with a full-time job, a dependent daughter and an active role in an environmental group: hers was less of an ideological position than a pragmatic one.

In summary, it would probably take an experienced trade unionist or a woman schooled in feminist politics and practice (via for example, participation in other women's groups in the union) to really make something of the role of 'women's rep'. Paradoxically, it is usually newer and often non-feminist women who are recruited to it. The result is that the 'women's rep' herself does not always have a sense of what she should or could be doing in the role as in the case of the two MSF women. Those who are concerned are likely to have to move themselves into mainstream positions of power and influence as in the case of the TGWU women. However, Beryl retained her 'women's rep' position and as a more experienced trade unionist, fully cognisant of the gendered politics of union life, she was now able to use the position to advance 'women's issues' when her position as a non-senior shop steward otherwise excluded her:

> With all this change [in management] a lot of the men felt it was their responsibility – there were no women involved in the negotiations at all and I felt that was really bad. We're hoping to organise union visits to other airports, so I will suggest that I go as the women's rep so that I can put women's view forward, because I feel that's important. Otherwise it will just be the [all male] senior stewards.

The above analysis indicates that the creation of 'women's reps' could point in the direction of incremental gendered transformation through a fairly subtle realignment of power, alternatively it could simply reinforce the marginalisation of women. The outcome seems contingent on the women who take up the positions actively pursuing gender-conscious or feminist strategies, rather than sitting back and waiting for the men to define the parameters of the role.

Women as representatives

This section gives a flavour of what the workplace representatives (three MSF, five TGWU) were doing in their unions generally two years after the women's schools. The analysis shows that there was evidence of gender conscious strategies and priorities being pursued by some of these women, although only three self-identified as feminists (one MSF, two TGWU). There were two main strands to this, the first concerned their emphasis on increasing women's participation and the second was their attention to workplace 'women's issues'. However, there were also some women who represented only or predominantly men, whose day-to-day union duties involved little consideration of female-gendered issues, but this did not necessarily result in a gender- neutral union identity.

Julie's Story

Julie was now on full-time union duties because of a major dispute within her employing local authority. This meant that she was taking a lead role in the dispute as deputy convenor. In the first interview Julie appeared nervous and lacking confidence in her role, whereas she said that she now worked with the convenor as an equal.

Julie, working in a skilled manual trade, represented an overwhelmingly male membership where women workers often reported social isolation. Since becoming involved with the union's women's groups Julie now organised monthly women's meetings to informally seek feedback from her few women members on workplace issues. This indicates her willingness, as a self-defined feminist, to utilise an explicitly feminist practice (women-only groups) to engage the female membership.

Julie had extended her participation beyond the workplace and was now a member of the union's national women's committee, which she found very interesting, as she explains:

'I think it's probably being with women from all different sectors, trade groups, to see how there's a group of women who want to get further in the union. They've fought to get women on union committees and they've pretty much been fighting sexism. It's just so inspiring.'

Over the two year period of the study, Julie's participation had developed in both measurable and subjective ways and it was clear that her involvement in women's groups had expanded her concept of what trade unionism was about.

However, she remained concerned not to lose sight of what she saw as class oppression, which meant that she defined her male membership as an oppressed social group:

'Regarding men, I mean at one stage I would have gone mad about pornography and stuff like that, but I think women have to realise that it's not just about our liberation. I mean I think the oppression of men hasn't really been recognised and it's absolutely major you know, of working class men.'

All the workplace representatives in the study were keen to encourage more women to participate in the union and to this end were using gender conscious, if not espousedly feminist, strategies. This involved personally identifying individual women whom they thought might be interested and developing practices to encourage them to participate. For example, Beryl (TGWU) had managed to recruit two cleaners as 'women's reps' because she was concerned that the wholly female cleaning staff had never been represented among the stewards and she felt little effort had been put into trying to involve them. The cleaners' exclusion from the union is an example of the way that gender and class intersect and combine to act as constraint and Beryl's intervention serves as an example of individual women using their agency to further women's interests generally. Elizabeth (MSF) was eager to share power by encouraging local women representatives to gain the confidence to deal with issues themselves rather than referring to her as chair of the branch. Helen and Fiona

(MSF), both mothers acutely aware of time constraints, had established some union roles as job share posts so as to appeal to women who were afraid of being engulfed by union participation. Once again these were all examples of the creative ways in which women contribute to incremental gendered transformation.

The literature has also highlighted the importance of female role models for encouraging women's participation (e.g. Kirton and Healy 1999). The women were generally reluctant to position themselves as role models, being modest about their achievements, but they all conceded that the presence of women encourages other women to become involved, as Hilary (TGWU) suggests:

> I think because I'm female, relatively young, I'm not very tall and I sit in these meetings and when I pipe up they think "she can do it and no one shot her down", so perhaps that's something other women may benefit from.

Suzanne (TGWU) had also identified two interested women and her experience of attempting to get them involved, highlights the contingent nature of women's participation:

> One of them has become a steward, but she has children so weekends are difficult for her. The other one unfortunately has had health problems that have made her take a back seat. She had more time to get involved at weekends because her children are grown up and just as that was getting off the ground she became ill. Once things start to interfere in their home life, it's still quite a big barrier for a lot of women.

The above examples reveal sensitivity to the realities of women's lives and how women make choices about which aspects of their lives to privilege at any given point in time. These women also show a concern to identify means of distributing union knowledge and increasing women's participation. Above all they did not position themselves as the experts on women, but were continually thinking of new ideas for involving more women. The practice of distributing knowledge is associated with feminist values (although not all these women self-identified as feminists) and is also an element of transformational leadership styles, which women often adopt in order to spread power and influence, rather than own it (Dorgan and Grieco 1993). This also demonstrates the intersection of politicised gender and union identities.

The literature on women in unions is also interested in whether women's presence in the ranks of representatives actually alters union agendas (e.g. Heery and Kelly 1988). Indeed, part of the feminist claim for measures to increase women's participation in democratic processes and structures rests on the belief that women do make a difference. There was evidence that the women used their positions to identify gender-specific issues, rather than simply respond to, membership concerns, in other words they acted to gender the union agenda. For example, in explaining why she would like to attend the women's school again, Beryl, a feminist, highlighted that 'women's issues' were a priority for her:

> One of my main things is the women here – how they're treated. I mean recruitment and selection for example – all that [good practice] seems to have fallen by the wayside

– we've got people coming in and they seem to be friends of friends and they only seem interested in promoting male graduates, instead of promoting women up from the floor. There are a lot of issues for women. The bus drivers have problems with their blouses because they're see-through and they're refusing to wear them.

In another example, Elizabeth (a non-feminist) (MSF) had instigated a job evaluation exercise for predominantly female secretaries, believing that there was significant under-valuation of the role. After two years of negotiations, this had resulted in a re-grading of most secretaries, an achievement of which Elizabeth was clearly proud.

The ability and willingness to identify pro-actively 'women's issues' and to bring these to the union agenda is highly significant. Firstly, bearing in mind generally low levels of (female) attendance, it is impossible for union representatives to rely solely on traditional consultation devices (i.e. meetings) in order to identify member concerns and to set the union bargaining agenda. Secondly, it also makes it harder for male officials to ignore women's concerns, which might be expressed in informal member-official communication, but be filtered out before reaching the union agenda. In this way, women's collective actions can help to break down women's internal exclusion.

When women represent women it is likely that they will unconsciously, if not consciously, identify with their membership and in doing so easily identify the issues of concern to the female membership, as was the case with Fiona, Helen and Elizabeth (MSF). It is interesting also to consider whether when women represent mostly men, their gender identity or feminist orientation has any bearing on the issues they take up or on the way they carry out their duties. There were three TGWU women who represented almost all men. None of these women reported any opposition to their election or to their carrying out their union duties, although as discussed earlier, this could be a function of the lesser willingness of men to become involved in unions, rather than indicating a change in union culture. It could also be that women have become more vocal in unions. Hilary (a non-feminist), for example, revealed somewhat contradictory views and presented an entirely different picture to Beryl (a self-identified feminist) of the same workplace. On the one hand she emphasised the absence of sexist attitudes in the union and workplace, on the other hand she felt that women might have to force change:

> Luckily we don't have any form of sexism here. Perhaps it's because we have a lot of female managers and female supervisors. It's not as if all the women here are only secretaries. I suppose that rubs off on the shop stewards. I can see the difference in the last ten years – the attitudes are changing. I'm not sure if it's that the attitudes of the senior men in the union are changing or whether it's the women who are forcing the attitudes to change. I'm sure it's the women who have said I'm just as good as you at doing that; just let me show you.

Mandy's activities as a steward representing almost all men were an example of the preparedness of non-feminist women to gender the union agenda even in the male dominated context. Mandy had negotiated the provision of smaller size footwear (as part of the uniform) with the tiny minority of women bus drivers in mind, overturning the previous requirement for women drivers to buy their own shoes. Mandy commented that her male branch secretary had felt that because there were so few women, this was not an issue worth putting effort into. Like Julie and Hilary though, Mandy was also keen to pursue 'equality for everyone' and did not confine her efforts to 'women's issues', pointing to a possible tension between gender and class-based union identities.

To summarise, the analysis of women as representatives points to the significance of feminist beliefs and values in underpinning the strategies and practices of trade union women, although there was no clear relationship with espousal of the feminist label, (mirroring other research, e.g. Kirton and Healy 1999; Parker 2002).

Final reflections on women's courses

Two years after the women's schools, interviewees who had sustained or developed their union participation were invited to offer their thoughts on the significance or impact for them of the women-only courses. All the women recalled fond memories of their course experiences and remained convinced that women's courses build women's confidence to participate. The impact for some had been profound and they were able to pinpoint specific ways in which they felt they had benefited. For some women, the benefit had been of a very personal nature, from which they had been able to draw strength as women. Deirdre (MSF) had returned to 'Women's Week' in 2001, she remarked:

> I broke down and cried at "Women's Week" last year, I felt that emotional. When you've never had praise in your life, it just feels so good to get it and there they are [the tutors] giving you so much. I mean I've been a battered wife and I know how women can be crushed so I want to support other women to get to where I am now.

Mandy believed that attending the women's school, as her first union course had given her confidence not only as a woman, also as a lesbian woman. She recalled a speech she had made at the end of a mixed-sex 'Equality for all' course, a year later:

> I got a standing ovation. They said it was the first time that anyone had spoken on that [lesbian and gay issues] at Eastbourne. Everybody on that course – well actually it wasn't everybody, but it feels like that when you're in a minority – there were four blokes and they were forever putting gays down, calling them queers. After a few days it gets really annoying, so I came out and said that I were gay. Then I got chosen for one of the speeches.

Mandy was clear that it was the women's course that had given her the confidence to publicly assert her identity as a lesbian woman. Other women felt that the experience of the women's school had been pivotal in their development as activists, as highlighted by Fiona. To continue her union learning, Fiona had been back to Women's Week twice since the first interview and completed all the available courses. She said she felt sad that for her Women's Week had come to an end, for now at least.

I couldn't imagine not being involved in the union now. It's amazing, it does bring you out of yourself. You feel more confident in situations outside of the union too. Going to Women's Week – it's made me much stronger. We know the tactics and the tricks to watch out for and we're not half as nervous as we were before. We are now a force to be reckoned with.

Some women had since participated in mixed courses for the first time and whilst they generally felt they had benefited from these, they were less enthusiastic. Helen (MSF), for example, talked (above) about the different (less interactive) teaching style of the male tutor of a mixed school she had attended. Overall, most of the women felt that women's schools served a special function, even the more sceptical supporters, because they had 'seen it with their own eyes'. For example, at the first interview Suzanne a very experienced activist of TGWU expressed only equivocal support for separate women's courses; she reflected on this again at the second interview:

I think having seen women coming through that route and actually taking part, I think I've probably changed my mind on that. I think what disturbed and I suppose still disturbs me is that they can become too dependent on women and not try to work with their male colleagues. I mean you do have to have a working relationship with men in the union as well. I think that some of them wouldn't go on mixed courses and that's a problem, I think. So it depends on the woman, but over these last two years, watching new women come through from the women's schools, I think they're very valuable.

Suzanne was also now a little more comfortable with feminist practices:

I mean I still strongly believe in women's equality, but I believe that women should be succeeding on their own ability, not because they've been given special help. Equality and fairness are important principles. I mean I'm involved in the women's committee and I will be going to the women's TUC, but the reason I go is in order to meet other women and to further my own knowledge about women's issues. I mean it is about the empowerment of women.

Elizabeth (MSF), however, retained her serious reservations about separate women's courses, but nevertheless conceded that there was a need for them:

I can understand why they're there – and that's not just on women, it's also on race issues – it's very difficult really, because what they're saying is that we should be equal on all things and then they have a black workers course or a women's course. It doesn't matter if they're black, male, female or blue with pink spots – people should go on courses because they're members. I know why they're there, but I don't like why they're there – I abhor the need for them to be there.

In summary, those who had previously supported the concept of women's courses continued to do so and in particular they continued to emphasise the value of women's courses to novice women. Some of the more ambivalent supporters were now a little less hesitant in their support for this form of women's separate organizing.

Summary

This chapter has explored how women's union participation develops over time. The putative barriers to women's participation according to the literature are the structure of women's employment, the gendered division of domestic labour and trade union culture (see Chapter 2). Significantly, this chapter has shown that the structure of women's employment and trade union culture were far more influential on patterns of participation, than were caring responsibilities. However, some women in the study found the inner strength and confidence to pursue alternative paths which led them into non-unionized employment and away from union participation, whilst others had poor experiences of workplace unions, which deterred them from going any further with their union careers. Significantly, some women had heavy domestic responsibilities, but managed to balance these with union roles. There were surprisingly few cases of women perceiving their domestic situations as a reason not to participate, although juggling the triple load might have influenced them to confine their participation to the low end of the hierarchy, thus stunting a vertical union career. There were also on occasion other reasons for breaking off or not starting a union career such as illness and disability or simple lack of interest.

It also seems that sustained participation favours stability in both personal and work circumstances, as none of the women who developed union careers had changed jobs or workplaces and most had had stability in their personal lives. However, their experiences were equally gendered: they were energetic, intelligent women who were unrecognised and unrewarded in their paid work, gaining enormous intrinsic rewards from union participation. They were treated with respect by co-workers and management and they were often more important in the workplace by virtue of the union role than because of their paid work role. Thus, from a policy perspective, women trapped in low skill work could constitute a huge untapped resource for unions, whilst from a conceptual perspective the intrinsic value of participation is far more important than previously suggested (e.g. by Klandermans 1992). Over time most interviewees became more attitudinally and/ or behaviourally committed to their union: their union identities had strengthened and in many cases so too had their gender identities. Therefore it is important that the opportunity to capitalise on the enthusiasm generated by women's schools is seized so that the investment in educating women is fully exploited towards trade union goals.

From the tracking of the interviewees, we can only conclude that life is messy and complicated, women's lives even more so than are men's because of the primary roles they assume in the home and family and because of the gender regime in employment. Thus it is necessary to emphasise again that women's union participation is shaped by a dynamic and complex interaction of socialisation in the family, workplace and union, together with gendered structural barriers to participation, all of which are mediated by the personal resources individual women are able to draw upon. It cannot be argued with any certainty, that the outcomes for the individual women in the study would have been different had they not attended the women's schools. However, their perception was overwhelmingly that their futures had been influenced by their experiences of women-only courses, even if in invisible (to others) and intangible ways. Mandy has the final word:

> I think it's brilliant. I think you get a hell of a lot from it. I wouldn't be where I am now if I hadn't been on them courses. I'd recommend it to anybody. (Mandy, TGWU).

Chapter 8

Making Sense of Women's Trade Union Careers

The broad aim of this book was to explore the making of women's trade union participation within the context of the existing gender democracy deficit (Cockburn 1995). The study sought to understand how women's trade union participation is shaped by their experiences of three interlocking social institutions – family, work and unions. The life history approach to the interviews with women trade union members revealed their routes to participation and the barriers they experienced and perceived to be in the way of union involvement. The main focus of the study was trade union women's engagement with one form of women's separate organizing – women-only courses. Education is a significant, but under-researched sphere of trade union activity, to the extent that from the literature we know very little about what unions are currently doing in the area and why (Kirton and Healy 2004). The research explored the social processes of women-only courses, investigating the ways in which women's gender and union identities are shaped by engagement with the gendered discourses of the courses. By re-interviewing participants approximately two years after they had attended women-only courses, the research was also able to explore the longer term influence of the courses on the trajectory of women's union careers.

The book has drawn upon a multi-disciplinary literature in order to locate the study in conceptual, contemporary and historical contexts. Chapter 1 outlined the conceptual approach of the book, which selectively draws on the traditions and strengths of a range of feminist and industrial relations theories appropriate to exploring the structure-agency dynamic in the making of women's trade union careers. Chapter 2 outlined female patterns of union membership and participation in Britain and discussed the main explanations for women's lesser participation and under-representation in union decision-making structures. It also discussed women's separate organizing as a strategy towards gender democracy. Chapter 3 situated the study in its historical context and revealed the longstanding existence of women's inequality in the British trade unions, thus linking past and present experiences. The history of women's challenge and resistance to external and internal exclusion via various forms of women's separate organizing (Boston 1987; Cunnison and Stageman 1995), places women as active agents from the birth of trade union organization. The historical account provides a vivid illustration of the structural nature of women's inequality. However, it also demonstrates that social structures are unstable and uneven in their effect when viewed historically. Women's inequality in unions is temporally persistent, but its forms and manifestations alter over time and can be destabilised by women's collective agency. This is evident from the experiences of the latter half of the twentieth century once women became more numerous and powerful within unions. In response to ongoing internal exclusion, women's separate organizing evolved into a proactive choice of a new generation of trade union women influenced by 'second wave' feminism (e.g. Cockburn 1991; 1995; Colgan and Ledwith 1996).

This concluding chapter identifies three interconnected key themes arising from the study: (i) the value and limitations of women's separate organizing; (ii) the shaping of women's gender and union identities; (iii) the making of women trade unionists. Finally, the chapter looks at the implications of the study for trade union policy and practice.

The value and limitations of women's separate organizing

Women's separate organizing is widely regarded as central to developing what Cockburn (1989) calls a long equality agenda (e.g. Briskin 1993; Colgan and Ledwith 2000; Healy and Kirton 2000; Humphrey 2002; McBride 2001). The research focus of the literature is generally on the structures of democracy – self-organised groups (e.g. Colgan and Ledwith 2000; Humphrey 2002; McBride 2001) and women's committees (e.g. Healy and Kirton 2000; McBride 2001, Parker 2002). Women-only courses are a weaker form of women's separate organizing to the extent that they have no direct influence on union policy-making (unlike women's committees, for example) and therefore no direct impact on union democracy, which possibly explains the lesser academic interest in them. However, from the research presented in this book it can be seen that the strength of women's courses lies in their potential to shape and strengthen the gender and trade union identities of participants. This then encourages women to develop union careers and then consciously or unconsciously to act to influence the gender democracy project.

The analysis demonstrated that the two unions' women's courses have broadly similar aims, namely to increase women's participation, but take somewhat different approaches, especially in relation to course content. MSF is more flexible in its approach to course content and emphasises the development of 'personal skills', which can be de-contextualised from the trade union environment if participants so choose. TGWU on the other hand is more prescriptive about content and explicitly situates the learning in the union context, placing a greater emphasis on imparting information and knowledge than on developing skills. However, in both unions women's courses are student-led and characterised by an 'active learning methods' approach (Croucher 2004), meaning that students drive the courses, with tutors facilitating learning rather than teaching. The outcome of the student-centred pedagogical approach is that the *processes* of the courses are similar and that in practice the women shape the actual content of discussions to a very large extent. There is also no clear discernible union by union pattern of outcomes; i.e. it was not the case that the majority of TGWU women developed their union careers in gender-aware ways, while the majority of MSF women did not, as perhaps might be assumed from the former union's explicitly union-focused course content. As shown in Chapter 7, the actual picture of longer term influences and outcomes was far more mixed and less union dependent, indicating that if the courses did have an influence the content was less important than the processes. Thus, one of the interesting findings from the study of two male-dominated unions is that women's experiences and perceptions of the influence of women-only courses, and their experiences and perceptions of barriers, constraints and opportunities in the union context were broadly similar.

The research drew on Briskin's (1993) influential conceptual typology of women's separate organizing. In summary, she argues that women's separate organizing can be informed by a variety of different political approaches, classified as (i) ghettoisation, (ii) a deficit model or (iii) a proactive politic. According to Briskin, proactive forms of separate organizing are preferable because they are more likely to contribute towards gendered transformation, because of the recognition that it is unions that must change, rather than women. Within this discussion Briskin (1993:96) positions some women's courses (those that aim to 'change' women by increasing their confidence and developing their assertiveness) as examples of a deficit approach because they send a message which blames the victim and assumes that being like men is the solution for women. Meanwhile, courses with a more feminist, politicised content (e.g. covering the history of women in unions, the family obstacles facing women) envisioning a transformed union movement, are placed within the proactive model of separate organizing.

The findings of this study show that in practice women-only courses are not either one or the other (deficit *or* proactive) in approach and content, but contain elements of both models. With regard to the deficit model, the research shows that women-only courses in the two unions do in some ways seek to 'correct' or 'change' women, for example, by building confidence and personal skills to participate. It is clear from the analysis that many women felt that the confidence they gained from the women-only courses could not be achieved in a mixed-sex, male dominated setting. Therefore they found the courses beneficial precisely because the constraint of the existing male dominated union hierarchy is a lived reality for women trade unionists (e.g. Cockburn 1991; Munro 1999; Rees 1990), which they need to have the personal resources to cope with before they will be in a position to challenge it. However, irrespective of the unions' possible intention to educate women to fit in or cope with the male-dominated context, the fact that the women gained personal resources, such as confidence and knowledge, undoubtedly increased their sense of self-efficacy and in many cases appeared to influence the orientation of their participation and involvement. Many women went on to develop alternative, transformational approaches to trade union work and to challenge the masculine hierarchy's control of agendas and practices. Thus indicating that the outcome of what might be deemed a deficit approach to educating women could be more radical than Briskin's (1993) typology implies and more so than the unions intend. This is because separate organizing cannot be understood as something unions *do to* women; it is a dynamic set of practices women actively shape and engage in. The implication then is that any single form of women's separate organizing might be informed by more than one political approach and therefore that attempts to classify actual practices might be futile.

The analysis has shown that the courses in MSF and TGWU also contained elements of a more proactive model. As Munro (2001) has noted, the dominant union discourse presents a limited range of issues as appropriate union business. In contrast, this research shows that discussions in the women-only educational setting take women physically, symbolically and intellectually, away from this limiting environment and provide a space where 'women's issues' can be legitimately privileged (see also Kirton and Healy 2004) and to which they bring their own gender-specific knowledge. Also the fact that many women consciously chose women-only courses over mixed-sex ones suggests a proactive approach on their part, that is women were not shunted off to women-only courses by male officers eager to 'correct' them. Women perceived the courses not simply as a shelter from the male-dominated context, but as a space where they could define 'the rules of the game' (as with other women-only spaces, e.g. McBride 2001; Parker 2002). Thus, to some extent the women's participation in the courses represented a vote in favour of separatism for it own sake, although this did not mean that they were unwilling to be involved in mixed-sex forums in the wider union.

The book has focused on the social processes rather than the content of the courses, because from observation and interviews it was clear that it was the social processes that had the most profound effect on the women. Young's work (2000) provides a useful conceptual framework for understanding the salience of the social processes of the women-only space of the courses. The analysis showed that in the context of the courses, the women invented what could be termed female-defined 'rules of the game'. This involved what Young (2000:56) has called more 'inclusive modes of political communication', including storytelling and expression of emotion. The significance of this is that this mode of communication constituted a form of consciousness-raising, from which it was clear that participants built a gendered understanding of their lived experiences as socially constructed and constrained. Deployment of a gender-conscious vocabulary enabled the women to express collectively their feelings about the male dominated context, for example, frustration, anger, bewilderment, etc, without undermining their sense of self and without blaming themselves. This was an empowering process because it politicised many of the women as they came to understand the social and cultural sources of their inequality. It also encouraged many to believe that they could gain control over their own lives as well as influence their collective social conditions, through union participation. In essence the women-only courses helped many participants learn to value themselves as women because their gender identity was not questioned or secondary to their trade union or class identity, as it often is in other union forums. Thus the courses were empowering because women gained authority to speak for themselves, an authority born of knowledge and confidence, which was taken forward by many women into their union, paid work and family/marriage careers.

The analysis has shown that the women had overwhelmingly positive experiences of women-only courses, although many held ambivalent views of women's separate organizing as a general principle (echoing other research, e.g. McBride 2001). This suggests a degree of discomfort with wider women's structures (particularly, although not uniquely among TGWU women), influenced by a combination of anti-feminist discourses, masculine constructions of union solidarity and strong class-based union identities. Thus, support for women-only courses, a relatively weak and institutionally powerless form of women's separate organizing cannot be taken to indicate support for more radical, influential forms, because it poses no direct or immediate threat to the traditional union *modus operandi*. Its power lies in what the women collectively and individually take from the course and how and if they subsequently use the sense of empowerment over time to alter union cultural practices. The nature and development of their union and gender identities is central to this.

The shaping of women's gender and union identities

The interest in this study in 'identity' was not as a self-contained concept, or for its own sake, rather in using it analytically as a means of exploring the identity formation processes of the courses, and for understanding and explaining the dynamics of women's union participation. Congruent with this objective identity was conceptualised as mediated by context; that is individuals choose to privilege different identities in different contexts, plus different identities are more or less salient in different contexts (Bradley 1996). For example, women who in the wider union context appeared to privilege their class identity, emphasising their solidarity with *all* union members, were comfortable with privileging their gender identity in the context of the women's courses.

It is clear from the analysis that the courses attempt to strengthen the women's *union* identity, so that they will want to participate and will see that participation could confer collective influence on the general conditions of working life. This is based on the belief that self-identification with a group promotes a commonality of interests (Kelly and Breinlinger 1996). However, it is not clear that the courses explicitly seek to develop more politicised *gender* identities, i.e. to encourage women to self-identify with women as an oppressed social group; although as indicated above, this does not mean that this is not the outcome. As with any educational process, especially student-centred pedagogic approaches, the providers and educators cannot entirely control the impact on learners individually or collectively. Indeed, the analysis of the providers' and educators' objectives revealed potential tensions surrounding the question of whether class-based union and gender identities are complementary and mutually reinforcing or whether they are opposing.

It is clear that the practices and discourses of the women's schools promote a greater awareness of gender and of trade union issues. The analysis shows that most women's union identities had strengthened following the course, when a strengthened commitment to the union and actual participation are taken as indicators. Further, many women's gender identities shifted following the course, so that many were conscious that they had developed a heightened awareness of women's inequality and its social causes. Through the narratives they told about their own lives during the courses and the knowledge they gained about women's position in society, many women came to see that they did count. Thus the courses constituted a safe space in which women could discover and re-discover their gender identities and recognise how this knowledge could become a powerful resource.

Activating a union identity is important to the extent that collective identification might promote/sustain participation (Kelly and Breinlinger 1996; Kelly 1998). Alongside this, activating a politicised gender identity might promote a critical stance that could encourage women to challenge the gendered cultural practices of local trade unions in pursuit of the gender democracy project. Equally a politicised gender identity might alienate women from masculine biased union politics and organization. However, it is important to emphasise that class-based union and gender identities are not always experienced as opposing or irreconcilable; rather it is a question of what underpins women's orientations and drives their actions in context. In this regard a number of issues emerge from the study.

First, it was apparent that more than one identity could be politicised, providing in Bradley's terms (1996) a base for constant action. For individual women, the lived experience of being, for example, a black, disabled or working class woman cannot be separated into different identity affiliations, where one might be privileged over another. It is evident that the women experienced an articulation of gender, class and race identities, rather than an additive disadvantage, pointing to the simultaneity of oppression on different grounds (Brewer 1997). However, it was also clear that a strong class-based identity could come into conflict with a gender identity particularly when the industrial relations context is hostile and there is a feeling of needing to 'stand together' that might involve dropping 'women's issues' from the union agenda.

Second, active and politicised gender identities became survival mechanisms for many women, imbuing them with a sense of greater personal efficacy achieved through adopting a more structural explanation of women's inequality, rather than an internalised one, but one where their individual and collective actions could have an impact. Thus the courses did not simply produce a greater awareness of female 'ways of being'; rather the courses showed how women's 'realities' and women's agency could become a powerful resource with which to resist and challenge the gendered union and employment hierarchy.

Third, it was significant that only a minority of women self-identified as feminists and this shaped, although did not determine the nature of their gender identity. For example, feminist women were more likely to have politicised gender identities, which informed the nature of their union identity and their more critical orientation to trade union policy and practice. Feminist women were also less likely to see their class and gender identities as clashing. Meanwhile, non-feminist women often had active, but not politicised gender identities, typically privileging their class-based union identity. Whilst these women were happy to criticise men in general, they were less happy to criticise fellow male trade unionists. All the women were conscious of women's collective inequality, agreeing that unions needed to tackle 'women's issues', but many had stronger and more politicised class-based union identities. This meant that many women were uncomfortable with the idea of *privileging* 'women's issues' in the wider union environment, even if they had found it a useful experience in the course context.

Fourth, the women's courses tend to present a limited range of 'women's issues' as salient to women's collective lived experiences, which is bound to exclude some women and some 'women's issues'. The courses tended to emphasise the material base of women's gender identities and a fairly traditional women's agenda; for example the gender pay gap, maternity pay, childcare etc. Whilst this undoubtedly politicised some women, it is a fairly narrow perspective and does not take adequate account of the diversity of women's subjective lived experiences based on other crosscutting identities such as age, race, class and sexuality. It is an approach which is therefore rightly subjected to criticism on grounds of its neglect of, for example, older women's concerns, lesbian issues, etc. At the same time it kindled a sense of injustice, which provided a basis for mobilising in some work and union contexts. However, in summary the course content was not as politicised (in feminist terms) as it might be.

It is clear from this and other research (e.g. Colgan and Ledwith 2002; McBride 2001) that for women collectively to challenge unions and to press for more action on women's internal and external inequality at workplace and branch levels involves their gender identities becoming politicised and a more constant base for action (Bradley 1996), but not necessarily at the expense of their class-based union identities. With regard to the role of women-only courses in this, the study suggests that there would need to be a clearer agenda on the part of the unions and the tutors that this was the goal, so that more politicised course content could be developed. At present, the *processes* of the women-only courses are on balance more important to the formation of the women's gender identities than the content. In summary, there would need to be a greater (feminist?) political will to develop a curriculum linking women's practical concerns with more strategic feminist approaches to challenging the existing gender hierarchy in the unions. Of course, even then, it is far from inevitable that women would adopt feminist strategies in their daily lives, but such an approach might enhance their ability to be more knowledgeable agents and open up more perceived 'choices'.

The making of women trade unionists

This study offers insights into the making of women trade unionists. It explores the variety of way in which women embark on a union career. It also explores the influence of one type of significant event in the shaping of a trade union careers. Finally, it investigates how women's union careers develop by examining in detail the social contexts in which women take the decision to participate and then how their careers unfold over time in those contexts. The study reveals that women's participation is far more complex than masculine linear models of union careers suggest.

With regard to the influences that propelled women into union membership/ participation in the first place, the majority of interviewees were from non-union family backgrounds, such that union and work influences, combined with the influence of the women's schools were overall more important than family influences. However, it is interesting to note that most of the women from union-minded backgrounds sustained or developed their participation over the two year period of the fieldwork. This highlights the fluid and emergent nature of union identities as not entirely fixed by prior beliefs and values, but continuously shaped by work, union and family contexts. Importantly it also highlights the way that various interventions, such as women-only courses and other experiences of unions can fashion orientations to participation.

Most of the interviewees embarked on the courses intending to become or stay active in their unions and as discussed above the courses appeared to have a significant positive impact on their union and gender identities, but not all the women sustained or developed participation over time. How could this be explained?

Turning first to the women whose union careers were 'stunted', their stories uncover the complexities of women's lives and the fact that personal, work or union contexts frequently interfere with the intention and willingness to participate becoming actualised. This did not mean, however, that the women-only courses had had any less profound an effect on these women than on those who developed their union careers. In fact some of these women felt so empowered following the course that they felt able to take greater control of their lives as individuals. This involved moving to what they considered to be better employment opportunities, rather than leading to stronger collective identification and therefore increased union participation. In other words once more choices open up to women, they do not necessarily jump in the 'right' direction from the point of view of the unions and some might choose individual mobility in pursuit of a positive social identity (Kelly and Breinlinger 1996). This is of course paradoxical given that the primary intention of women-only courses is to empower women to participate in the unions.

Another significant and ironic finding was that the women who ceased to participate largely consisted of 'atypical' women (meaning childfree, partner free) with few domestic constraints, who according to existing literature are most, rather than least, likely to participate (Colgan and Ledwith 1996; Kirton and Healy 1999; Lawrence 1994). This then stood in contrast to other studies, which tend to emphasise motherhood and the burden of domestic labour as major barriers to women's participation (e.g. Lawrence 1994; Walton 1991). In this research the structure of women's employment and trade union culture emerged as more important determinants of participation patterns, and more significant barriers, than the gendered division of domestic labour. It has to be acknowledged though that the division of domestic labour is to a large extent negotiable within individual households, whereas, as the study shows, an individual woman has greater difficulty acting on embedded gendered power relations within the workplace and union contexts.

Nevertheless, the stories of this group of women highlight the fragile nature of women's participation, which can easily be broken by constraints imposed (perceived and actual) by work, union, home and family. In short, the study demonstrates that women's relationship with trade union participation is complex, dynamic and fluid and likely to alter over the life course, but not necessarily in ways advanced by, for example, Cunnison's (1987) somewhat simplistic three-phase model with its emphasis on the constraints of child rearing. This research shows very clearly that women make their own union careers, but the choices and opportunities are mediated by structural, ideological and cultural barriers found within the union, work and family contexts.

What can be learnt from the stories of the majority of women in the study who developed their union careers over the two-year period of the fieldwork? One of the surprising and important findings was the high level of sustained involvement of mothers in the 'right' conditions, which were unionised employment, an encouraging and enabling local union culture, a morally and practically supportive partner/family. However, it is important not to become too optimistic about the changing nature of gender relations in the home, as many of the women, especially mothers, in the study complied with the prevailing household gender regime by becoming more organised and efficient such that trade union participation seldom intruded into the domestic domain. To emphasise, many of the women talked about how 'lucky' they were to have partners who 'helped' them in the home and family.

Turning to consider whether women acted on the existing union structures to transform them or to reproduce them, the picture was mixed. Layder (1993:91) suggests that 'social forms are reproduced over time because people generally replicate the habits, traditions, rules and stocks of knowledge that sustain these social forms in the first place'. This is a somewhat pessimistic outlook for feminists seeking social change. However, as Layder (ibid.) goes on to say 'social production takes place at the same time as social reproduction' because of the efforts of the participants involved. This highlights the possibility in the context of this research of women breaking the vicious circle of gender inequality through their own individual and collective actions or by utilising social change strategies (Kelly and Breinlinger 1996). There were many examples of women using their position, power and influence to alter union practices, arrangements and agendas, but there were also some examples of the women simply complying with and unwittingly reproducing existing ones.

The study leaves no doubt that contexts structure choices and influence behaviour regardless of the strength of identity positions. The qualitative nature of this research allowed a deeper understanding of the contexts, which framed the participation and identities of the interviewees. The conclusion, which must be drawn, is that the interviewees' union participation is grounded in the particular conditions of the specific workplace, union and family circumstances of each woman. In this respect, the level of participation of the interviewees is worthy of comment i.e. most privileged their participation at workplace/branch level, although some did participate in regional and national structures. The analysis showed that their priorities were a function of individual decision-making in the context of the perceived and actual barriers and constraints, underlining the structure-agency dynamic and the possibility for agency to both reproduce and transform.

In exploring the women's union career trajectories over time, union participation as an alternative career emerges very strongly. This is a theme neglected by the literature, which emerges in this study largely because of the multiple and life history interview method. In this regard, the intrinsic value of participation is emphasised by the women in this study, challenging the notion that people participate largely for instrumental reasons (e.g. Klandermans 1992). Many of the women who developed their union careers over time were in relatively low level employment, which provided little intrinsic satisfaction. In contrast, their union careers represented an outlet for their personal abilities, from where they could influence the conditions of their working lives and command the respect of co-workers and management. Given women's concentration in low-level employment, there is clearly a gendered dimension to the phenomenon of union as alternative career as women are more likely to find their skills and intellectual capabilities under-utilised, class-based occupational variation notwithstanding. For other women, who were partner free and free of caring responsibilities, the union also seemed to be an alternative to a family or 'marriage' career, where some found a satisfying social life. Finally, there were some women for whom union participation seemed to represent a parallel career. These were professional women who saw the union as a vehicle for pushing professional issues, especially for women (see also Healy and Kirton 2002). Thus the study highlights the importance of gendering the analysis of participation and the value of qualitative methodologies for unpacking different meanings attached to union careers.

Implications for trade union strategy and policy

If unions are to continue to invest in women-only courses it is self evident that they must meet union objectives, which were broadly defined as increasing women's participation. This was not always the outcome for this group of women: some women sustained and developed their union careers, others did not. It is clear that although the findings of a qualitative study can never be taken as generalisable, they are indicative. This could lead unions to question the utility of women-only courses. However, it cannot be emphasised enough that it is clear from the research that women-only courses have an enormous impact on participants, which could be taken as a sign of their 'success', even without firm evidence to support the fact that they increase women's participation, particularly if the broader purposes of trade union education are still valued. Many women regarded women-only courses as the making of them and most had a stronger attachment to trade unionism afterwards.

From the research it is also clear that there is a strong case on educational grounds for women's courses. Looking at the alternative – mixed-sex courses – the documentary evidence showed that women are proportionally represented among participants in MSF and TGWU. In practice though with small course groups, *actual* numbers of women participants can be very small indeed and it is not unusual for a woman to be a lone female participant on a mixed-sex course. This inevitably creates a gendered dynamic within courses, which as the reflective accounts of the tutors and students showed, acts as a deterrent for some women, hindering learning, particularly those who are less experienced trade union activists, and/or those who are unused to male dominated domains. All this is recognised by the two unions and provides an ongoing rationale for women-only education, which the unions' directors of education and tutors marshal as an argument. However, it is also a reason for not seeing individual women's attendance of women-only courses as one-off, or as a 'stepping stone' to mixed-sex courses. The study indicates that even many experienced women prefer women-only courses and believe that they learn far more in the women-only space, suggesting that separate organizing is a pro-active choice (Briskin 1993) on the part of many women, which they believe strengthens them individually and collectively.

Whatever the 'evidence', it is unlikely in the current internal and external climates that British unions would cease to provide women-only courses. Indeed there is widespread rhetorical policy commitment to the principle of women's separate organizing in the trade union movement even though some members construct it as divisive (e.g. Greene and Kirton 2002; McBride 2001). Despite both male and female detractors, it would be a retrograde and risky step to dismantle the structures, which have given women voice and variable degrees of power and influence in the unions over the last twenty years or so. Doing so would send the wrong signals to women at a time when unions need women more than ever.

The complexities of the gender democracy/equality project inside trade unions and extending this beyond the 'show case' of the national executive is an ongoing project. Women's courses can assist by finding ways of attracting less experienced trade unionists and cementing the trade union and gender identities of the more experienced in order to sustain their participation. In addition, despite the apparent success of women-only courses in empowering many women to participate, the contexts women return to following the courses are critical in shaping their union career trajectories. Thus, this form of intervention will always have limited success in terms of sustaining and developing women's trade union careers, while there remain cultural and structural barriers in the sites of actual participation. It is clear that the unions need to develop ways of tackling this problem.

The study has explored the shaping and making of women's trade union participation within the contexts of work, union and family and shown that various significant others, events, experiences and influences shape the contours and the paths of women's trade union careers. Women-only courses emerge as a significant event, experience and influence. This is an important finding of the research because significant experiences that promote union involvement are usually assumed to be located at the level of the workplace (e.g. Kelly 1998; Morris and Fosh 2000; Watson 1988) often relating to the engendering of the feelings of 'them' and 'us' believed necessary for willingness to participate (e.g. Kelly 1998). The research has also uncovered some of the gendered social processes of inclusion and exclusion within the union context, which simultaneously and paradoxically herald and circumscribe gendered transformation. Women trade unionists and feminist authors have been talking for more than a century about gender inequalities within trade unions: from this study it looks as though this discussion will continue well into this century.

Appendix

Research Methods

Four main research methods were employed in the study: (i) in-depth interviews with key respondents (directors of education and course tutors) and with course participants; (ii) observation of courses; (iii) analysis of documentary data and materials; (iv) a survey of course participants. A schedule of the fieldwork is presented in Table A1.

Analytical emphasis was given to the interviews with course participants. Individual biographies of course participant interviewees are provided in Tables A2 and A3. Course participant interviewees were recruited to the study at national women's schools in the two unions. It was a deliberate research strategy to attempt to achieve a diversity of demographic and occupational characteristics among interviewees, as well as both experienced and inexperienced activists. Of particular note is that most course participant interviewees were interviewed twice: the first interviews took place shortly after attendance of the women's schools I observed and the second interviews were two years' after the schools. The interviews took a life history approach in order to explore how the women understood and experienced various life stages. An interview guide was used consisting of open-ended questions encouraging interviewees to talk from their own interpretations and experiences. First interviews started with the interviewee's work, family and union history. Questioning then turned to the woman's experiences and perceptions of trade union education with special attention to the recently attended women's school. Questions were also asked about present workplace and union involvement. Second interviews explored whether and how the woman had become more involved in the union and any more recent experiences of union education were also discussed. This second meeting was also used to gain a broader understanding of the women's politics, attitudes and orientations to trade unionism and feminism.

Table A1 Schedule of fieldwork

Year	Observation	Survey Work	Organization Interviews	Participant Interviews
1999	**TGWU** National Women Members' School	1st Survey of participants at **TGWU** National Women Members' School – 57 returns.	1st Interview with Director of Education, **TGWU** 1st Interview with Director of Education, **MSF**	First interviews with 15 **TGWU** women
2000	**MSF** Women's Week	1st Survey of participants at **MSF** Women's Weeks – 37 returns.	1st Interview with Education Officer, **MSF** 2nd Interview with Education Officer, **MSF**	First interviews with **TGWU** women First interviews with 14 **MSF** women
2001	**TGWU** National Women Members' School	2nd Survey of participants of **TGWU** National Women Members' School – 42 returns.	2nd Interview with Director of Education, **TGWU** Interviews with **TGWU** tutors,	Second interviews with 12 **TGWU** women
2002	**MSF** Women's Week	2nd Survey of participants at **MSF** Women's Week – 30 returns.	Interviews with **MSF** tutors	Second interviews with 11 **MSF** women

Table A2 Individual biographies of MSF interviewees

Pseudonym / Age / Race / Ethnicity	Employment Sector	Occupation	Union Position(s)	Partner Status / Dependent Children	Highest Level Qualification
Kim / 38 / White	Manufacturing	Sales Manager	Women's Officer	Partner-free / None	HND
Susan / 36 / Black-Caribbean	Insurance	Clerical Work	None	Partner-free / None	HND
Barbara / 35 / White	Public/Voluntary	Advice Worker	None	Partner-free / None	Masters Degree
Sarah / 43 / White	NHS	Speech Therapist	None	Partner-free / None	Degree
Deirdre / 47 / White	Unemployed/Disabled	Previously Care Worker	Branch Chair	Married / None	State Enrolled Nurse
Kate / 30 / White	University	Laboratory Technician	Rep, Safety Rep	Partnered / None	Degree
Elizabeth / 56 / White	Union	Regional Centre Manager	Branch Chair	Divorced, Partner-free / None	'O' Levels
Fiona / 34 / White, Irish	Manufacturing	Clerical Work	Rep	Married / Two	'O' Levels
Afsana / 35 / Black-Asian	Voluntary	Community Worker	None	Divorced, Partner-free / Three	NVQ 3
Vera / 46 / White	NHS	Medical Officer	None	Divorced, Partner-free / None	Degree
Kamaljit / 29 / Black-Asian	Voluntary	Sexual Health Trainer	Rep	Partnered / None	Degree
Christine / 38 / Black-Caribbean	Voluntary	Day Centre Manager	Rep	Partner-free / None	Degree
Linda / 48 / White	University	Laboratory technician	Rep	Married / One	HND
Helen / 35 / White, Irish	Manufacturing	Clerical work	Rep	Divorced, Partner-free / Three	'O' Levels

Table A3 Individual biographies of TGWU interviewees

Pseudonym / Age / Race / Ethnicity	Employment Sector	Occupation	Union Position(s)	Partner Status / Dependent Children	Highest Level Qualification
Mary / 53 / White, Irish	Airline	Clerical Work	Shop Steward, Branch Secretary	Married / One	'O' Levels
Sally / 44 / White	Airline	Clerical Work	Shop Steward	Partnered / None	'O' Levels
Bernadette / 37 / Black-Caribbean	Public / Voluntary	Policy Officer	None	Married / Two	'A' Levels
Judy / 36 / Black-Caribbean	Unemployed / Disabled	Previously Bus Driver	None	Partner free/ None	'O' Levels
Delia / 32 / White	Insurance	Clerical Work	None	Divorced, Partner-free / None	'O' Levels
Mandy / 40 / White	Transport	Bus Driver	Shop Steward	Partner-free / None	'A' Levels
Beryl / 47 / White	Airport	Clerical Work	Shop Steward, Women's Officer	Married / None	'O' Levels
Diane / 32 / White	Catering / NHS	Kitchen Supervisor	None	Married / Two	Degree
Jane / 47 / White	Transport	Bus Driver	Women's Rep, Shop Steward	Married / None	None
Hilary / 32 / White	Airport	Clerical Work	Shop Steward, Branch Administrator, Education Officer	Married / One	Degree

Julie / 39 / White	Local Authority	Carpenter	Shop Steward, Deputy Branch Convenor	Partner-free / None	Degree
Evelyn / 45 / White	Voluntary / Advice Centre	Advice Worker	None	Divorced, Partner-free / One	Degree
Melanie / 30 / White	Union	Clerical Work	Shop Steward	Partner-free / None	HND
Molly / 48 / White	School	Secretary	Shop Steward, Safety Rep	Married / Three	'O' Levels
Suzanne / 40 / White	Manufacturing	Laboratory Technician	Senior Shop Steward	Married / Two	HNC

Bibliography

Acker, J. (1989), 'The Problem with Patriarchy', *Sociology*, **23**(2): 235–240.

Aldred, C. (1981), 'Men and the unions – just a side issue?', *Trade Union Studies Journal*, **Autumn**: 9–10.

Alvesson, M. and Billing, Y. (1997), *Understanding Gender and Organizations*, London, Sage.

Anthias, F. and Yuval–Davis, N. (1993), *Racialised Boundaries: Race, Nation, Gender, Colour and Class and the Anti–racist Struggle*, London, Routledge.

Barrett, M. (1992), 'Words and things: materialism and method in contemporary feminist analysis', *Destablising Theory*, Barrett, M. and Phillips, A., Cambridge, Polity Press.

Barrett, M. and Phillips, A. (1992), *Destablising Theory*, Cambridge, Polity Press.

Bassett, P. and Cave, A. (1993), 'All for one: the future of the unions', *Fabian Pamphlet*.

Batten, P. (2000), Education and Training: Regional Quarterly Report, 30 September– 21 December 2000, Region 1, London, TGWU.

Beale, J. (1982), *Getting It Together*, London, Pluto.

––––––– (1982a), 'What can we all learn from women's courses?', *Trade Union Studies Journal*, **Winter**: 20–21.

Beechey, V. and Perkins, T. (1987), *A Matter of Hours – Women, Part–time Work and the Labour Market*, Cambridge, Polity Press.

Blanden, J. and Machin, M. (2003), 'Cross-generation correlations of union status for young people in Britain', *British Journal of Industrial Relations*, **41**: 3, 391– 415.

Boston, S. (1987), *Women Workers and the Trade Unions*, London, Lawrence and Wishart.

Bradley, H. (1996), *Fractured Identities*, Cambridge, Polity Press.

––––––– (1997), 'Gender and Change in Employment: Feminisation and its Effects', *The Changing Shape of Work*, Brown, R., Basingstoke, Macmillan: 87–102.

––––––– (1999), *Gender and Power in the Workplace: Analysing the Impact of Economic Change*, Basingstoke, Macmillan.

Bradley, H., Erickson, M., Stephenson, C. and Williams, S. (2000), *Myths at Work*, Cambridge, Polity Press.

Bradley, H., Healy, G. and Mukherjee, N. (2002), 'A Double Disadvantage? Minority Ethnic Women in Trade Unions', Report funded by ESRC Future of Work Programme, Universities of Bristol and Hertfordshire.

––––––– (2005), 'Multiple Burdens: Problems of Work/Life Balance for Ethnic Minority Trade Union Activist Women', Houston, D. *Future of Work Life Balance*, Basingstoke, Palgrave.

Brew, K. and Garavan, T. (1995), 'Eliminating Inequality: Women–only Training', *Journal of European Industrial Training*, **19**(7): 13–19.

Brewer, R. (1997), 'Theorizing Race, Class, and Gender: the New Scholarship of Black Feminist Intellectuals and Black Women's Labor', *Materialist Feminism*, Hennessy, R. and Ingraham, C., London, Routledge: 236–247.

Bridgford, J. and Stirling, J. (2000), *Trade Union Education in Europe*, Brussels, European Trade Union College.

Bright, D. and MacDermott, T. (1982), 'Trade Union Tutors and their Students', *Employee Relations* **4**(3): 11–15.

Briskin, L. (1993), 'Union Women and Separate Organizing', *Women Challenging Unions*, Briskin, L. and McDermott, P., Toronto, University of Toronto Press: 89–108.

——— 'The equity project in Canadian unions: confronting the challenge of restructuring and globalisation', *Gender, Diversity and Trade Unions*, Colgan, F. and Ledwith, S., London, Routledge: 28–47.

Brook, K. (2002), 'Trade Union Membership: an Analysis of Data from the Autumn 2002 LFS', *Labour Market Trends* (July): 343–54.

Brown, W. and Lawson, M. (1973), 'The Training of Trade Union Officers', *British Journal of Industrial Relations*, **11** (3): 431–438.

Bulger, C. and Mellor, S. (1997), 'Self-efficacy as a mediator of the relationship between perceived union barriers and women's participation in union activities', *Journal of Applied Psychology*, **82**(6): 935–944.

Calas, M. and Smircich, L. (1996), 'From "the woman's point of view": feminist approaches to organization studies', *Handbook of Organization Studies*, Clegg, S., Handy, C. and Nord, W., London, Sage: 218–257.

Carter, B. (1997), 'Restructuring State Employment: Labour and non-Labour in the Capitalist State', *Capital & Class*, **63**.

——— (2000), 'Adoption of the organising model in British trade unions: some evidence from Manufacturing, Science and Finance (MSF)', *Work, Employment and Society*, **14**(1): 117–136.

Catlett, J. (1986), 'After the Goodbyes: a Long-Term Look at the Southern School for Union Women', *Labor Studies Journal*, **Winter**: 300–311.

Charles, N. and Hintjens, H. (1998), 'Gender, ethnicity and cultural identity: women's "places"', *Gender, ethnicity and political ideologies*, Charles, N. and Hintjens, H., London, Routledge: 1–26.

Cobble, D. and Bielski Michal, M. (2002), 'On the edge of equality? Working women and the US labour movement', *Gender, Diversity and Trade Unions*, Colgan, F. and Ledwith, S., London, Routledge: 232–256.

Cockburn, C. (1989), 'Equal Opportunities: the Short and the Long Agenda', *Industrial Relations Journal*, **20**(3): 213–225.

——— (1991), *In the Way of Women*, Basingstoke, Macmillan.

——— (1994), 'Play of Power: Women, men and equality initiatives in a trade union', *Anthropology of Organizations*, Wright, S., London, Routledge: 94–114.

——— (1995), *Strategies for Gender Democracy*, Luxembourg, European Commission.

Colgan, F. (1999), 'Recognising the lesbian and gay constituency in UK trade unions: moving forward in UNISON?', *Industrial Relations Journal* **30**(5): 444–63.

Colgan, F. and Ledwith, S. (1996), 'Sisters Organising – Women and their Trade Unions', *Women in Organizations*, Ledwith, S. and Colgan, F., Basingstoke, Macmillan: 152–185.

——— (2000), 'Diversity, Identities and Strategies of Women Trade Union Activists', *Gender, Work and Organization*, **7**(4): 242–257.

——— (2002), 'Gender and diversity: Reshaping union democracy', *Employee Relations*, **24**(2): 167–189.

——— (2002a), 'Gender, diversity and mobilisation in UK trade unions', *Gender, Diversity and Trade Unions*, Colgan, F. and Ledwith, S. London, Routledge: 154–185.

Colling, T. and Dickens, L. (2001), 'Gender Equality and Trade Unions: a new Basis for Mobilisation?', *Equality, Diversity and Disadvantage in Employment*, Noon, M. and Ogbonna, E., Basingstoke, Palgrave: 136–155.

Cook, A., Lorwin, V. and Kaplan Daniels, A. (1992), *The Most Difficult Revolution: Women and Trade Unions*, Ithaca, Cornell University Press.

Crain, M. (1994), 'Gender and Union Organizing', *Industrial and Labor Relations Review*, **47**(2): 227–247.

Croucher, R. (2004), 'The impact of trade union education: a study in three countries in Eastern Europe', *European Journal of Industrial Relations*, 10:1, 90–109.

Cully, M., S. Woodland, et al. (1999), *Britain at Work*, London, Routledge.

Cunnison, S. (1987), 'Women's Three Working Lives and Trade Union Participation', *Women and the Life-Cycle*, Allat, P., Keil, T., Bryman, A. and Bytheway, B., London, Macmillan: 135–148.

Cunnison, S. and Stageman, J. (1995), *Feminising the Unions*, Aldershot, Avebury.

Curtin, J. and Higgins, W. (1998), 'Feminism and Unionism in Sweden', *Politics and Society*, **26**(1): 69–93.

Dickens, L. (1997), 'Gender, Race and Employment Equality in Britain: Inadequate Strategies and the Role of Industrial Relations Actors', *Industrial Relations Journal*, **28**(4): 282–289.

Dickens, L., Townley, B. and Winchester, D. (1988), *Tackling Sex Discrimination through Collective Bargaining*, Manchester, Equal Opportunities Commission.

Dorgan, T. and Grieco, M. (1993), 'Battling against the odds: the emergence of senior women trade unionists', *Industrial Relations Journal*, **24**(2): 151–164.

Drake, B. (1984), *Women in Trade Unions*, London, Virago.

Elliot, R. (1980), 'Women in Unions: the Contribution of Trade Union Education', *Trade Union Studies Journal*, **Autumn**: 3–6.

ETUC (2002) *Women in unions: Making the difference*, Brussels, ETUC.

Fagan, C. and Burchell, B. (2002), *Gender, jobs and working conditions in the European Union*, Dublin, European Foundation for the Improvement of Living and Working Conditions.

Farnham, D. and Giles, L. (1995), 'Trade Unions in the UK: trends and counter-trends since 1979', *Employee Relations*, **17**(2): 5–22.

Flax, J. (1992), 'Beyond equality: gender, justice and difference', *Beyond equality and difference*, Bock, G. and James, S., London, Routledge: 193–210.

Fosh, P. (1993), 'Membership participation in workplace trade unionism: the possibility of union renewal', *British Journal of Industrial Relations*, **31**(4): 577–592.

Franzway, S. (2000), 'Women Working in a Greedy Institution: Commitment and Emotional Labour in the Union Movement', *Gender, Work and Organization*, **7**(4): 258–268.

Giddens, A. (1984), *The Constitution of Society*, Cambridge, Polity Press.

Gottfried, H. (1998), 'Beyond Patriarchy? Theorising Gender and Class', *Sociology*, **32**(3): 451–468.

Grayson, J. (1985), 'Power, Sex and the Unions: a new look at strategies for anti-sexist teaching', *Trade Union Studies Journal*, **Summer**: 8–12.

Greene, A. M. and Kirton, G. (2002), 'Advancing gender equality: the role of women-only trade union education', *Gender, Work and Organization*, **9**(1): 39–59.

Hakim, C. (1991), 'Grateful Slaves and Self-made Women: Fact and Fantasy in Women's Work Orientations', *European Sociological Review*, **7**(2): 101–118.

Hansen, L. (2002), 'Rethinking the industrial relations tradition from a gender perspective. An invitation to integration', *Employee Relations*, **24**(2): 190–210.

Hartley, J. (1992), 'Joining a Trade Union', *Employment Relations*, Hartley, J. and Stephenson, G., London, Blackwell: 163–183.

Healy, G. (1999), 'Structuring Commitments in Interrupted Careers: the case of teachers', *Gender Work and Organization*, **6**(4): 185–281.

Healy, G., Bradley, H., Mukerjee, N. (2003) 'Getting in – Getting Active: the Experience of Minority Ethnic Women in Trade Unions', Working Paper No.29, ESRC Future of Work Programme, University of Leeds.

———— (2004), 'Individualism and collectivism revisited: a study of black and minority ethnic women', *Industrial Relations Journal*, 35: 5, 451–466.

Healy, G. and Kirton, G. (2000), 'Women, Power and Trade Union Government in the UK', *British Journal of Industrial Relations* **38**(3): 343–360.

———— (2002), 'Professional and highly qualified women in two contrasting trade unions', *Gender, Diversity and Trade Unions*, Colgan, F. and Ledwith, S., London, Routledge: 186–204.

Hearn, J. and Parkin, W. (1993), 'Organizations, Multiple Oppressions and Post Modernism', *Postmodernism and Organizations*, Hassard, J. and Parker, M., London, Sage.

Heery, E. and Kelly, J. (1988), 'Do Female Representatives Make a Difference? Women FTOs and Trade Union Work', *Work, Employment and Society* **2**(4): 487–505.

———— (1990), 'A Cracking Job for a Woman – a Profile of Women Trade Union Officers', *Industrial Relations Journal*, **20**(3): 192–202.

Heery, E., Kelly, J. and Waddington, J. (2003), 'Union Revitalization in Britain', *European Journal of Industrial Relations* **9**(1): 79–97.

Heery, E. and Abbott, B. (2000), 'Trade unions and the insecure workforce', *The Insecure Workforce*, Heery, E. and Salmon, J., London, Routledge, 155–180.

Hennessy, R. and Ingraham, C. (1997), *Materialist Feminism*, London, Routledge.

Hicks, S. and Palmer, T. (2004), 'Trade Union Membership', *Labour Market Trends*, **112**(3): 3.

Holford, J. (1993), *Union Education in Britain: a TUC Activity*, Nottingham, University of Nottingham.

hooks, b. (1989), *Talking Back*, London, Sheba.

Howell, C. (1996), 'Women as the Paradigmatic Trade Unions? New Work, New Workers and New Trade Union Strategies in Conservative Britain', *Economic and Industrial Democracy*, **17**(5): 511–541.

Humphrey, J. (2002), *Towards a politics of the rainbow*, Aldershot, Ashgate.

Hunt, G. and Rayside, D. (2000), 'Labor Union Response to Diversity in Canada and the United States', *Industrial Relations*, **39**(3): 401–444.

Hyman, R. (1994), 'Theory and Industrial Relations', *British Journal of Industrial Relations*, **33**(2): 165–180.

Jenkins, R. (1996), *Social Identity*, London, Routledge.

Jewson, N. and Mason, D. (1986), 'The theory and practice of equal opportunities policies: liberal and radical approaches', *Sociological Review*, **34**(2): 307–334.

Jones, S. (2002), 'A woman's place is on the picket line. Towards a theory of community industrial relations', *Employee Relations*, **24**(2): 151–166.

Kanter, R. M. (1977), *Men and Women of the Corporation*, New York, Basic Books

Kelly, J. (1998), *Rethinking Industrial Relations: Mobilization, Collectivism and Long Waves*, London, Routledge.

Kelly, C. and Breinlinger, S. (1996), *The Social Psychology of Collective Action*, London, Taylor and Francis.

Kelly, J. and Heery, E. (1994), *Working for the Union*, Cambridge, Cambridge University Press.

Kelly, J. and Kelly, C. (1994), 'Who Gets Involved in Collective Action?: Social Psychological Determinants of Individual Participation in Trade Unions', *Human Relations*, **47** (1) 63–88.

Kelly, J. and Waddington, J. (1995), 'New Prospects for British Labour', *Organization*, **2**(3/4 Aug/November): 415–426.

Kerr, A. (1992), 'Why Public Sector Workers Join Unions: An Attitude Survey of Workers in the Health Service and Local Government', *Employee Relations*, **14**(2): 39–45.

Kirton, G. (1999), 'Sustaining and Developing Womens Trade Union Activism: A Gendered Project', *Gender, Work and Organization*, **6**(4): 213–223.

——— (2005), 'The influences on women joining and participating in unions', *Industrial Relations Journal* 36(5): 386–40.

Kirton, G. and Greene, A. M. (2002), 'The Dynamics of Positive Action in UK Trade Unions: The Case of Women and Black Members', *Industrial Relations Journal*, **33**(2): 157–172.

——— (2002a), 'New directions in managing women's trade union careers: online learning', *Women in Management Review*, **17**(3/4): 171–179.

Kirton, G. and Healy, G. (1999), 'Transforming Union Women: the Role of Women Trade Union Officials in Union Renewal', *Industrial Relations Journal*, **30**(1): 31–45.

———— (2004) 'Shaping Women's Trade Union Identities: a Case Study of Women-only Courses in MSF and TGWU', *British Journal of Industrial Relations*, **42**(2): 303–324.

Klandermans, B. (1992), 'Trade Union Participation' *Employment Relations*, Hartley, J. and Stephenson, G., London, Blackwell: 184–199.

Labour Research (1988), 'Educating Rita to sort out the boss', *Labour Research,* (January): 19–20.

———— (2000), 'Women everywhere but at the top', *Labour Research* (March): 17–19.

———— (2002), 'Women in unions face glass ceiling', *Labour Research*: 10–12.

———— (2004), 'Women's rise in union patchy', *Labour Research* (March): 10–12.

Lawrence, E. (1994), *Gender and Trade Unions*, London, Taylor and Francis.

Layder, D. (1993), *New Strategies in Social Research*, London, Polity Press.

Ledwith, S., Colgan, F., Joyce, P. and Hayes, M. (1990), 'The Making of Women Trade Union Leaders', *Industrial Relations Journal*, **21**(2): 112–125.

Ledwith, S. and Colgan, F. (2002), 'Tackling gender, diversity and trade union democracy: a worldwide project?', *Gender, Diversity and Trade Unions*, Colgan, F. and Ledwith, S., London, Routledge: 1–27.

Lee, G. (1987), 'Black Members and their Unions', *The Manufacture of Disadvantage*, Lee, G. and Loveridge, R., Milton Keynes, Open University Press: 144–157.

Marsden, R. (1982), 'Industrial Relations: a critique of empiricism', *Sociology*, **16**: 232–50.

Maynard, M. (1994), ' "Race", gender and the concept of "difference" in feminist thought', Afshar, H. and Maynard, M., *The Dynamics of 'Race' and Gender*, London: Taylor & Francis: 9–25.

McBride, A. (2001), *Gender Democracy in Trade Unions*, Aldershot, Ashgate.

McIlroy, J. (1980), 'Education for the Labour Movement: UK Experience Past and Present', *Labor Studies Journal*, **4**(3): 198–213.

———— (1982), 'Sexism and Trade Union Education', *Trade Union Studies Journal*, **Summer**: 2–3.

Metcalf, C. (2000), 'Fighting for Equality', *CentrePiece, The Magazine for Economic Performance*, www.centrepiece–magazine.com/summer00/metcalf.htm

Metochi, M. (2002), 'The influence of leadership and member attitudes in understanding the nature of union participation', *British Journal of Industrial Relations*, **40**(1): 87–111.

Millar, J. (1930), *Why Trade Union Education?* Amalgamated Union of Upholsterers, London.

Miller, D. (1983), 'Student Centred Learning in Trade Union Education', *Trade Union Studies Journal*, **Summer**: 2–3.

Morris, H. and Fosh, P. (2000), 'Measuring Trade Union Democracy: The Case of the UK Civil and Public Services Association', *British Journal of Industrial Relations*, **38**(1): 95–114.

MSF (2000), 'Women's Week: Negotiating Skills for Women', Course Handbook, September.

———— (2000a), 'Women's Week: Skills for Organising', Course Handbook, June.

————— (2002), 'Women's Week: Developing Women's Leadership', Course Handbook, June.

————— (2002a), 'Women's Week: Assertiveness for Women, Course Handbook, June.

Munro, A. (1999), *Women, Work and Trade Unions*, London, Mansell.

————— (2001), 'A Feminist Trade Union Agenda? The Continued Significance of Class, Gender and Race', *Gender, Work and Organization*, **8**(4): 454–471.

Munro, A. and Rainbird, H. (2000), 'The New Unionism and the New Bargaining Agenda: UNISON – Employer Partnerships on Workplace Learning in Britain', *British Journal of Industrial Relations*, **38**(2): 223–240.

————— (2000a), 'UNISON's Approach to Lifelong Learning', *Redefining Public Sector Unionism*, Terry, M., London, Routledge: 175–187.

Nicholson, G., Ursell, G. and Blyton, P. (1981), *The Dynamics of White-collar Unionism*, London, Academic Press.

Parker, J. (2002), 'Women's groups in British unions', *British Journal of Industrial Relations*, **40**(1): 23–48.

————— (2003), *Women's Groups and Equality in British Trade Unions'*, New York, Edwin Mellen Press.

Pedler, M. (1974), 'The Training Implications of the Shop Steward's Leadership Role', *Industrial Relations Journal*, **5**(1): 57–69.

Phillips, A. (1991), *Engendering Democracy*, Oxford, Polity Press.

————— (1992), 'Universal Pretensions in Political Thought', *Destabilising Theory*, Barrett, M. and Phillips, P., Cambridge, Polity Press.

Phizacklea, A. and Miles, R. (1987), 'The British Trade Union Movement and Racism', *The Manufacture of Disadvantage*, Lee, G. and Loveridge, R., Milton Keynes, Open University Press: 112–125.

Pierce, S. (1981), 'Women's Issues on Trade Union Courses', *Trade Union Studies Journal*, **Spring**: 9–11.

Pollert, A. (1996), 'Gender and Class Revisited; or the Poverty of Patriarchy', *Sociology*, **30**(4): 639–659.

Pringle, R. and Watson, R. (1992), 'Women's Interests and the Post-structuralist State', *Destabilising Theory*, Barrett, M. and Phillips, A., Cambridge, Polity Press.

Procter, I. and Padfield, M. (1999), 'Work orientations and women's work: a critique of Hakim's theory of the heterogeneity of women', *Gender, Work and Organization*, **6**(3): 152–162.

Purcell, K. (1979), 'Militancy and Acquiescence amongst Women Workers', *Fit Work for Women*, Burman, S., Oxford, Blackwell: 112–133.

Rees, T. (1990), 'Gender, power and Trade Union Democracy', Fosh, P. and Heery, E., *Trade Unions and their Members – Studies in Union Democracy and Organization*, Basingstoke, Macmillan: 177–205.

————— (1992), *Gender and the Labour Market*, London, Routledge.

Reinelt, C. (1994), 'Fostering Empowerment, Building Community: the Challenge for State-funded Feminist Organizations', *Human Relations*, **47**(6): 685–705.

Salmon, J. (1983), 'Trade Union Education: its Past and Future', *Industrial Relations Journal*, **15**(2): 72–90.

SERTUC (1987), 'Moving Towards Equality', London, Southern and Eastern Region TUC.

———— (2000), 'New Moves Towards Equality – New Challenges', London, Southern and Eastern Region TUC.

Sinclair, D. (1995), 'The Importance of Sex for the Propensity to Unionise', *British Journal of Industrial Relations*, **33**(2): 239–252.

———— (1996), 'The Importance of Gender for Participation in and Attitudes to Trade Unionism', *Industrial Relations Journal*, **27**(3): 239–252.

Smith, T. (1982), 'Trade Union Education: its past and future', *Industrial Relations Journal*, **15**(2): 72–90.

Sneade, A. (2001), 'Trade union membership 1999–2000: an analysis of data from the Certification Officer and the Labour Force Survey', *Labour Market Trends*, **September**: 433–441.

Soldon, N. (1978), *Women in British trade unions 1874–1976*, Dublin, Gill and Macmillan.

Sommerville, J. (1997), 'Social Movement Theory, Women and the Question of Interests', *Sociology*, **31**(4): 673–695.

Stabile, C. (1997), 'Feminism and the Ends of Postmodernism', *Materialist Feminism*, Hennessy, R. and Ingraham, C., London, Routledge: 395–408.

Sudano, L. (1998). 'Women Union Leaders: Mongrels, Martyrs, Misfits or Models for the Future?', Pocock, B., *Strife, Sex and Politics in Labour Unions*, New South Wales: Allen and Unwin: 149–171.

Tajfel, H. and Turner, J. C. (1986), 'The Social Identity Theory of Intergroup Behaviour', Worchel, S. and Austin, W. G., *Psychology of Intergroup Relations*, Chicago, Nelson Hall.

Terry, M. (1995), 'Trade Unions: Growth, Structure and Policy', *Industrial Relations: Theory and Practice in Britain*, Edwards, P., Oxford, Blackwell: 203–228.

———— (1996), 'Negotiating the Government of Unison: Union Democracy in Theory and Practice', *British Journal of Industrial Relations*, **34**: 87–111.

TGWU (1992), Education Guidelines, London, TGWU.

———— (1998), Home Study Course, London, TGWU.

———— (1999), Encouraging women's participation in the T&G, London, TGWU.

———— (1999a), 'Women at Work', National Women Members' School, Course Handbook.

———— (1999b), 'Women beyond the Workplace', National Women Members' School Course, Handbook.

———— (1999c), 'Women in Europe', National Women Members' School, Course Handbook.

———— (1999d), 'Recruitment and Organization for Women', National Women Members' School, Course Handbook.

———— (2001), 'Understanding the Union and Maximising Women's Involvement', National Women Members' School, Course Handbook.

———— (2001a), 'Public Speaking, Using the Media and Promoting the Union in the Community', National Women Members' School, Course Handbook.

———— (2001b), 'Campaigning and Bargaining for Women', National Women Members' School, Course Handbook.

———— (2001c), 'New Employment Rights and Organising Women Workers', National Women Member's School, Course Handbook.

————(2001d), 'Women and Pensions', National Women Members' School, Course Handbook.

Thompson, P. (1993), 'Postmodernism: Fatal Distraction', *Postmodernism and Organizations*, Hassard, J. and Parker, M., London, Sage.

Trebilcock, A. (1991), 'Strategies for strengthening women's participation in trade union leadership', *International Labour Review*, 130:4, 407–26.

TUC (1926), First Annual Report of Women's Trade Union Conference, London, TUC.

———— (1931), Report of the Annual Conference of Unions Catering for Women Workers, London, TUC.

———— (1934), Report of the Annual Conference of Unions Catering for Women Workers, London, TUC.

———— (1936), Report of the Annual Conference of Union Catering for Women Workers, London, TUC.

———— (1938), Report of the Annual Conference of Unions Catering for Women Workers, London, TUC.

———— (1950), Report of the Annual Conference of Unions Catering for Women Workers, London, TUC.

———— (1951), Report of the Annual Conference of Unions Catering for Women Workers, London, TUC.

———— (1952), Report of the Annual Conference of Unions Catering for Women Workers, London, TUC.

———— (1953), Report of the Annual Conference of Unions Catering for Women Workers, London, TUC.

———— (1954), Report of the Annual Conference of Unions Catering for Women Workers, London, TUC.

———— (1956), Report of the Annual Conference of Unions Catering for Women Workers, London, TUC.

———— (1958), Report of the Annual Conference of Unions Catering for Women Workers, London, TUC.

———— (1960), Report of the Annual Conference of Unions Catering for Women Workers, London, TUC.

———— (1965), Report of the Annual Conference of Unions Catering for Women Workers, London, TUC.

———— (2001), General Council Report, London, TUC.

TUEEC (1920), 'Adult Education and the Trade Unionist', London, Trade Union Education Enquiry Committee, TUC.

Virdee, S. and Grint, K. (1994), 'Black Self–Organization in Trade Unions', *Sociological Review*, **42**(2): 202–226.

Wacjman, J. (2000), 'Feminism Facing Industrial Relations', *British Journal of*

Industrial Relations, **38**(2): 183–201.

Waddington, J. and Whitston, C. (1997), 'Why do people join trade unions in a period of membership decline?' *British Journal of Industrial Relations*, **35**(4): 515–546.

Waddington, J. and Kerr, A. (2002), 'Unions fit for young workers?' *Industrial Relations Journal*, **33**(4): 298–315.

Walby, S. (1986), *Patriarchy at Work*, Cambridge, Polity Press.

———— (1989), 'Theorising Patriarchy', *Sociology*, **23**(2): 213–234.

———— (1990), *Theorising Patriarchy*, Oxford, Blackwell.

———— (1992), 'Post–Post–Modernism? Theorising Social Complexity', *Destabilising Theory*, Barrett, M. and Phillips, A., Cambridge, Polity Press.

———— (1997), *Gender Transformations*, London, Routledge.

Walters, D. (1996), 'Trade Unions and the Training of Health and Safety Representatives in Europe', *Employee Relations*, **18**(6): 50–68.

Walters, S. (2002), 'Female Part-time Workers' Attitudes to Trade Unions in Britain', *British Journal of Industrial Relations*, **40**(1): 49–68.

Walton, J. (1991), 'Women Shop Stewards in a County Branch of NALGO', *International Perspectives on Labour and Gender Ideology*, Redclift, N. and Sinclair, M., London, Routledge: 149–172.

Watson, D. (1988), *Managers of Discontent*, London, Routledge.

Windebank, J. (2001), 'Dual-Earner couples in Britain and France: gender divisions of domestic labour and parenting work in different welfare states', *Work, Employment and Society*, **15**(2): 269–290.

Woodland, S. and Cully, M. (1997). 'Swings, roundabouts and slides: changes in union membership, 1995–96', Paper presented to BUIRA Conference, Bath University.

Young, I. M. (1990), *Justice and the Politics of Difference*, Princeton, Princeton University Press.

———— (1997), *Intersecting Voices. Dilemmas of Gender, Political Philosophy and Policy*, Princeton, New Jersey, Princeton University Press.

———— (2000), *Inclusion and Democracy*, Oxford, Oxford University Press.

Yuval-Davis, N. (1998), 'Women, empowerment and coalition politics', Charles, N. and Hintgens, C., *Gender, ethnicity and political ideologies*, London, Routledge: 168–189.

Index